ICSEA 2022

The Seventeenth International Conference on Software Engineering Advances

October 16 - 20, 2022

Lisbon, Portugal

ICSEA 2022 Editors

Lugi Lavazza, University of Insubria at Varese, Italy

Printed from e-media with permission by:

Curran Associates, Inc.
57 Morehouse Lane
Red Hook, NY 12571

Some format issues inherent in the e-media version may also appear in this print version.

Printed with permission by Curran Associates, Inc. (2023)

International Academy, Research, and Industry Association (IARIA)
412 Derby Way
Wilmington, DE 19810

Phone: (408) 893-6407
Fax: (408) 527-6351

petre@iaria.org

Additional copies of this publication are available from:

Curran Associates, Inc.
57 Morehouse Lane
Red Hook, NY 12571 USA
Phone: 845-758-0400
Fax: 845-758-2633
Email: curran@proceedings.com
Web: www.proceedings.com

Table of Contents

ICSEA 2022

Forward

The Seventeenth International Conference on Software Engineering Advances (ICSEA 2022), held between October 16th and October 20th, 2022, continued a series of events covering a broad spectrum of software-related topics. The conference covered fundamentals on designing, implementing, testing, validating and maintaining various kinds of software. Several tracks were proposed to treat the topics from theory to practice, in terms of methodologies, design, implementation, testing, use cases, tools, and lessons learned. The conference topics covered classical and advanced methodologies, open source, agile software, as well as software deployment and software economics and education.

Other advanced aspects are related to on-time practical aspects, such as run-time vulnerability checking, rejuvenation process, updates partial or temporary feature deprecation, software deployment and configuration, and on-line software updates. These aspects trigger implications related to patenting, licensing, engineering education, new ways for software adoption and improvement, and ultimately, to software knowledge management.

There are many advanced applications requiring robust, safe, and secure software: disaster recovery applications, vehicular systems, biomedical-related software, biometrics related software, mission critical software, E-health related software, crisis-situation software. These applications require appropriate software engineering techniques, metrics and formalisms, such as, software reuse, appropriate software quality metrics, composition and integration, consistency checking, model checking, provers and reasoning.

The nature of research in software varies slightly with the specific discipline researchers work in, yet there is much common ground and room for a sharing of best practice, frameworks, tools, languages and methodologies. Despite the number of experts we have available, little work is done at the meta level, that is examining how we go about our research, and how this process can be improved. There are questions related to the choice of programming language, IDEs and documentation styles and standard. Reuse can be of great benefit to research projects yet reuse of prior research projects introduces special problems that need to be mitigated. The research environment is a mix of creativity and systematic approach which leads to a creative tension that needs to be managed or at least monitored. Much of the coding in any university is undertaken by research students or young researchers. Issues of skills training, development and quality control can have significant effects on an entire department. In an industrial research setting, the environment is not quite that of industry as a whole, nor does it follow the pattern set by the university. The unique approaches and issues of industrial research may hold lessons for researchers in other domains.

We take here the opportunity to warmly thank all the members of the ICSEA 2022 technical program committee, as well as all the reviewers. The creation of such a high-quality conference program would not have been possible without their involvement. We also kindly thank all the authors who dedicated much of their time and effort to contribute to ICSEA 2022. We truly believe that, thanks to all these efforts, the final conference program consisted of top-quality contributions. We also thank the members of the ICSEA 2022 organizing committee for their help in handling the logistics of this event.

We hope that ICSEA 2022 was a successful international forum for the exchange of ideas and results between academia and industry and for the promotion of progress in software engineering advances.

ICSEA 2022 Chairs

ICSEA 2022 Steering Committee

Herwig Manaert, University of Antwerp, Belgium
Radek Koci, Brno University of Technology, Czech Republic
Sébastien Salva, University of Clermont Auvergne | LIMOS Laboratory | CNRS, France
José Carlos Metrôlho, Polytechnic Institute of Castelo Branco, Portugal
Luigi Lavazza, Università dell'Insubria – Varese, Italy
Hironori Washizaki, Waseda University / National Institute of Informatics / SYSTEM INFORMATION, Japan
Roy Oberhauser, Aalen University, Germany

ICSEA 2022 Publicity Chairs

Sandra Viciano Tudela, Universitat Politecnica de Valencia, Spain
Jose Luis García, Universitat Politecnica de Valencia, Spain

ICSEA 2022
Committee

ICSEA 2022 Steering Committee

Herwig Manaert, University of Antwerp, Belgium
Radek Koci, Brno University of Technology, Czech Republic
Sébastien Salva, University of Clermont Auvergne | LIMOS Laboratory | CNRS, France
José Carlos Metrôlho, Polytechnic Institute of Castelo Branco, Portugal
Luigi Lavazza, Università dell'Insubria – Varese, Italy
Hironori Washizaki, Waseda University / National Institute of Informatics / SYSTEM INFORMATION, Japan
Roy Oberhauser, Aalen University, Germany

ICSEA 2022 Publicity Chairs

Sandra Viciano Tudela, Universitat Politecnica de Valencia, Spain
Jose Luis García, Universitat Politecnica de Valencia, Spain

ICSEA 2022 Technical Program Committee

Tamer Abdou, Ryerson University, Canada
Morayo Adedjouma, CEA Saclay Nano-INNOV - Institut CARNOT CEA LIST, France
Ammar Kareem Obayes Alazzawi, Universiti Teknologi PETRONAS, Malaysia
Washington H. C. Almeida, CESAR School, Brazil
Eman Abdullah AlOmar, Rochester Institute of Technology, USA
Sousuke Amasaki, Okayama Prefectural University, Japan
Talat Ambreen, International Islamic University, Islamabad, Pakistan
Amal Ahmed Anda, University of Ottawa, Canada
Daniel Andresen, Kansas State University, USA
Jean-Paul Arcangeli, UPS - IRIT, France
Francesca Arcelli Fontana, University of Milano Bicocca, Italy
Héber H. Arcolezi, Inria & École Polytechnique (IPP), Palaiseau, France
Benjamin Aziz, University of Portsmouth, UK
Takuya Azumi, Saitama University, Japan
Gilbert Babin, HEC Montréal, Canada
Jorge Barreiros, ISEC - Polytechnic of Coimbra / NOVA LINCS, Portugal
Marciele Bergier, Universidade do Minho | Research Center of the Justice and Governance, Portugal
Silvia Bonfanti, University of Bergamo, Italy
Mina Boström Nakicenovic, Paradox Interactive, Sweden
Khadija Bousselmi Arfaoui, University of Savoie Mont Blanc, France
José Carlos Bregieiro Ribeiro, Polytechnic Institute of Leiria, Portugal
Uwe Breitenbücher, University of Stuttgart, Germany
Antonio Brogi, University of Pisa, Italy
Carlos Henrique Cabral Duarte, Brazilian Development Bank (BNDES), Brazil
Carlos A. Casanova Pietroboni, National Technological University - Concepción del Uruguay Regional Faculty (UTN-FRCU), Argentina

Olena Chebanyuk, National Aviation University, Ukraine
Fuxiang Chen, DeepSearch Inc., Korea
Dickson Chiu, The University of Hong Kong, Hong Kong
Rebeca Cortazar, University of Deusto, Spain
André Magno Costa de Araújo, Federal University of Alagoas, Brazil
Mónica Costa, Polytechnic Institute of Castelo Branco, Portugal
Yania Crespo, University of Valladolid, Spain
Luís Cruz, Delft University of Technology, Netherlands
Beata Czarnacka-Chrobot, Warsaw School of Economics, Poland
Giovanni Daián Róttoli, Universidad Tecnológica Nacional (UTN-FRCU), Argentina
Darren Dalcher, Lancaster University, UK
Andrea D'Ambrogio, University of Rome Tor Vergata, Italy
Guglielmo De Angelis, CNR - IASI, Italy
Thiago C. de Sousa, State University of Piauí, Brazil
Manuel De Stefano, University of Salerno, Italy
Lin Deng, Towson University, USA
Fatma Dhaou, University of Tunis el Manar, Tunisia
Jaime Díaz, Universidad de La Frontera, *Chile*
Dragos Laurentiu Dobrean, Babes-Bolyai University, Cluj Napoca, Romania
Diogo Domingues Regateiro, Instituto de Telecomunicações | Universidade de Aveiro, Portugal
Dimitris Dranidis, CITY College, University of York Europe Campus, Greece
Imke Helene Drave, RWTH Aachen University, Germany
Arpita Dutta, National University of Singapore, Singapore
Holger Eichelberger, University of Hildesheim | Software Systems Engineering, Germany
Ridha Ejbali, National Engineering School of Gabes (ENIS) / University of Gabes, Tunisia
Gledson Elias, Federal University of Paraíba (UFPB), Brazil
Fernando Escobar, University of Brasilia (UNB), Brazil
Kleinner Farias, University of Vale do Rio dos Sinos, Brazil
Thomas Fehlmann, Euro Project Office AG, Zurich, Switzerland
Alba Fernandez Izquierdo, Universidad Politécnica de Madrid, Spain
David Fernandez-Amoros, Universidad Nacional de Educación a Distancia (UNED), Spain
Estrela Ferreira Cruz, Instituto Politécnico de Viana do Castelo | ALGORIMTI research centre - Universidade do Minho, Portugal
Harald Foidl, University of Innsbruck, Austria
Jonas Fritzsch, University of Stuttgart | Institute of Software Engineering, Germany
Jicheng Fu, University of Central Oklahoma, USA
Stoyan Garbatov, OutSystems SA, Portugal
Jose Garcia-Alonso, University of Extremadura, Spain
Wided Ghardallou, ENISO, Tunisia / Hail University, KSA
Giammaria Giordano, University of Salerno, Italy
Gregor Grambow, Aalen University, Germany
Jiaping Gui, NEC Labs America, USA
Chunhui Guo, California State University, Los Angeles, USA
Zhensheng Guo, Siemens AG, Germany
Bidyut Gupta, Southern Illinois University, Carbondale, USA
Huong Ha, University of Newcastle, Singapore
Shahliza Abd Halim, UniversityTeknologi Malaysia, Malaysia
Atsuo Hazeyama, Tokyo Gakugei University, Japan

Qiang He, Swinburne University of Technology, Australia
Jairo Hernán Aponte, Universidad Nacional de Colombia, Columbia
LiGuo Huang, Southern Methodist University, USA
Rui Humberto Pereira, ISCAP/IPP, Portugal
Waqar Hussain, Monash University, Australia
Emanuele Iannone, University of Salerno, Italy
Gustavo Illescas, Universidad Nacional del Centro-Tandil-Bs.As., Argentina
Irum Inayat, National University of Computer and Emerging Sciences, Islamabad, Pakistan
Florije Ismaili, South East European University, Republic of Macedonia
Angshuman Jana, IIIT Guwahati, India
Marko Jäntti, Center for Measurement and Information Systems (CEMIS), Finland
Judit Jász, University of Szeged, Hungary
Laid Kahloul, Biskra University, Algeria
Hermann Kaindl, Vienna University of Technology, Austria
Yasushi Kambayashi, NIT - Nippon Institute of Technology, Japan
Ahmed Kamel, Concordia College, Moorhead, USA
Chia Hung Kao, National Taitung University, Taiwan
Dimitris Karagiannis, University of Vienna, Austria
Dimitra Karatza, iov42, UK
Vikrant Kaulgud, Accenture, India
Siffat Ullah Khan, University of Malakand, Pakistan
Reinhard Klemm, Avaya Labs, USA
Radek Koci, Brno University of Technology, Czech Republic
Christian Kop, University of Klagenfurt, Austria
Blagovesta Kostova, EPFL, Switzerland
Eberhard Kranich, Euro Project Office, Duisburg, Germany
Akrivi Krouska, University of Piraeus, Greece
Bolatzhan Kumalakov, Al-Farabi Kazakh National University, Kazakhstan
Tsutomu Kumazawa, Software Research Associates Inc., Japan
Rob Kusters, Open University, The Netherlands
Alla Lake, LInfo Systems, LLC - Greenbelt, USA
Jannik Laval, University Lumière Lyon 2 | DISP lab EA4570, Bron, France
Luigi Lavazza, Università dell'Insubria - Varese, Italy
Ahmed Lekssays, Università degli studi dell'Insubria, Varese, Italy
Maurizio Leotta, University of Genova, Italy
Abderrahmane Leshob, University of Quebec at Montreal (UQAM), Canada
Zheng Li, University of Concepción, Chile
Panos Linos, Butler University, USA
Alexandre Marcos Lins de Vasconcelos, Universidade Federal de Pernambuco, Recife, Brazil
David H. Lorenz, Open University of Israel, Israel
Stephane Maag, Télécom SudParis, France
Silvana Togneri Mac Mahon, Dublin City University, Ireland
Frédéric Mallet, Université Cote d'Azur | Inria Sophia Antipolis Méditerranée, France
Herwig Mannaert, University of Antwerp, Belgium
Krikor Maroukian, Microsoft, Greece
Johnny Marques, Aeronautics Institute of Technology (ITA), Brazil
Célia Martinie, Université Paul Sabatier Toulouse III, France
Rohit Mehra, Accenture Labs, India

Kristof Meixner, Christian Doppler Lab CDL-SQI | Institute for Information Systems Engineering | Technische Universität Wien, Vienna, Austria
Vojtech Merunka, Czech University of Life Sciences in Prague / Czech Technical University in Prague, Czech Republic
José Carlos M. M. Metrolho, Polytechnic Institute of Castelo Branco, Portugal
Sanjay Misra, Covenant University, Nigeria
Mohammadsadegh Mohagheghi, Vali-e-Asr University of Rafsanjan, Iran
Miguel P. Monteiro, Universidade NOVA de Lisboa, Portugal
Fernando Moreira, Universidade Portucalense, Portugal
Óscar Mortágua Pereira, University of Aveiro, Portugal
Ines Mouakher, University of Tunis El Manar, Tunisia
Kmimech Mourad, Higher Institute for Computer Science and Mathematics of Monastir, Tunisia
Lucilene F. Mouzinho da Silva, Federal Institute of Maranhão, Brazil
Sana Ben Hamida Mrabet, Paris Nanterre University / LAMSADE - Paris Dauphine University, France
Kazi Muheymin-Us-Sakib, Institute of Information Technology (IIT) | University of Dhaka, Bangladesh
Marcellin Nkenlifack, University of Dschang, Cameroon
Marc Novakouski, Carnegie Mellon Software Engineering Institute, USA
Roy Oberhauser, Aalen University, Germany
Shinpei Ogata, Shinshu University, Japan
Thomas Olsson, RISE Research Institutes of Sweden, Sweden
Safa Omri, Daimler AG / Karlsruhe Institute of Technology, Germany
Flavio Oquendo, IRISA (UMR CNRS) - University of South Brittany, France
Marcos Palacios, University of Oviedo, Spain
Harsha Perera, Monash University, Australia
Beatriz Pérez Valle, University of La Rioja, Spain
Quentin Perez, IMT Mines Alès, France
Monica Pinto, University of Málaga, Spain
Aneta Poniszewska-Maranda, Institute of Information Technology | Lodz University of Technology, Poland
Valeria Pontillo, University of Salerno, Italy
Pasqualina Potena, RISE Research Institutes of Sweden AB, Sweden
Evgeny Pyshkin, University of Aizu, Japan
Claudia Raibulet, University of Milano-Bicocca, Italy
Aurora Ramírez, University of Córdoba, Spain
Raman Ramsin, Sharif University of Technology, Iran
Fernando Reinaldo Ribeiro, Polytechnic Institute of Castelo Branco, Portugal
Catarina I. Reis, ciTechCare - Center for Innovative Care and Health Technology | Polytechnic of Leiria, Portugal
Wolfgang Reisig, Humboldt University, Berlin, Germany
Michele Risi, University of Salerno, Italy
Simona Mirela Riurean, University of Petrosani, Romania
Nelson Rocha, University of Aveiro, Portugal
José Raúl Romero, Universidad de Córdoba, Spain
António Miguel Rosado da Cruz, Polytechnic Institute of Viana do Castelo, Portugal
Adrian Rutle, Western Norway University of Applied Sciences, Norway
Renaud Rwemalika, SnT - University of Luxembourg, Luxembourg
Ines Bayoudh Saadi, ENSIT - Tunis University, Tunisia
Nyyti Saarimäki, Tampere University, Finland

Copyright Information

A Smart Manufacturing Data Lake Metadata Framework for Process Mining

Michalis Pingos
Department of Electrical Engineering, Computer Engineering and Informatics
Cyprus University of Technology
Limassol, Cyprus
email: michalis.pingos@cut.ac.cy

Andreas S. Andreou
Department of Electrical Engineering, Computer Engineering and Informatics
Cyprus University of Technology
Limassol, Cyprus
email: andreas.andreou@cut.ac.cy

Abstract— **The fourth industrial revolution consists of a new level of organization and control of the entire production process. The smart manufacturing ecosystem and especially Cyber Physical Systems are evolving rapidly. They constitute an environment with multiple heterogeneous sources that produce high volumes of data. This data needs to be stored in a storage system that can handle raw, unprocessed, relational, and non-relational data types, such as Data Lakes, in order to be processed when needed. This paper introduces a Data Lake-based metadata framework, which utilizes the concept of blueprints to characterize the data sources and the data itself to facilitate process mining tasks. The applicability and effectiveness of the proposed framework is validated through a real-world smart manufacturing case-study, namely a poultry meat production factory, which offers operational support and business workflow analysis.**

Keywords: Smart Manufacturing; Data Lakes; Heterogeneous Data Sources; Metadata Mechanism; Data Blueprints; Process Mining.

I. INTRODUCTION

Industry 4.0 is based on a number of new and innovative technological developments, such as Cyber Physical Systems (CPSs), Internet of Things (IoT), Cloud Computing, Cognitive Computing, robotics, Augmented Reality (AR) technology and intelligent tools [1], which contribute to the production of personalized products according to customer needs by digitization of the entire product production cycle [2].

Factories of the future will consist of a CPS or a set of CPSs that will interact with each other. A CPS consists of mechanisms controlled or monitored by computer algorithms, integrated into the Internet and its users. CPSs change the way people interact with machines and workers will need to be skilled and will need to be aware of the functions of coordinated intelligent machines from a central control point and of the data they produce [3].

The main challenges of Industry 4.0 are the need for: (i) constant availability of all data and information in a smart factory in real-time; (ii) interoperability of all entities that contribute to production (customer, services, production systems, etc.); and (iii) extraction of the optimal value-added flow at any time from the data [5].

A smart factory is an environment that consists of Big Data sources, such as data warehouses, Data Lakes (DLs), and databases, whether on-premises or on the cloud, that can produce massive volumes of textual content (unstructured, semi-structured, and structured), multimedia content (images, video, and audio), utilizing a variety of platforms (enterprise, social media, and sensors) during the production cycle. Despite the great and drastic solutions proposed in recent years in the area of Big Data Processing and Systems of Deep Insight, treating Big Data produced by multiple heterogeneous data sources remains a challenging and unsolved problem [4].

Nowadays, in the era of Big Data, with huge amounts of information produced and consumed, data is considered as the "power" of businesses only if is properly processed to offer mainly decision support. Most companies have a lot of unused data that can be used for process mining. This is a side-effect of the widespread digitization and automation of business processes, which leaves digital traces of real process executions as a byproduct. To the best of our knowledge, the integration of DL with process mining activities has not received much attention in research literature yet. As DLs appear to be a promising technique for temporal Big Data storing, the present work, apart from the goals described below, intends to cover this gap as well.

This paper introduces a new approach to handle Big Data in terms of storing and retrieval, which intends to serve best process mining activities that use this data. More specifically, a novel metadata mechanism is proposed that provides the ability to characterize and describe data sources, data items and process related information which are stored in a DL by means of blueprinting. The proposed approach is an extension of prior work on the topic [14], which builds upon the notions of DL and blueprints [16] to add the following contribution: (a) a separate class of blueprints to account for the information related to process mining activities in a smart manufacturing environment (processes, events, machines); (b) the actions to store, retrieve and process data produced by various sources (e.g., sensors) and relate to workflows and mining activities (e.g., events, sequencing, dependencies, etc.); (c) an extension to the DL architecture where we introduce the notion of data puddles to be used for storing smaller portions of data according to some formatting criterion; and (d) the successful application of the framework on a real-world industrial case study, which, on one hand it is quite rare in literature to report a real business customer to study, and on the other hand it yielded some very interesting findings.

The remainder of the paper is structured as follows: Section II discusses related work and the technical background in the areas of Smart Manufacturing, DLs, and Business Process Mining (BPM). Section III presents the DL source description framework and discusses its main components that prepare the relevant data for process mining. This is followed by Section IV that presents an experimental validation of the proposed framework on a real-world case, namely that of poultry meat production. Finally, Section V concludes the paper and highlights future work directions.

II. TECHNICAL BACKGROUND

Nowadays, industries are being transformed with the rise of disrupting technologies and this transformation is called Industry 4.0 or Smart Manufacturing. Industry 4.0 aims to construct an open and smart manufacturing platform for industrial information applications based on a range of disrupting technologies.

As previously mentioned, Smart Manufacturing consists of new scientific trends worldwide, such as IoT, Big Data analytics, cloud computing, Artificial Intelligence (AI), CPS and other new generation information disrupting technologies. All these technologies are related to the recent technological developments where Internet and its supporting technologies serve as a backbone to integrate human and machine agents, materials, products, production lines and processes, within and beyond organizational boundaries, to form a new kind of intelligent, connected, and agile value chain [6].

The vision of smart manufacturing envisages the use of smart technologies, such as information technology, sensor networks, process analysis, and production management and control software, to improve efficiency on agility, asset utilization and sustainability [7].

Industry 4.0 aims at digitizing engineering, production and manufacturing with the goal of:

- A seamless integration device, sensors, machines, as well as software and IT systems
- Increased flexibility thanks to pushing more intelligence from centralized planning systems to the edge
- Increased efficiency due to automated data exchange and analysis within the value chain

The most popular advantages of Smart Manufacturing are [8]:

- Optimization
- Customization
- Cost reduction
- Efficiency
- Customer Experience

The aforementioned information technologies, which are the backbone of smart manufacturing, generate a large volume of heterogeneous data, structured, semi-structured and unstructured. Big data analysis models and algorithms may be executed to organize, analyze and mine this raw data to obtain valuable knowledge. This manufacturing data is collected usually in real-time and sometimes automatically by IoT devices. Manufacturers aim to find a way to increase the efficiency, manage the storage of all this data and visualize it to improve and increase productivity and quality of products.

Most of the work on Big Data integration has been focused on the problem of processing very large amounts of data, extracting information from multiple, possibly conflicting data sources, reconciling the values and providing unified access to data residing in multiple, autonomous data sources.

Various studies addressed isolated aspects of data source management relying on schema mapping and semantic integration of different sources [9][10]. Those studies focused primarily on the construction of a global schema or a knowledge base to describe the domain of the data sources. Most of the proposed techniques examine user queries and return tables related to specific keywords presented in the query; however, keyword-based techniques fail to capture the semantics of natural language, i.e., the intentions of the users, and thus they can only go as far as giving relevant hints.

DL is a storage repository that can store large amounts of structured, semi-structured, and unstructured data. With this Big Data storage architecture, data holders can store every type of data in its native format without the need to structure or clean them until it needed. Every data element in a DL needs to be given a unique identifier and tagged with a set of metadata information [15].

Process mining is an emerging research discipline that helps organizations discover and analyze business processes based on raw event data. Basically, it sits between computational intelligence and data mining on one hand, and process modeling and analysis on the other [12]. Many researchers are developing new and more powerful process mining techniques and software vendors are incorporating these in their software and especially for Big Data [13]. Generally, process mining techniques based on the business log files produced. In our paper we are trying to utilize also Big Data produced by a manufacturing environment as a goal to transform them by the metadata mechanism to participate also in the process mining. This is very important in a world in which data is produced by a vast number of heterogeneous data sources.

There are three types of process mining activities, discovery, conformance checking, and enhancement. These activities use an existing process model produced based on event logs (see Figure 2). Companies and organizations tend to produce their log files according to their own data standards. Therefore, a standardization model is needed, to unify and formalize the description of all business entities in the enterprise under analysis, allowing to efficiently monitor and extract knowledge from event logs. In our case, this standardization is provided through the theory of Blueprint Models.

The target here is to build a unified DL-based business information standardization model, which is tailored to the needs of manufacturing organizations and consists of a

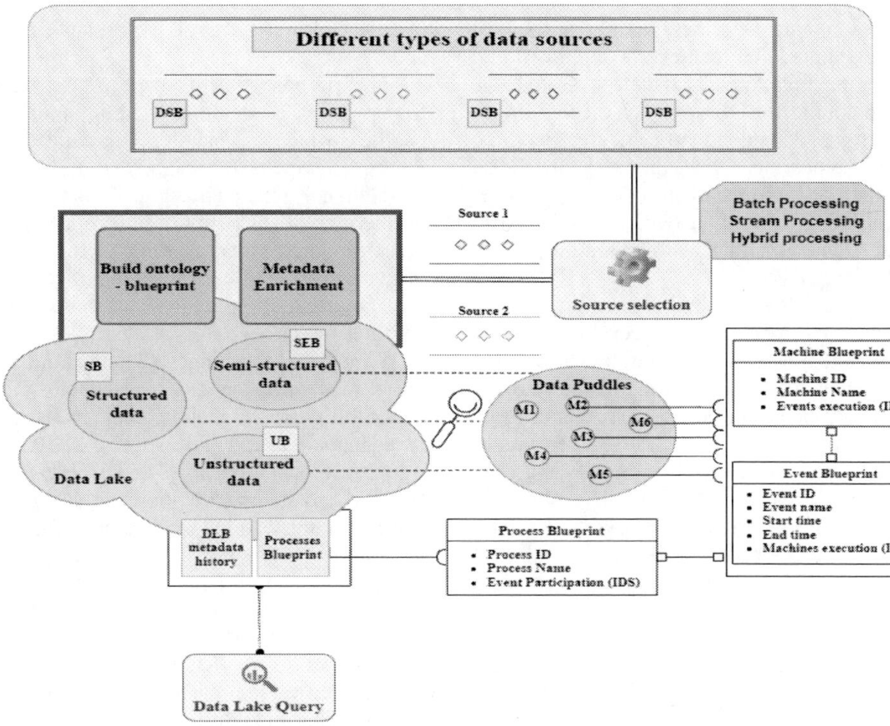

Figure 1. The architectural structure of the proposed approach

number of blueprint entities. These blueprints essentially describe an environment that produces large amounts of different types of data in a specific, disciplined form, including the data sources and their outputs, as well as the business processes. The entities in the business process related blueprints essentially describe and correlate the process information stored in the DL, offering also links to events interacting in chronological order and based on dependencies. These special blueprints codify, integrate, and contextualize business data and processes. They provide parameterized solution-aware patterns that represent operational processes and inter-relate a variety of data of diverse data types, critical functional, sensor, and performance factors in business production. These smart manufacturing intelligence blueprints are built using ontologies and utilizing a dedicated blueprint processing data mechanism along with event logs to facilitate efficient execution of process discovery, conformance checking, and model enhancement.

III. METHODOLOGY

As mentioned above, an extended, unified standardization framework for smart manufacturing and business process related data residing in a DL is introduced in this work, which utilizes a semantic metadata enrichment mechanism via Blueprints [14]. The latter utilizes the 5Vs Big Data characteristics and ontologies to assist data processing (storing and retrieval) in DLs with pond architecture, with emphasis on organizing and preparing data to facilitate process mining.

According to the proposed pond architecture, a DL consists of a set of data ponds, and each pond hosts / refers to a specific data type: structured, semi-structured and unstructured. Each pond contains a specialized storage and data processing system depending on the data type [11].

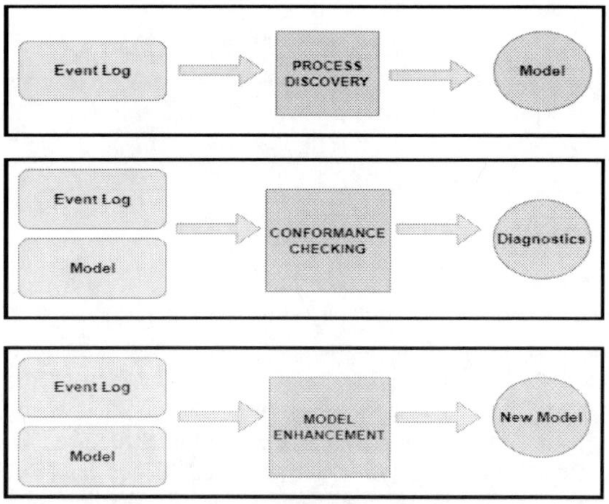

Figure 2. The three types of process mining activities

Process mining is performed mainly by using timestamped data logs. In a DL, however, there are various types of unstructured and semi-structured data, such as images, video, and sounds that may lack time information. Furthermore, structured data as well may not be ready to participate in process mining activities, mainly because it does not have timestamps. To achieve a uniform and constrained approach to the way related data is stored, we will adopt the data blueprint for DL approach created in our previous work (see Figure 1) and extend it by creating three new manufacturing blueprints that describe the data produced by machines and processes in a factory. This is performed by enriching the metadata manufacturing semantics of the DL framework that will prepare the data to be used by process mining tasks.

As mentioned above, this paper builds upon an existing framework [14] which is based on a metadata semantic enrichment mechanism that uses the notion of blueprints [16] to produce and organize meta-information related to each source producing data to be hosted in a DL. In this context, each data source is described via two types of blueprints as shown in Figure 3, which essentially utilize the 5Vs Big Data characteristics Volume, Velocity, Variety, Veracity and Value. The first includes information that is stable over time, such as, the name of the source and its velocity of data production. The second involves descriptors that vary as data is produced by the source in the course of time, such as the volume and date/time of production. The combination of these blueprints creates the Data Source Blueprint (DSB).

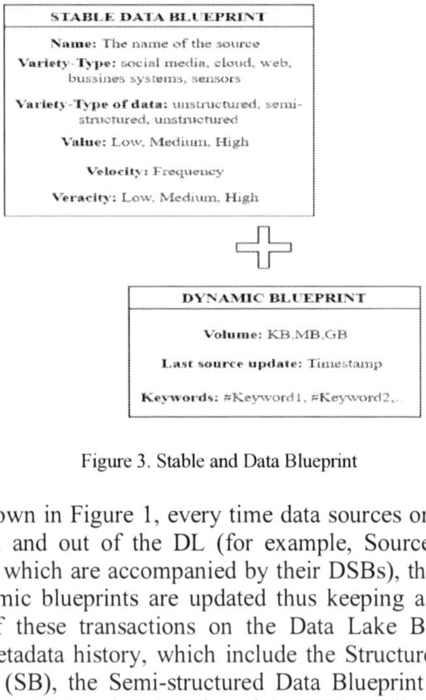

Figure 3. Stable and Data Blueprint

As shown in Figure 1, every time data sources or data is pushed in and out of the DL (for example, Source 1 and Source 2, which are accompanied by their DSBs), the stable and dynamic blueprints are updated thus keeping a sort of history of these transactions on the Data Lake Blueprint (DLB) metadata history, which include the Structured Data Blueprint (SB), the Semi-structured Data Blueprint (SEB), and the Unstructured Data Blueprint (UB) residing in the data ponds.

Essentially, the description of the sources helps to treat and manage many, multiple, and different types of data sources and to contribute to the DLs' metadata enrichment before and after these sources become its members. When a data source becomes part of the DL, the metadata schema is utilized, describing the whole DL ontology. The filtering and retrieval of data is based on this metadata mechanism which involves attributes from the 5Vs, such as last source updates and keywords.

The purpose of this paper is to extend the proposed framework via creating in the ponds the so-called data puddles, which are smaller, pre-build datasets as shown in Figure 1, which store data that machines produce in the production line (Machine and Event Blueprints). Furthermore, the existing framework is extended to include a process-related blueprint which provides information about the participation of each machine in various processes during production, that is, which machine executes each event within a process cycle.

To test that the proposed framework works properly and that it meets the needs of a real factory, we investigated its applicability to a major local industrial player, namely Paradisiotis Group (PARG) [17]. PARG is one of the most significant local companies and experts in the field of poultry farming and trading of poultry meat in Cyprus. It offers a wide selection of high-quality products that meet the needs of modern consumers for convenience in cooking and healthy eating. The business processes and the manufacturing data of the factory are, of course, confidential, and therefore, this paper reports only a part of the processes with not so many details, associated with a masked and downgraded version of the data. Nevertheless, the case-study is more than enough to demonstrate the basic principles of the proposed framework and prove its applicability and usefulness.

Every process in the manufacturing cycle consists of events and each event is executed by a machine that participates in a specific blueprint. Figure 4 describes an example of a process followed during the production of chicken nuggets at the PARG factory. First, the ingredients are prepared consisting of 85% chicken breast meat and 15% chicken skin. These ingredients are pushed into a flaker machine that cools down the raw material to a uniform temperature ranging between -2°C and 0°C and then shapes it to blocks. Subsequently, the blocks are chopped in smaller pieces of 8mm size by a mincing machine. Then, these minced pieces are mixed with dry ingredients (such as spices) and water, for 3-5 minutes and the end-product created consists of chicken nuggets formed to have a net weight of 40g each. Finally, the chicken nuggets are deep fried and packaged with appropriate labeling.

The process analyzed above is practically followed for all pre-fried products, such as drumsticks and meatballs, with the only difference being in the forming, with size and shape changing accordingly depending on the product. In addition, for fresh products, such as burgers, the forming event is omitted and another event is added before downcooling, namely the deboning of raw material which is executed by the Tappler machine (out of scope of the present study). In all these processes, the material is pushed from machine to machine via conveyors.

If we analyze the process of producing chicken nuggets depicted in Figure 4, we may derive that the following seven events take place:

- Downcooling *(ID: 12)*
- Chopping 8m *(ID: 4)*

- Mixing *(ID: 7)*
- Forming *(ID: 5)*
- Frying *(ID: 2)*
- Packaging *(ID: 3)*
- Labeling *(ID: 9)*

This process consists of events that are carried-out by machines which produce data during execution. To prepare this data for process mining, we use the process blueprint that provides information about production and is part of the manufacturing DL, as shown in Figure 1, as well as a machine blueprint and an event blueprint, which describe the data that machines produce during the production cycle.

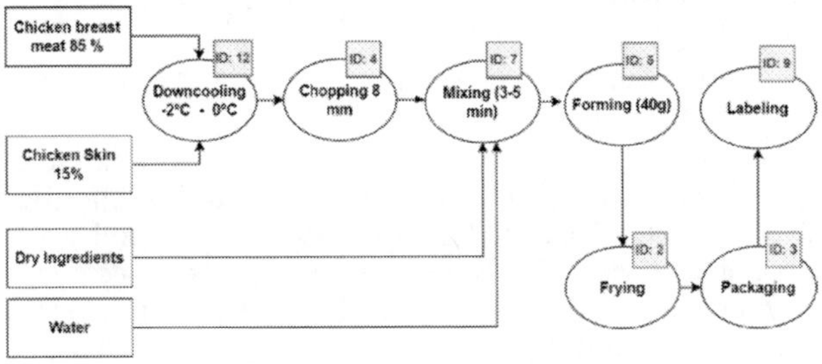

Figure 4. PARG chicken nuggets manufacturing process

As we can see on the previously described process, 10 machines (3 of which perform the same task) participate in the chicken nuggets production:

- Flaker *(ID, Type: FL2, Downcooling)*
- Mincer *(ID, Type: MC1, Chopping)*
- Mixer *(ID, Type: MX3, Mixing)*
- Former *(ID, Type: FRM1, Forming)*
- Fryer *(ID, Type: FR4, Frying)*
- Labeler *(ID, Type: LB1, Labeling)*
- Packager *(ID, Type: PC3, Labeling)*
- Conveyors (x3) *(ID, Type: CV1, CV2, CV3 Conveyor)*

These machines execute multiple events in a specific order during the production of nuggets. The type of machine that executes a specific event is stored in the Manufacturing Blueprint thus being able to check the availability of machines of this type.

The Process Blueprint captures the *Process ID*, the *Process name* and *Events participation*. For example, the chicken nuggets process blueprint is described as follows:

- Process ID: 100
- Process Name: Nuggets production
- Events execution: 12, 4, 7, 5, 2, 3, 9

The Event Blueprint consists of *Event ID*, *Event name*, *Start Time*, *End Time*, *Expected execution time*, *Executed by* (Machine Type) and *Dependencies*, the latter describing what other event has to be executed before the current event may start. For example, the Mixing event is described by the following Event Blueprint:

- Event ID: 7
- Event name: Mixing nuggets ingredients
- Start time: Timestamp
- End time: Timestamp
- Expected execution time: 4 minutes
- Executed by (ID, Type): MX
- Dependencies: 12, 4

Furthermore, the Event Blueprint captures the *Expected execution time* of the event to be able to check for abnormalities in case the execution of the event is delayed for some reason. This is performed through the analysis of the start and end times, the resources utilized, the roles etc., so as to trace the causes of this delay.

The Machine Blueprint captures *Machine ID*, *Machine Type*, *Machine name* and the *IDs* of the machines that may execute the specific event.

Essentially, the proposed information structure for the description of the data sources that exist in a smart factory efficiently supports the management of multiple data formats. It also allows data to be prepared for process mining through the metadata semantic enrichment that requires events to be timestamped and set in chronological order according to the process executed. Finally, sources that produce unstructured and semi-structured data that are stored in the relevant pond of the proposed approach may also be linked with the rest of the event information and provide added value to the analysis of a certain process. For example, data from a sensor installed on some machine in the production line (e.g., counting packages in the case of chicken nuggets) is coupled with photos captured of a certain spot (e.g., when packaging or labeling) to allow for assessing productivity or the level of defects, offering a complete root-cause analysis.

IV. EXPERIMENTATION

To demonstrate the applicability and effectiveness of the proposed framework, we will use the chicken nuggets production process of the PARG factory described in the previous section. The target here is twofold: First, to demonstrate how the proposed approach was used in practice for the PARG case-study and highlight some interesting findings. Second, to make a short assessment of different DL structures, including the proposed one, according to specific metrics and present the results that show the superiority of this approach.

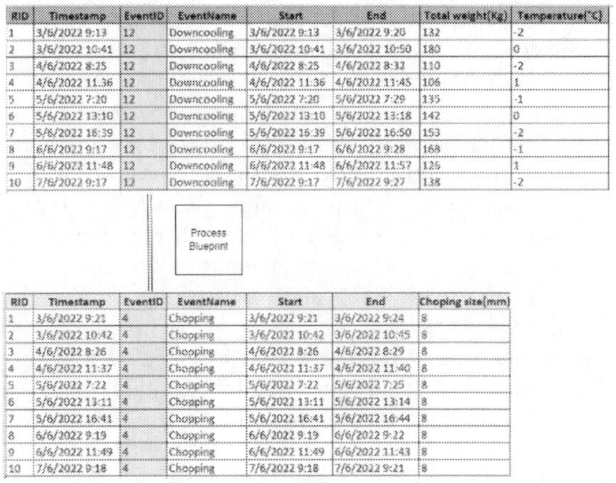

RID	Timestamp	EventID	EventName	Start	End	Total weight(Kg)	Temperature(°C)
1	3/6/2022 9:13	12	Downcooling	3/6/2022 9:13	3/6/2022 9:20	132	-2
2	3/6/2022 10:41	12	Downcooling	3/6/2022 10:41	3/6/2022 10:50	180	0
3	4/6/2022 8:25	12	Downcooling	4/6/2022 8:25	4/6/2022 8:32	110	-2
4	4/6/2022 11.36	12	Downcooling	4/6/2022 11:36	4/6/2022 11:45	106	1
5	5/6/2022 7:20	12	Downcooling	5/6/2022 7:20	5/6/2022 7:29	135	-1
6	5/6/2022 13:10	12	Downcooling	5/6/2022 13:10	5/6/2022 13:18	142	0
7	5/6/2022 16:39	12	Downcooling	5/6/2022 16:39	5/6/2022 16:50	153	-2
8	6/6/2022 9:17	12	Downcooling	6/6/2022 9:17	6/6/2022 9:28	168	-1
9	6/6/2022 11:48	12	Downcooling	6/6/2022 11:48	6/6/2022 11:57	126	1
10	7/6/2022 9:17	12	Downcooling	7/6/2022 9:17	7/6/2022 9:27	138	-2

RID	Timestamp	EventID	EventName	Start	End	Choping size(mm)
1	3/6/2022 9:21	4	Chopping	3/6/2022 9:21	3/6/2022 9:24	8
2	3/6/2022 10:42	4	Chopping	3/6/2022 10:42	3/6/2022 10:45	8
3	4/6/2022 8:26	4	Chopping	4/6/2022 8:26	4/6/2022 8:29	8
4	4/6/2022 11:37	4	Chopping	4/6/2022 11:37	4/6/2022 11:40	8
5	5/6/2022 7:22	4	Chopping	5/6/2022 7:22	5/6/2022 7:25	8
6	5/6/2022 13:11	4	Chopping	5/6/2022 13:11	5/6/2022 13:14	8
7	5/6/2022 16:41	4	Chopping	5/6/2022 16:41	5/6/2022 16:44	8
8	6/6/2022 9:19	4	Chopping	6/6/2022 9:19	6/6/2022 9:22	8
9	6/6/2022 11:49	4	Chopping	6/6/2022 11:49	6/6/2022 11:43	8
10	7/6/2022 9:18	4	Chopping	7/6/2022 9:18	7/6/2022 9:21	8

Figure 5. Indicative data for PARG's chicken nuggets production process

Figure 5 presents an excerpt of the data produced by the Flaken and Mincing machines at PARG factory during the manufacturing process presented in Figure 4. This data is stored in the structured data pond of Figure 1. More specifically, each dataset produced by the two different machines is stored using a different puddle within the data pond. During this process other formats of data is generated as well, such as video and images (omitted due to size limitations) and, since these constitute unstructured and XML-based data (semi-structured), data is stored in the respective pond and distinct puddles, respectively.

As presented in the previous sections, according to the process blueprint describing process with ID100, the execution of events is in sequence 12, 4, 7, 5, 2, 3, and 9. In order to retrieve the data for this specific process, the following SPARQL query should be executed:

```
SELECT ? DLsources
  WHERE {
      ? process ID <has ID> 100 }
```

Running this query on the DL blueprint triggers first the retrieval of information on event execution from the process blueprint. Using this information as the basis, all relevant data for this process is retrieved and mapped depending on the order in which events are executed by machines. As shown in Figure 1, the process blueprint is connected with the event blueprint, which provides the expected execution time of each event by a machine, as well as the type of machine that executes this event, while the machine blueprint describes the events that can be executed by each machine. This information was combined with the data retrieved from the appropriate puddles residing in the specific pond of the DL and were made ready for use in the process mining activities that followed, the latter yielding some interesting results. For confidentiality purposes, we report here two of them very abstractly.

A few delays were encountered in some of the steps, which were revealed during this analysis by comparing the expected with the actual execution time. This led to further investigating these delays through the start and end times of the relevant events. It was noticed that optimization in the way the sequence of the execution of tasks (events) by the machines had ample room for improvement in terms of timing: There were delays in commencing operation from a machine after the previous task was finished. This was partly attributed to roles and resources within the production line, as various tasks were shared amongst employees and, in some cases, multitasking was an issue. All the above were communicated to the senior management of PARG who acknowledged their value for future actions.

The analysis was also supported by unstructured data (images of the production line) which was acknowledged by all parties involved (analysts, managers, workers) to have played a crucial role in identifying bottlenecks. Therefore, as the proposed framework allows for utilizing both unstructured and semi-structured data for process mining, it was considered a significant benefit.

The second experimental aim is to investigate in general the readiness of the manufacturing data residing in a DL to participate in process mining tasks, when the DL has the following structure:

- without the proposed metadata enrichment mechanism
- with the metadata mechanism without a pond architecture
- with metadata mechanism and a pond architecture
- with metadata mechanism, and with pond and puddle architecture (the proposal of this paper)

The following characteristics/metrics are utilized for each DL structure:

- Granularity
- Ease of storing/retrieval
- Process mining readiness
- Expandability

We define *Granularity* [14] as the ability to refine the type of information that needs to be retrieved for a specific factory process. This ability is expressed by the number of fine-grained levels the DL mechanism supports for defining the information sought. *Ease of storing/retrieval* refers to the ability of the DL structure to store or retrieve data in the DL in a simple and easy way. It is assumed here that the retrieval action is efficient enough to return the desired parts of the information sought. This characteristic is reflected on the number of steps that need to be executed for the process of storing and retrieving data items to be completed. Moreover, we define *Expandability* as the ability to expand the structure of the DL and the metadata mechanism with further functional characteristics or other supporting techniques and approaches, such as visual querying and blockchain. Obviously, the more open the mechanism for expansion, the better. Finally, *Process mining readiness* is reflected in the number of steps that need to be executed after the query is executed for the data to be fed to process mining activities. The aforementioned characteristics are evaluated using a Likert linguistic scale, including the values Low, Medium, and High. Table 1 provides a definition of Low, Medium and High for each characteristic introduced.

TABLE I. DEFINITION OF LOW, MEDIUM, AND HIGH OF EACH ASSESMENT CHARACTERISTIC

Characteristic	**Low**	**Medium**	**High**
Granularity	1 level	2 levels	3 or more levels
Ease of storing /retrieval	5 or more actions	3-4 actions	2 actions maximum
Expandability	No or limited	Normal	Unlimited
Process mining readiness	4 – 5 actions	2 – 3 actions	1 action maximum

As an example, let us now assume that the PARG factory's DL owner wants to retrieve all data present in the DL relevant to the process of chicken nuggets production presented in the previous section so as to feed it to the process mining stages of discovery, conformance checking, and model enhancement. Note that the PARG factory consists of hundreds of production processes. In order to retrieve the data, the following SPARQL query should be formed and executed:

SELECT ? Dlsources
WHERE { process ID <has ID> 20 }

TABLE 2. EVALUATION AND COMPARISON OF DL STRUCTURES

Approach	Granu-larity	Ease of storing /retriev.	Process mining readin.	Expanda-bility
Without metadata mechanism	Low	Low	Low	Low
With metadata mechanism without pond architecture	Medium	Medium	Low	Unlimited
With metadata mechanism with pond architecture	High	High	Medium	Unlimited
With metadata mechanism with pond and puddle architecture	High	High	High	Unlimited

The metadata mechanism with pond architecture (third from top in Table 2) may be considered as the benchmark of our comparison [14]. It presents High *Granularity*, High *Ease of storing/retrieval* using the stable and dynamic data source blueprint descriptions, with a Medium *Process Mining Readiness*, and High *Expandability*. These values are attributed as follows: High *Granularity* is achieved using keywords that essentially describe the sources and the blueprint values. This enables the user to define details at the level of the properties offered, enabling the retrieval of data based on fine-grained query-like information. The High *Ease of storing/retrieval* is achieved by the DL metadata history which stores the blueprint description of the DL as each time data sources are pushed into it. This helps the mechanism to place the sources to a specific pond according to the structure of the data involved (structured, semi-structured and unstructured). This source distribution in the DL also facilitates simple and *Easy Storing and Retrieval* of the information stored. In addition, the implementation of this DL architecture is based on the Hadoop ecosystem and hence this provides High *Expandability*. Finally, the metadata mechanism provides Medium Level of *Process Mining Readiness* due to the lack of defining dependencies and describing the process, events and machines in the production line.

It is logical that, as we move to the upper structural forms of Table 2, the evaluation of the selected characteristics gets worse: Assuming that PARG's DL has an architecture without metadata, a SPARQL query could not be executed at all. In addition, with this structure, all the data is pushed to the DL without any management policy and as a result the DL is highly likely to transform into a Data Swamp, while at the same time it would take quite a few actions (more than five) to retrieve data because all datasets will need to be visited and checked if they are related to the specific process. *Process Mining Readiness* is Low as no clear separation of events, type, dependencies etc., exists, let alone the fact that data needs to be timestamped. Finally, in the absence of a management mechanism, *Expandability* may be characterized as Low. Taking into consideration now that the PARG DL has a structure with the proposed metadata enrichment mechanism but without a pond architecture, the data is pushed to the DL following a metadata policy. As a result, this DL can be characterized with Medium *Granularity* due to the fact that the metadata mechanism provides 2 levels of Granularity, which are provided by the metadata mechanism and the pond the data is stored in, with Low to Medium *Ease of storing/retrieval* as the data is pushed to the DL with its metadata. Therefore, in order to retrieve it, one needs to access and process the metadata to check if a certain piece of information is related to the specific process examined. This DL structure could be characterized also with Low *Process Mining Readiness* because, after executing a query, the data is not separated according to its type and an additional task to separate and timestamp it should be performed, along with proper definition of any dependencies. Finally, it can be characterized with *Unlimited Expandability* as the metadata mechanism allows for practically any extension.

The proposed metadata mechanism with pond and puddle architecture can be characterized similarly to the previous benchmark (3rd row in Table 2), but with High *Process Mining Readiness*. By extending the mechanism reported in [14] and introducing the process blueprint that captures the specific events triggered while a process is executed, the event blueprint that captures the type of machines that participate in a process and the machines blueprint that captures the events that specific machines can trigger, results in a data environment ready to perform process mining readiness. Furthermore, by extending data ponds with data puddles where each puddle stores data from each machine on PARG factory, enables a query to provide the requested data of a specific process to be separated according to its format types.

Table 2 sums up all the information of the short comparison between the DL structures made in this section. It is evident that the proposed mechanism outperforms all alternatives in terms of the *Process mining readiness* characteristic as a result of the extensions made in the blueprints.

V. CONCLUSIONS

This paper proposed a novel smart manufacturing DL framework for process mining utilizing a semantic enrichment mechanism via metadata blueprints [14]. The framework utilizes the 5Vs Big Data characteristics and blueprint ontologies to assist data processing (storing and retrieval) in DLs, the latter being organized with a pond architecture that hosts different types of data, structured, semi-structured and unstructured, enhanced by data puddles. The puddles consist of data produced by machines in the production line and essentially prepare the data in the ponds for process mining activities.

The applicability of the framework was demonstrated and assessed through a real-world case-study on a local poultry meat production factory. The process of producing chicken nuggets was modeled with relevant data captured, stored and processed. Process mining revealed delays and bottlenecks in the sequencing of the execution of events by machines and personnel which may be avoided by optimizing task sharing amongst roles. The senior management of the factory greatly appreciated the support of the proposed approach for decision support with respect to production control.

Furthermore, a short comparison with different DL structures was performed revealing the high potential of the proposed approach as it offers a more complete characterization of the data sources and covers a set of key features reported in literature. Especially, the inclusion of data paddles can greatly enhance the management of manufacturing data that can later participate in process mining activities, such as discovery, conformance checking, and model enhancement utilizing all available data types.

Future research steps will include the full implementation of the proposed mechanism in cooperation with the industrial partner using the metadata model described in this work and extending its application in the context of structured, semi-structured and unstructured data present in the processes of the factory. This will allow the evaluation of the proposed framework in more detail and performing further process mining steps utilizing real-world manufacturing data. As a result, investigation of how to improve privacy, security, and data governance in DLs will be made feasible, also by extending it to include blockchain technology characteristics and smart contracts.

ACKNOWLEDGMENT

This paper is part of the outcomes of the Coordination and Support Actions (CSA) Twinning project DESTINI. This project has received funding from the European Union's Horizon 2020 research and innovation program under grant agreement No.945357.

REFERENCES

[1] F. Tao, Q. Qi, A. Liu, and A. Kusiak, "Data-driven smart manufacturing," J. Manuf. Syst., vol. 48, pp. 157–169, 2018.J. Clerk Maxwell, A Treatise on Electricity and Magnetism, 3rd ed., vol. 2. Oxford: Clarendon, pp. 68–73, 1892.

[2] P. Zheng et al., "Smart manufacturing systems for Industry 4.0: Conceptual framework, scenarios, and future perspectives," Front. Mech. Eng., vol. 13, no. 2, pp. 137–150, 2018. L. Wang, M. Törngren, and M. Onori, "Current status and advancement of cyber-physical systems in manufacturing," J. Manuf. Syst., vol. 37, pp. 517–527, 2015.

[3] J. Wan et al., "Software-Defined Industrial Internet of Things in the Context of Industry 4.0," IEEE Sens. J., vol. 16, no. 20, pp. 7373–7380, 2016.D. Kornack and P. Rakic, "Cell Proliferation without Neurogenesis in Adult Primate Neocortex," Science, vol. 294, pp. 2127-2130, Dec. 2001, doi:10.1126/science.1065467.

[4] M. Farid, A. Roatiş, I. F. Ilyas, H. F. Hoffmann, and X. Chu, "CLAMS: Bringing quality to data lakes," Proc. ACM SIGMOD Int. Conf. Manag. Data, vol. 26-June-20, pp. 2089–2092, 2016.

[5] S. Erol, A. Jäger, P. Hold, K. Ott, and W. Sihn, "Tangible Industry 4.0: A Scenario-Based Approach to Learning for the Future of Production," Procedia CIRP, vol. 54, pp. 13–18, 2016.

[6] G. Shao, S. J. Shin, and S. Jain, "Data analytics using simulation for smart manufacturing," Proc. - Winter Simul. Conf., vol. 2015-Janua, no. Smlc 2012, pp. 2192–2203, 2015.

[7] N. Petersen, M. Galkin, C. Lange, S. Lohmann, and S. Auer, "Monitoring and automating factories using semantic models," Lect. Notes Comput. Sci. (including Subser. Lect. Notes Artif. Intell. Lect. Notes Bioinformatics), vol. 10055 LNCS, pp. 315–330, 2016.

[8] T. Wuest, D. Weimer, C. Irgens, and K. D. Thoben, "Machine learning in manufacturing: Advantages, challenges, and applications," Prod. Manuf. Res., vol. 4, no. 1, pp. 23–45, 2016.

[9] M. J. Cafarella, A. Halevy, and N. Khoussainova, "Data integration for the relational web," Proc. VLDB Endow., vol. 2, no. 1, pp. 1090–1101, 2009.

[10] J. Fan, M. Lu, B. C. Ooi, W. C. Tan, and M. Zhang, "A hybrid machine-crowdsourcing system for matching web tables," Proc. - Int. Conf. Data Eng., pp. 976–987, 2014.

[11] P. N. Sawadogo, É. Scholly, C. Favre, É. Ferey, S. Loudcher, and J. Darmont, "Metadata Systems for Data Lakes: Models and Features," in Communications in Computer and Information Science, 2019, vol. 1064, pp. 440–451.

[12] W. M. P. van der Aalst et al., "Business process mining: An industrial application," Inf. Syst., vol. 32, no. 5, pp. 713–732, 2007.

[13] W. M. P. Van Der Aalst and S. Dustdar, "Process mining put into context," IEEE Internet Comput., vol. 16, no. 1, pp. 82–86, 2012.

[14] M. Pingos and A. Andreou, "A Data Lake Metadata Enrichment Mechanism via Semantic Blueprints," In Proceedings of the 17th International Conference on Evaluation of Novel Approaches to Software Engineering - ENASE, ISBN 978-989-758-568-5; ISSN 2184-4895, pages 186-196. DOI: 10.5220/0011080400003176, 2022.

[15] P. Sawadogo and J. Darmont, "On data lake architectures and metadata management," J. Intell. Inf. Syst., vol. 56, no. 1, pp. 97–120, 2021.

[16] M. P. Papazoglou and A. Elgammal, "The manufacturing blueprint environment: Bringing intelligence into manufacturing," 2017 Int. Conf. Eng. Technol. Innov. Eng. Technol. Innov. Manag. Beyond 2020 New Challenges, New Approaches, ICE/ITMC 2017 - Proc., vol. 2018-Janua, pp. 750–759, 2018.

[17] "Home - Paradisiotis Group," Paradisiotis Group (PARG). [Online]. Available: https://paradisiotis.com/. [Accessed: 13-Jul-2022].

VR-Git: Git Repository Visualization and Immersion in Virtual Reality

Roy Oberhauser[0000-0002-7606-8226]
Computer Science Dept.
Aalen University
Aalen, Germany
e-mail: roy.oberhauser@hs-aalen.de

Abstract—**The increasing demand for software functionality necessitates an increasing amount of program source code that is retained and managed in version control systems, such as Git. As the number, size, and complexity of Git repositories increases, so does the number of collaborating developers, maintainers, and other stakeholders over a repository's lifetime. In particular, visual limitations of Git tooling hampers repository comprehension, analysis, and collaboration across one or multiple repositories with a larger stakeholder spectrum. This paper contributes VR-Git, a Virtual Reality (VR) solution concept for visualizing and interacting with Git repositories in VR. Our prototype realization shows its feasibility, and our evaluation results based on a case study show its support for repository comprehension, analysis, and collaboration via branch, commit, and multi-repository scenarios.**

Keywords – Git; virtual reality; visualization; version control systems; software configuration management.

I. INTRODUCTION

In this digitalization era, the global demand for software functionality is increasing across all areas of society, and with it there is a correlating necessity for storing and managing the large number of underlying program source code files that represent the instructions inherent in software. Program source code is typically stored and managed in repositories within version control systems, currently the most popular being Git. Since these repositories are often shared, various cloud-based service providers offer Git functionality, including GitHub, BitBucket, and GitLab. GitHub reports over 305m repositories [1] with over 91m users [2]. Even within a single company, the source code portfolio can become very large, as exemplified with the over 2bn Lines Of Code (LOC) accessed by 25k developers at Google [3]. Over 25m professional software developers worldwide [4] continue to add source code to private and public repositories.

To gain insights into these code repositories, various command-line, visual tools, and web interfaces are provided. Yet, repository analysis can be challenging due to the potentially large number of files involved, and the added complexity of branches, commits, and users involved over the history of a repository. Furthermore, the analysis can be hampered by the limited visual space available for analysis. It can be especially difficult for those stakeholders unfamiliar with a repository, or for collaborating with stakeholders who may not be developers but have a legitimate interest in the code development. Possible scenarios include someone transferred to the development team (ramp-up), joining an open-source code project, quality assurance activities, forensic or intellectual property analysis, maintenance activities, defect or resolution tracking, repository fork analysis, etc.

Virtual Reality (VR) is a mediated visual environment which is created and then experienced as telepresence by the perceiver. VR provides an unlimited immersive space for visualizing and analyzing models and their interrelationships simultaneously in a 3D spatial structure viewable from different perspectives. As repository models grow in size and complexity, an immersive digital environment provides additional visualization capabilities to comprehend and analyze code repositories and include and collaborate with a larger spectrum of stakeholders.

As to our prior work with VR for software engineering, VR-UML [5] provides VR-based visualization of the Unified Modeling Language (UML) and VR-SysML [6] for Systems Modeling Language (SysML) diagrams. This paper contributes VR-Git, a solution concept for visualizing and interacting with Git repositories in VR. Our prototype realization shows its feasibility, and a case-based evaluation provides insights into its capabilities for repository comprehension, analysis and collaboration.

The remainder of this paper is structured as follows: Section 2 discusses related work. In Section 3, the solution concept is described. Section 4 provides details about the realization. The evaluation is described in Section 5 and is followed by a conclusion.

II. RELATED WORK

With regard to VR-based Git visualization, Bjørklund [7] used a directed acyclic graph visualization in VR using the Unreal Engine, with a backend using NodeJS, Mongoose, and ExpressJS, with SQLite used to store data. GitHub Skyline [8] provides a VR Ready 3D contribution graph as an animated skyline that can be annotated.

For non-VR based Git visualization, RepoVis [9] provides a comprehensive visual overview and search facilities using a 2D JavaScript-based web application and Ruby-based backend with a CouchDB. Githru [10] utilizes graph reconstruction, clustering, and context-preserving squash merge to abstract a large-scale commit graph, providing an interactive summary view of the development history. VisGi [11] utilizes tagging to aggregate commits for a coarse group graph, and Sunburst Tree Layout diagrams to visualize group contents. It is interesting to note that the paper states "showing all groups at once overloads the available display space, making any two-dimensional visualization cluttered and uninformative. The use of an interactive model is important for clean and focused visualizations." UrbanIt [12] utilizes an iPad to support mobile Git visualization aspects, such as an evolution view. Besides the web-based visualization interfaces of Git cloud providers, various desktop Git tools, such as Sourcetree and Gitkracken, provide typical 2D branch visualizations.

In contrast, VR-Git maps familiar 2D visual Git constructs and commit content to VR to make its usage relatively intuitive without training. In contrast to other approaches that apply clustering, aggregating, merging, metrics, or data analytics, our concept preserves the chronological sequence of commits and retains their content details in support of practical analysis for Software Engineering (SE) tasks. To reduce visual clutter, detailed informational aspects of an element of interest can be obtained via the VR-Tablet. By not storing the data in a database, it avoids issues regarding storage format, transformation, and synchronization.

III. Solution Concept

Our VR-Git solution concept is shown relative to our other VR solutions in Figure 1. VR-Git is based on our generalized VR Modeling Framework (VR-MF) (detailed in [13]). VR-MF provides a VR-based domain-independent hypermodeling framework addressing four aspects requiring special attention when modeling in VR: visualization, navigation, interaction, and data retrieval. Our VR-SE area includes VR-Git and the aforementioned VR-UML [5] and VR-SysML [6]. Since Enterprise Architecture (EA) can encompass SE models and development and be applicable for collaboration in VR. Our other VR modeling solutions in the EA area include: VR-EA [13] for visualizing EA ArchiMate models; VR-ProcessMine [14] for process mining and analysis; and VR-BPMN [15] for Business Process Modeling Notation (BPMN) models. VR-EAT [16] integrates the EA Tool (EAT) Atlas to provide dynamically-generated EA diagrams, while VR-EA+TCK [17] integrates Knowledge Management Systems (KMS) and/or Enterprise Content Management Systems (ECMS).

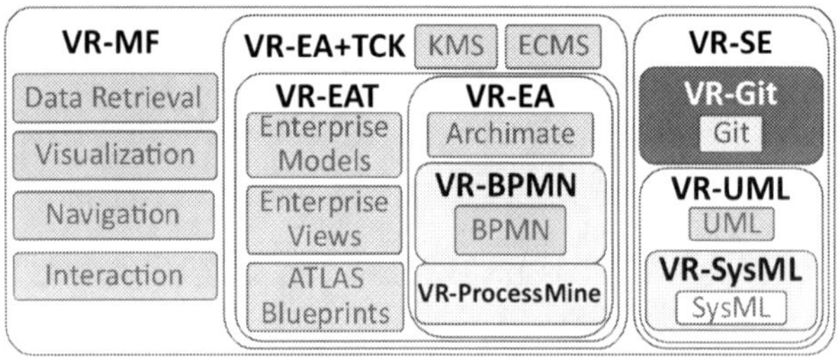

Figure 1. Conceptual map of our various VR solution concepts.

In support of our view that an immersive VR experience can be beneficial for a software analysis, Müller et al. [18] compared VR vs. 2D for a software analysis task, finding that VR does not significantly decrease comprehension and analysis time nor significantly improve correctness (although fewer errors were made). While interaction time was less efficient, VR improved the user experience, was more motivating, less demanding, more inventive/innovative, and more clearly structured.

A. Visualization in VR

A hyperplane is used to intuitively represent and group the commits related to a repository. Each commit is then represented by a vertical *commit plane*. These commit planes are then sequenced chronologically on the hyperplane as a set of planes. Since VR space is unlimited, we can thus convey the sequence of all commits in the repository. Each 2D plane then represents each file involved in that commit as a tile. These are then colored to be able to quickly determine what occurred. Green indicates a file was added, red a file removed, and blue that a file was modified. On the left side of the hyperplane, a transparent *branch plane* (branch perspective) perpendicular to the hyperplane and the commit planes depicts branches as an acyclic colored graph to indicate which branch is involved with a commit. This allows the user to travel down that side to follow a branch, see to which branch any commit is related, and to readily detect merges. In accordance, the commit planes are also slightly offset in height since they dock to a branch, thus "deeper" or "higher" commits indicate how close or far they were relatively from the main branch. Via the anchor, commit planes can be manually collapsed (hidden), expanded, or moved to, for example, compare one commit with another side-by-side. In order to view the contents of a file, when a file tile is selected, a *content plane* (i.e., code view) extends above the commit plane to display the file contents.

B. Navigation in VR

One navigation challenge arising from the immersion VR offers is supporting intuitive spatial navigation while reducing potential VR sickness symptoms. Thus, we incorporate two navigation modes in our solution concept: the default uses gliding controls for fly-through VR, while teleporting instantly places the camera at a selected position either via the VR controls or by selection of a commit in our VR-Tablet. While teleporting is potentially disconcerting, it may reduce the likelihood of VR sickness induced by fly-through for those prone to it.

C. Interaction in VR

As VR interaction has not yet become standardized, in our concept we support user-element interaction primarily through VR controllers and a *VR-Tablet*. The VR-Tablet is used to provide detailed context-specific element information based on VR object selection, menu, scrolling, field inputs, and other inputs. It includes a *virtual keyboard* for text entry via laser pointer key selection. As another VR interaction element, we provide the aforementioned corner *anchor sphere* affordance, that supports moving, collapsing / hiding, or expanding / displaying hyperplanes or commit planes.

IV. Realization

The logical architecture for our VR-Git prototype realization is shown in Figure 2. Basic visualization, navigation, and interaction functionality in our VR prototype is implemented with Unity 2020.3 and the OpenVR XR

Plugin 1.1.4, shown in the Unity block (top left, blue). Scripts utilize Libgit2Sharp [19] to access the Git commit history of one or more repositories from within Unity. To avoid redundancy, only realization aspects not explicitly mentioned in the evaluation are described in this section.

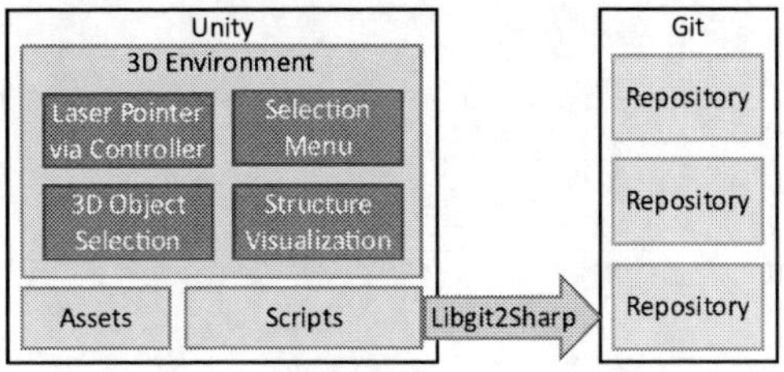

Figure 2. VR-Git logical architecture.

An anchor (ball) is placed on one corner of a hyperplane and is an affordance in order to move or expand/collapse an entire hyperplane (see Figure 3). The anchors are also placed at the left bottom corner of all commit planes and colored and aligned with the branch with which they are associated.

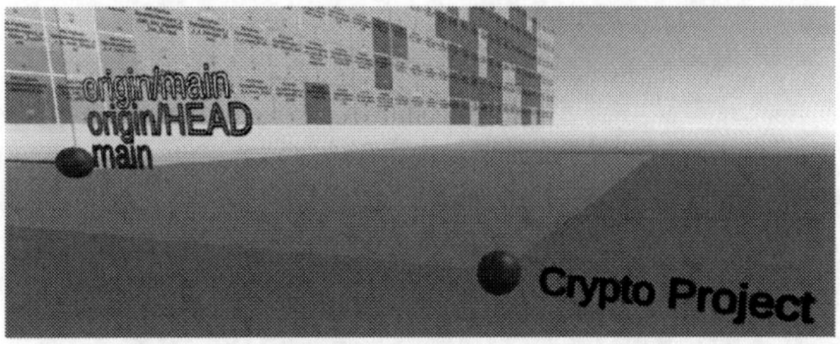

Figure 3. Hyperplane anchor for a repository.

Projects can be selected via the VR-Tablet and provide a teleporting capability to the hyperplane, as shown in Figure 4.

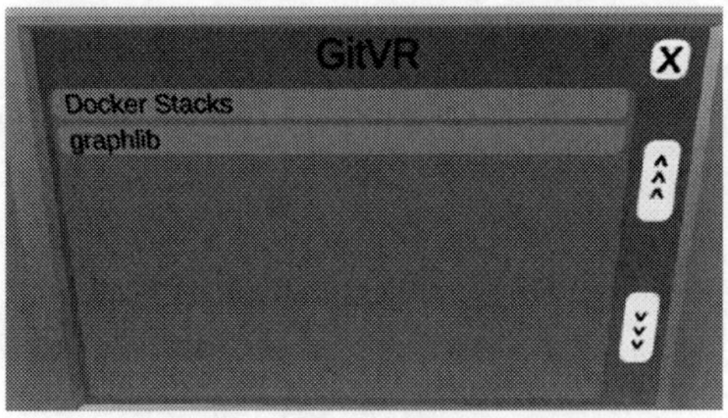

Figure 4. Project list in VR-Tablet.

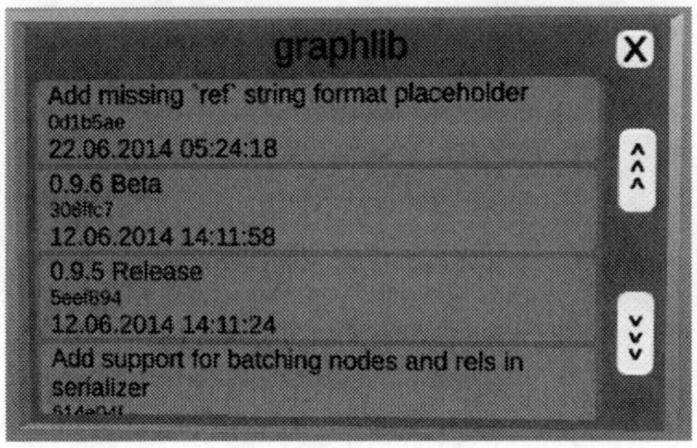

Figure 5. Git commit messages in VR-Tablet.

Figure 5 shows a list of Git commit messages including their commit ID (Secure Hash Algorithm 1 (SHA-1)) and the date and timestamp in the VR-Tablet. This can also be used to teleport to a specific commit plane.

V. EVALUATION

The evaluation of our solution concept is based on the design science method and principles [20], in particular, a viable artifact, problem relevance, and design evaluation (utility, quality, efficacy). We use a case study based on common Git repository comprehension and analysis scenarios: branch analysis, commit analysis, and multi-repository analysis. Various Git repositories were used to evaluate the prototype.

A. Branch Analysis Scenario

To support branch analysis, at the front of the hyperplane oriented to the left side, an invisible branch graph plane is rendered perpendicular to the hyperplane and a color-coded list of all the branches can be seen next to the first commit plane (see Figure 6). These colored labels can be used for orientation. By selecting a branch label, the user can be teleported to the first commit of that branch. The branches could also be referenced in the VR-Tablet in case one forgets, and can be used for teleporting as well. We chose to repeat the branch labels throughout the graph to reduce the textual visual clutter.

Figure 6. VR-Git branch overview.

The branch perspective of the hyperplane (its left side) shows a contiguous color-coded graph of the branches as shown in Figure 7, with commit plane heights offset based on the branch to which they are associated. This can provide a quick visual cue as to how relatively close or far the commit is from the main branch. Figure 8 shows a merge of two branches.

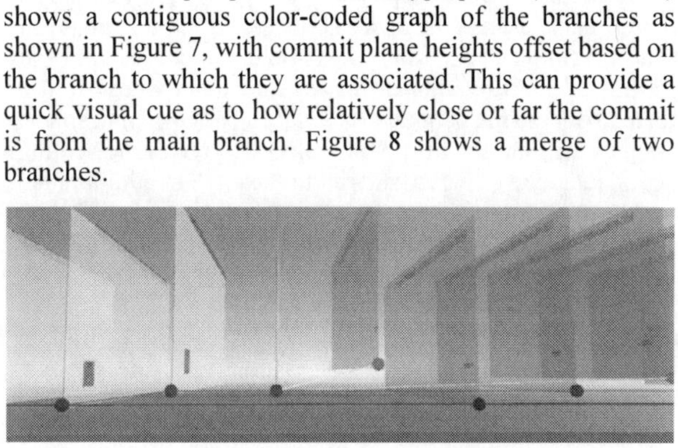

Figure 7. VR-Git branch tree graph.

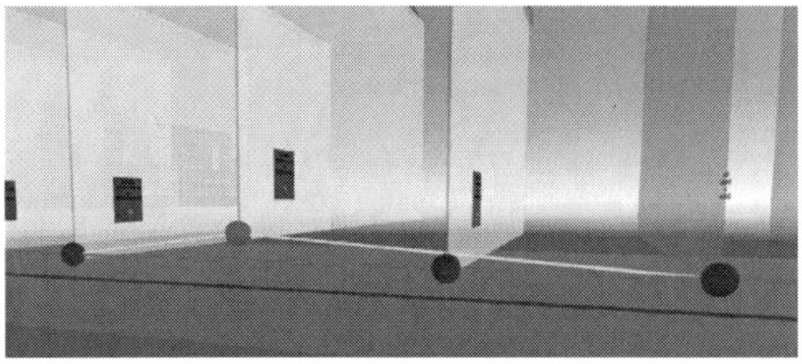

Figure 8. Branch merge.

As a reference, in Figure 9 we see the terminal output in Git. In comparison, VR-Git provides equivalent branch information, providing the labels and also using different branch colors and spatial offsetting to indicate which branch a commit relates to. To reduce visual clutter, commit messages are not shown on the planes, but rather the VR-Tablet (Figure 5) includes the commit messages, timestamp, and commit ID (SHA). Note that the commit ID is also shown at the top of each commit plane to both differentiate and identify them.

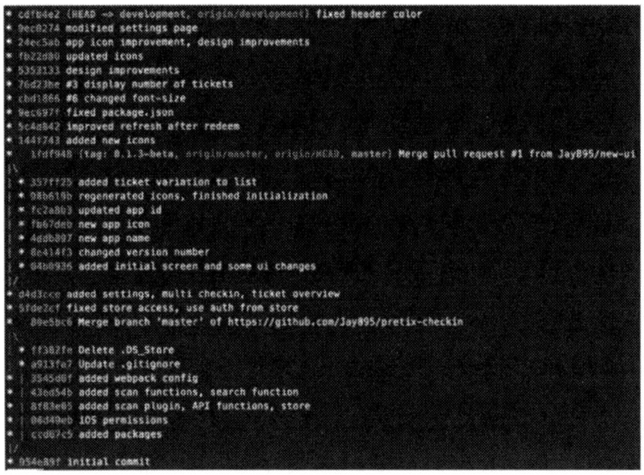

Figure 9. Example Git log terminal output

B. Commit Analysis Scenario

Git commits are a snapshot of a repository. In a typical commit analysis, a stakeholder is interested in what changed with a commit, i.e., what files were added, deleted, or modified. To readily indicate this, as shown in Figure 10, tiles labeled with the file pathname are placed on the commit plane to represent changed files, with colors of green representing files added, blue changed, and red for deleted. In addition, the number of lines of text are shown at the bottom or a tile, with positive numbers in green indicating the number of lines added, and negative red values below it for the lines removed.

Figure 11 shows how commits that affect a large number of files can be readily determined. This can be helpful in analysis to quickly hone in on commit with the greatest impacts.

Figure 12 depicts how VR can visually scale with commits affecting a very large number of files. As we see, there is no issue displaying the data, and VR navigation and the VR-Tablet can be used to analyze the commit further.

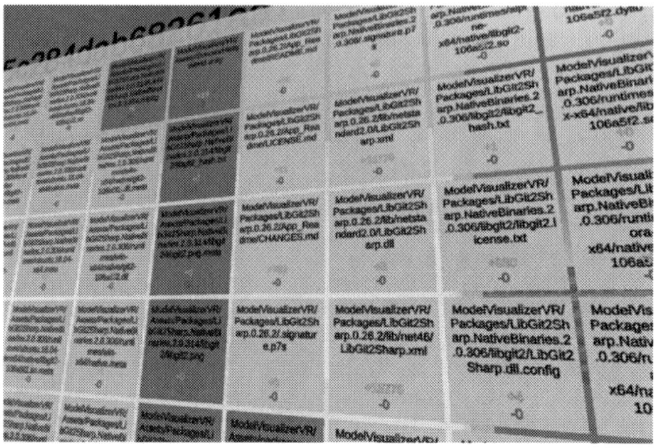

Figure 10. Commit files added (green), changed (blue), deleted (red); number of lines affected indicated in each tile at the bottom.

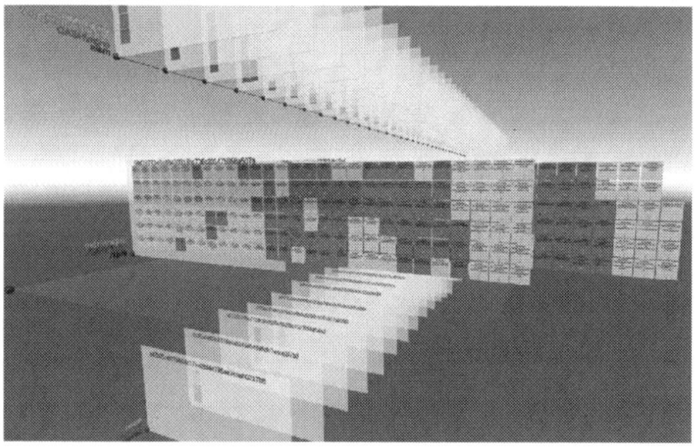

Figure 11. VR-Git showing commits affecting a large number of files.

Figure 12. VR-Git commit visual scaling example for a very large file set.

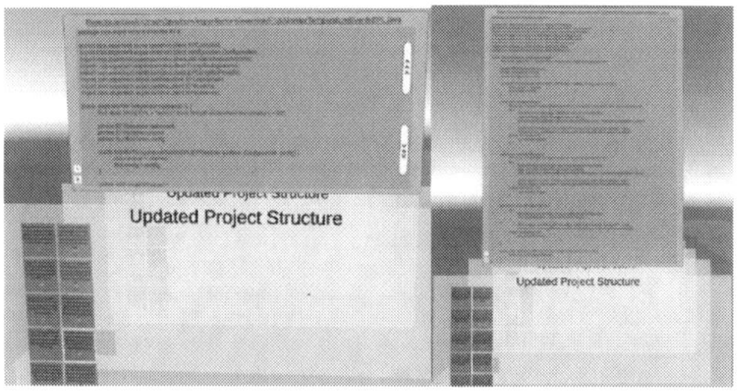

Figure 13. Code View: collapsed and scrollable (left) and expanded (right).

By selecting a specific tile (file), a file *contents plane* (i.e., code view), shown in Figure 13, pops up above the plane displaying the contents of that file for that commit. Since file contents can be too lengthy and wide for practical depiction in our VR-Tablet, we chose to display the plane above the commit plane, providing a clear association. The contents are initially scrollable, and can be expanded with the plus icon to show the entire file contents if desired. Since VR is not limited, one can navigate by moving the VR camera to any part of the code plane to see the code there.

C. Multi-Repository Analysis Scenario

To support multiple repository analysis, hyperplanes are used to represent each separate repository. Via the anchors, these can be placed where appropriate for the user. Figure 14 shows how branch and commit comparisons can be made from the branch perspective, with visual cues being offered by the tiles. Here, one can see how the branches developed with their commits.

On the other hand, Figure 15 shows a larger visual depiction of three repositories and readily indicates which ones involved more commits, and via the extended commit planes where large commits were involved.

D. Discussion

In summary, the evaluation showed that these primary comprehension and analysis scenarios were supported by the solution concept and our prototype. Branch comprehension and analysis were supported via the branch plane. Commit comprehension and analysis were supported via the commit planes, which readily showed the number of files involved in a commit (based on the number of tiles) and via their color if they were added, removed, or changed. The metrics in each tile show the number of lines affected. Multi-repository analysis showed the potential of VR to display and compare multiple repositories, where the limitless space can be used to readily focus and hone-in on the areas of interest or differences between repositories. This type of visual, immersive multi-repository analysis could support fork analysis, intellectual property analysis and tracking, forensic analysis, etc.

VI. Conclusion

VR-Git contributes an immersive software repository experience for visually depicting and navigating repositories in VR. It provides a convenient way for stakeholders who may not be developers yet have a legitimate interest in the code development to collaborate. This can further the onboarding of maintenance or quality assurance personnel. The solution concept was described and a VR prototype demonstrated its feasibility. Based on our VR hyperplane principle, repositories are enhanced with 3D depth and color. Interaction is supported via a virtual tablet and keyboard. The unlimited space in VR facilitates the depiction and visual navigation of large repositories, while relations within and between artifacts, groups, and versions can be analyzed. Furthermore, in VR additional related repositories or models can be visualized and analyzed simultaneously and benefit more complex collaboration and comprehension. The sensory immersion of VR can support task focus during comprehension and increase enjoyment, while limiting the visual distractions that typical 2D display surroundings incur. The solution concept was evaluated with our prototype using a case study based on typical Git comprehension and analysis scenarios: branch analysis, commit analysis, and multi-repository analysis. The results indicate that VR-Git can support these analysis scenarios and thus provide an immersive collaborative environment to involve and include a larger stakeholder spectrum in understanding Git repository development.

Future work includes support for directly invoking and utilizing Git within VR, including further visual constructs, integrating additional informational and tooling capabilities, and conducting a comprehensive empirical study.

Acknowledgment

The authors would like to thank Jason Farkas and Marie Bähre for their assistance with the design, implementation, and evaluation.

References

[1] GitHub repositories [Online]. Available from: https://web.archive.org/web/20220509204719/https://github.com/search 2022.07.25

[2] GitHub users [Online]. Available from: https://web.archive.org/web/20220529205506/https://github.com/search 2022.07.25

[3] C. Metz, "Google Is 2 Billion Lines of Code—And It's All in One Place," 2015. [Online]. Available from: http://www.wired.com/2015/09/ google-2-billion-lines-codeand-one-place/ 2022.07.25

[4] Evans Data Corporation. [Online]. Available from: https://evansdata.com/press/viewRelease.php?pressID=293 2022.07.25

[5] R. Oberhauser, "VR-UML: The unified modeling language in virtual reality – an immersive modeling experience," International Symposium on Business Modeling and Software Design, Springer, Cham, 2021, pp. 40-58.

[6] R. Oberhauser, "VR-SysML: SysML Model Visualization and Immersion in Virtual Reality," International Conference of Modern Systems Engineering Solutions (MODERN SYSTEMS 2022), IARIA, 2022, pp. 59-64.

[7] H. Bjørklund, "Visualisation of Git in Virtual Reality," Master's thesis, NTNU, 2017.

[8] GitHub Skyline [Online]. Available from: https://skyline.github.com 2022.07.25

[9] J. Feiner and K. Andrews, "Repovis: Visual overviews and full-text search in software repositories," In: 2018 IEEE Working Conference on Software Visualization (VISSOFT), IEEE, 2018, pp. 1-11.

[10] Y. Kim et al., "Githru: Visual analytics for understanding software development history through git metadata analysis," IEEE Transactions on Visualization and Computer Graphics, 27(2), IEEE, 2020, pp.656-666.

[11] S. Elsen, "VisGi: Visualizing git branches," In 2013 First IEEE Working Conference on Software Visualization, IEEE, 2013, pp. 1-4.

[12] A. Ciani, R. Minelli, A. Mocci, and M. Lanza, "UrbanIt: Visualizing repositories everywhere," In 2015 IEEE International Conference on Software Maintenance and Evolution (ICSME), IEEE, 2015, pp. 324-326.

[13] R. Oberhauser and C. Pogolski, "VR-EA: Virtual Reality Visualization of Enterprise Architecture Models with ArchiMate and BPMN," In: Shishkov, B. (ed.) BMSD 2019. LNBIP, vol. 356, Springer, Cham, 2019, pp. 170–187.

[14] R. Oberhauser, "VR-ProcessMine: Immersive Process Mining Visualization and Analysis in Virtual Reality," The Fourteenth International Conference on Information, Process, and Knowledge Management (eKNOW 2022), IARIA, 2022, pp. 29-36.

[15] R. Oberhauser, C. Pogolski, and A. Matic, "VR-BPMN: Visualizing BPMN models in Virtual Reality," In: Shishkov, B. (ed.) BMSD 2018. LNBIP, vol. 319, Springer, Cham, 2018, pp. 83–97. https://doi.org/10.1007/978-3-319-94214-8_6

[16] R. Oberhauser, P. Sousa, and F. Michel, "VR-EAT: Visualization of Enterprise Architecture Tool Diagrams in Virtual Reality," In: Shishkov B. (eds) Business Modeling and Software Design. BMSD 2020. LNBIP, vol 391, Springer, Cham, 2020, pp. 221-239. https://doi.org/10.1007/978-3-030-52306-0_14

[17] R. Oberhauser, M. Baehre, and P. Sousa, "VR-EA+TCK: Visualizing Enterprise Architecture, Content, and Knowledge in Virtual Reality," In: Shishkov, B. (eds) Business Modeling and Software Design. BMSD 2022. Lecture Notes in Business Information Processing, vol 453, pp. 122-140. Springer, Cham. https://doi.org/10.1007/978-3-031-11510-3_8

[18] R. Müller, P. Kovacs, J. Schilbach, and D. Zeckzer, "How to master challenges in experimental evaluation of 2D versus 3D software visualizations," In: 2014 IEEE VIS International Workshop on 3Dvis (3Dvis), IEEE, 2014, pp. 33-36

[19] Libgit2Sharp. [Online]. Available from: https://github.com/libgit2/libgit2sharp 2022.07.25

[20] A.R. Hevner, S.T. March, J. Park, and S. Ram, "Design science in information systems research," MIS Quarterly, 28(1), 2004, pp. 75-105

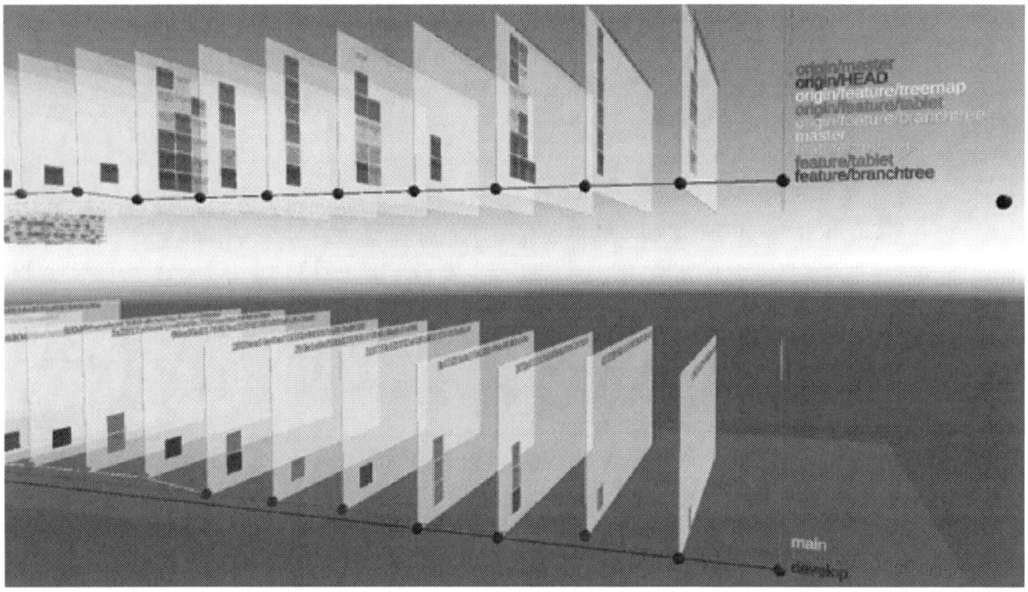

Figure 14. Dual repository comparison with a branch focus.

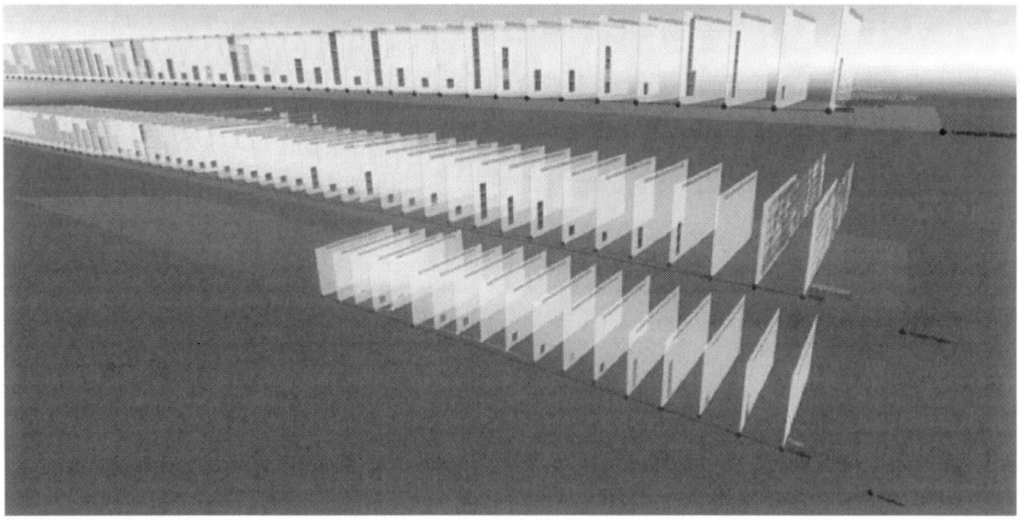

Figure 15. Multiple repositories from a wide perspective.

Offline and Online Active Learning: Lessons in Teaching Software Engineering to Multicultural Groups

Simona Vasilache
Faculty of Engineering, Information and Systems
University of Tsukuba
Tsukuba, Japan
e-mail: simona@cs.tsukuba.ac.jp

Abstract—**The past two years have seen a huge increase in university courses offered online, due to the impact of the Covid-19 pandemic. At the same time, as the active learning approach is one of the most pursued approaches in teaching engineering disciplines, new strategies of implementing it online had to be pursued. Whereas the benefits of active learning have often been highlighted, the question arises whether the (sudden) transition to online teaching can remain successful in its pursuit of active learning, especially in multicultural groups. This short paper will be based on the experience of teaching an undergraduate software engineering course to a multicultural group of students. It will describe the active learning strategies employed during offline classes and will highlight the changes made once the course was suddenly switched to an online format, providing important lessons for software engineering instructors.**

Keywords-software engineering; active learning; culturally-responsive teaching; multicultural students.

I. Introduction

Software engineering has always been considered a discipline necessitating a hands-on approach. The concept of active learning is often applied in teaching this discipline, as a means to impart to students the practicalities of developing a software application. Researchers agree that projects using "active methodologies" help students to "develop deeper knowledge and apply it in a practical way according to a work plan" [1]. A lot has been said about active learning and its benefits in the past few years. During traditional "passive" classes, students listen to experts who impart their knowledge [2]. When active learning is used, students "must do more than just listen: they must read, write, discuss, or be engaged in solving problems" [3], engaging in analysis, synthesis, and evaluation" [3].

The 2020 Covid-19 pandemic forced many academic institutions to move their courses to an online format; this sudden shift, taking place with no preparation, was termed Emergency Remote Teaching (ERT) [9]. As the name suggests, this was different than the well-established online class teaching method, which took years of work and gradual improvements until it reached a well-established teaching format. Its purpose - as a response to crisis - was to provide temporary access to instruction quickly and reliably [9]. Whereas implementing active learning has its own predefined challenges, the sudden move to ERT brought with it its own set of challenges. This short paper will highlight some of these challenges, along with lessons learned in teaching software engineering to a multicultural group of students at a national university in Japan, during an introductory level course. The structure of the paper is as follows: Section II describes the details of the course, whereas Section III shows how active learning was implemented; Section IV provides conclusions and directions for future work.

II. Course Description

A. Basic Course Description

This paper highlights the experiences of teaching an introductory software engineering course at the University of Tsukuba in Japan. The course is offered as an elective for master's students in the computer science department, which covers the majority of the class participants. Every year, however, a number between 2 and 5 students belonging to other departments enroll in this course, as well. Stretching over 10 weeks and awarding two credits upon completion, the course introduces basic principles, methodologies, theories and notations used by software engineers during various phases of software development. The language of instruction is English, and the class participants are a mixture of local Japanese students and international students enrolled in graduate school at the university.

B. Format and Number Changes

This course has been offered since 2016 and its need emerged from the necessity of providing more graduate school courses in English. Figure 1 illustrates the changes in numbers and format, along with a brief overview of the style and type of activities used during classes.

For the first 4 years (until 2019), the course was provided in the classical face-to-face format. It started with 15 students in its first year, followed by 26, 35 and 66 students enrolled in subsequent years, respectively. With the sudden change in online format, or to be more precise, ERT format (due to the Covid-19 pandemic), the number reduced to 35 students in 2020, followed by an increase to 53 students in 2021. At the time of writing this paper, the current 2022 edition of the course is taking place online, with 66 participants. Whereas the previous two years were held in the ERT format, a third year can already be considered beyond ERT.

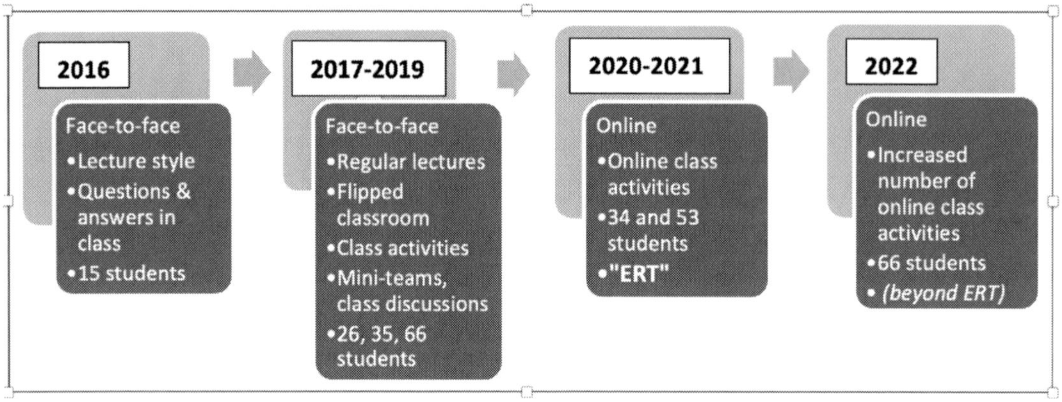

Figure 1. Software engineering course format over the years

III. Implementing Active Learning

A. Active Learning in Face-to-face Settings

In its first four years, the course was held in the classical face-to-face format. In its first edition, 15 students enrolled in the class. Such a low number of participants allowed rather easy interactions between the instructor and the students. However, the novelty of the course, along with the inexperience of the instructor at the time did not facilitate implementing active learning on a large scale. The simple method of constantly asking students to answer various questions in class was, however, implemented. Although it was observed that the international students (making up most of the class, i.e., 9 out of the total of 15 students) were more active in answering the questions and generally interacting with the teacher, efforts were made to involve the Japanese students, as well. It is important to mention that, at the time, lectures in Japanese classroom generally meant passive participation of students: the teacher would stand in front of the classroom and teach while students simply listened. This is still often the case in many Japanese classrooms and the root causes stem form cultural characteristics. There is ample research on this topic (e.g., [4]), but it is essential to emphasize that things are slowly, but steadily improving: more and more (higher and even secondary education) institutions in Japan encourage active participation of students in class and active learning in general.

In the subsequent two years, flipped classroom was attempted (one time each year, experimentally), in order to observe its impact on overall class performance. At the end of the course, a questionnaire was administered and the students were asked about their preference for different class styles: lecture style, discussion style, combination (of lecture and discussions) and flipped. As shown in our previous work [5], the experimental flipped classroom was the least popular with the students. However, it was perceived as both more challenging and more enjoyable ([5]).

At the same time, class activities were introduced, along with the creation of mini-teams which were given tasks to solve during classes. Our previous works ([6] and [7]) show how collaborative learning was used and the lessons learned during this time. In 2019, with 66 students enrolled, a micro-project was introduced, along with an increase in class activities (often more than one within one class). The feedback gathered from the students at the end of the class, as well as through questionnaires administered by the instructor, showed that the course in 2019 was quite successful. As one student stated, *"the lecturer changed the students' silence into discussion and projects"*. This implies that the course was successful in persuading the students more inclined to be silent in class to participate more. Furthermore, some students believe that they learned things that could prove useful not only in software engineering, but in other fields, as well (to quote one other student, *"the principles that I learned in the class changed the way I approach problem solving in general"*).

Overall, as active learning was implemented on an increasingly larger scale, the instructor felt that every year more progress was being made. However, as described in the next section, the course format in 2020 suffered a major change.

B. Online Active Learning

As explained earlier, the Covid-19 pandemic brought with it a sudden transition to online teaching all over the world, at various levels of education. According to Whittle at al., the focus was shifted towards "the method of delivering instruction rather than the learning goals" [8] and this made implementing active learning more challenging. In the software engineering class, in the spring of 2020, the number of enrolled students was almost half that of the previous year (34 students, as opposed to 66 in 2019). In the author's opinion, this was brought upon by the uncertainties regarding the online environment, along with the (too optimistic, as it turned out) expectation of return to a face-to-face format in the near future. (This would have meant that the students could enroll in the class later, once the class returned to the regular format.) Furthermore, the number of students dropping the class in the first couple of weeks was more than 10 (in our university, the students have around two weeks to decide the classes they register for, allowing them some time to observe, before making a decision). As discussed in [7], these students felt that combining the difficulties of sudden online learning with the requirement of being active participants (in a multicultural class) represented a hurdle impossible to overcome.

This was the first year when active learning was attempting during online, ERT-style classes. The classes were held online, synchronously, using MSTeams [10] and Zoom [11]. All class materials were placed on *manaba* (which is the learning management system employed by our university [12]). Several international students were still abroad at the beginning of the course (they could not arrive in time or were not allowed to enter Japan, due to the pandemic restrictions). In order to accommodate the time differences and different locations, the classes were also available on demand: each lecture was recorded, and the recordings were placed on MSStream [13] (with links to them placed in *manaba*). At the end of the course, the instructor administered a questionnaire, to find out the students' opinions and perceptions regarding online classes, active learning and specifics of the course they had just taken (the results were summarized in our previous work in [6]).

The teacher continued to make efforts to involve all students in the learning process. Although conversations online were more difficult to implement than in a classroom, the instructor asked questions and attempted to engage all students in the discussions. Each class started with a "light" topic for discussion, usually a piece of technology-related news, which acted as a warm-up activity.

Various class activities were adapted to an online format. Instead of teams created in a classroom, organized by desks, the instructor created breakout rooms in Zoom; each such room acted as a group, and they held discussions and performed various tasks given in class.

Dealing with a multicultural classroom (with 6 Japanese students and 28 from 4 other countries) meant that cultural differences had a strong impact on discussions. Often the same students responded to questions every time in the main meeting. However, within the breakout rooms, it was easier to involve the less communicative (or less confident) students. The most obvious reason is the number of peers present: breakout rooms consisted of only 5-7 students (as opposed to over 30 in the main meeting), which made it easier to overcome the lack of confidence, particularly with regard to language skills (English was not the mother tongue for most students). Most students agreed that active participation in an online setting may be more difficult, as can be seen from the following two responses.

- *"I feel like when classes are held online, people will be very hesitant to participate unless they are picked on directly."*

- *"I think the online environment keeps many people silent, or because they don't speak and no one can see so they keep silent. Such discussions are not very effective and there will be problems in the allocation of discussion time."*

However, one participant expressed a different opinion, stating that asynchronous work allows different modalities of work:

- *"I think that online classes can result in *more* discussion than face-to-face classes because students can work asynchronously and in different modalities. I don't need to see someone or hear them to discuss, there are other ways of communication."*

Moreover, when questioned about the class activities, about 90% of the students stated that they found them useful (a lot or in a moderate amount), whereas about 80% found them enjoyable (a lot or in a moderate amount).

As mentioned earlier, when it comes to group tasks, the implementation was adapted to the online format. Not all activities could be carried out online, thus some of them had to be completely eliminated (e.g., the agile game "paper airplanes" [14]). The most challenging part proved to be collaborating to perform a task and express the results in writing. At first, a generic request was made by the instructor in each breakout room, for one student to share their document (which could be in various formats), listen to the other group members' opinions and take notes (draw diagrams, write text, etc.). Often, no student was willing to take the initiative, to guide the discussions or to share their own screen. In later classes, the instructor designated a student to be the "sharing" member, and this proved to be a more effective strategy of involving students.

Overall, despite the initial worries that the classes would be less interactive than usual, the instructor believes that active learning was implemented to an acceptable level, considering the circumstances. The following year saw the software engineering class held online again.

In 2021, a number of 53 students enrolled in the class - an increase from the first online class. Taking into account the fact that students often consult with their seniors on which classes to enroll in, a larger number of students might hint to the impression that the online edition was rather successful and the students this year were encouraged to take it. Not only more international students enrolled (37, from 9 different countries), but the number of Japanese students increased, as well (from 6 to 16 participants).

The format used was very similar to the one from the previous year: classes were held online, synchronously, they were recorded and made available offline for the students. By now, the instructor had a better idea of what could work in an online setting, and she organized even more class activities. At the suggestion of one of the students, an online document was shared, with sections available for each group in the breakout room. This way anyone could edit the document, and anyone could see what other groups are working on.

As usual, the instructor gathered feedback from the students with regard to the current class. At this point, 40% of the students stated that they preferred online classes, whereas almost 25% preferred face-to-face classes. Interestingly, 30% of the students responded that this depends on the class they are taking. One participant stated that *"No matter what kind of classroom form, the activity of the classroom is very important.* ". Another student responded with *"I think "Class Activity" are interesting. But I am Japanese and not good at English. If I could speak English very well, I would have been able to participate more actively.* ". Moreover, *"The class with discussion activity should be Face-to-Face."* and *"Face-to-face classes are more interactive and engaging"*, supporting the idea that class activities may be perceived as more successful in a classroom setting.

The participants were asked which format they consider more successful for class activities/discussions. About 43% considered that they are more successful if held face-to-face, approx. 27% stated that they are about the same, and just over 13% believed that they are more successful if online (the remaining ~17% responded that they do not know).

When asked to compare online classes with face-to-face classes in terms of cultural differences, almost 49% of the students considered that cultural differences are more visible in face-to-face classrooms and about 15% thought that they are more visible in online classes. 20% of the students found no difference between the two (with the remaining 16% stating that they do not know). Last, but not least, the students were asked whether they find the class activities useful/valuable on one hand and enjoyable on the other hand. The results are summarized in Table 1.

TABLE I. CLASS ACTIVITIES: ENJOYABLE VS. VALUABLE/USEFUL

	A lot	*Moderately*	*A little*	*Not at all*
Enjoyable	24.44%	53.33%	20.00%	2.22%
Valuable/useful	32.11%	60.00%	8.89%	0%

We can observe that more than three quarters of the students find these activities enjoyable and more than 90% find them valuable (either a lot or moderately). These results show us that, despite the cultural differences and the difficulties inherent to online environments, the students generally found the active learning implementation not only useful, but also rather enjoyable. The instructor's observations are in line with these results: based on the impressions gathered in class, she felt that the course was successful and that the activities and discussions played an important role in this success.

IV. CONCLUSION AND FUTURE WORK

This paper described the experiences of teaching an introductory software engineering course to a group of multicultural students. It highlighted the approaches used by the class instructor to implement active learning, both in the face-to-face format and the online setting. Based on the instructor's observations and the feedback obtained from the students, it was concluded that active learning could successfully be carried out, despite the challenges brought upon by the sudden switch to an online format. In future work, the instructor plans to gather comprehensive feedback from the students and incorporate all the lessons learned in the previous years, to be prepared for implementing this course in either format necessary.

REFERENCES

[1] V. M. F. Fonseca and J. Gomez, "Applying active methodologies for teaching software engineering in computer engineering", IEEE Revista Iberoamericana de Tecnologias del Aprendizaje, vol. 12, no. 4, pp.182-190, 2017.

[2] S. Sandrone, G. Scott, W. J. Anderson, and K. Musunuru, "Active learning-based STEM education for in-person and online learning", Cell, vol. 184, no. 6, pp.1409-1414, 2021.

[3] C. C. Bonwell and J. A. Eison, "Active Learning: Creating Excitement in the Classroom", 1991 ASHE-ERIC Higher Education Reports. ERIC Clearinghouse on Higher Education, The George Washington University, 1991.

[4] H. Mercier, M. Deguchi, J. B. Van der Henst, and H. Yama, "The benefits of argumentation are cross-culturally robust: The case of Japan", Thinking & Reasoning, vol. 22, no. 1, pp. 1-15, 2016.

[5] S. Vasilache, "From an International Classroom to a Distributed Work Environment: Student Perspectives on Global Software Engineering", Proceedings of International Conference on Teaching and Learning for Engineering (TALE 2018), Dec. 2018, pp. 825-828.

[6] S. Vasilache, "Suddenly Online: Active Learning Implementation Strategies During Remote Teaching of a Software Engineering Course", In: Auer M.E., Hortsch H., Michler O., Köhler T. (eds) Mobility for Smart Cities and Regional Development - Challenges for Higher Education, ICL 2021, Lecture Notes in Networks and Systems, vol 389. Springer, Cham, pp. 395-402, 2021.

[7] S. Vasilache, "A Taste of Distributed Work Environments: Emergency Remote Teaching and Global Software Engineering", In: Stephanidis C., Antona M., Ntoa S. (eds) HCI International 2021 - Posters. HCII 2021, Communications in Computer and Information Science, vol 1421, Springer, Cham, pp. 624-628, 2021.

[8] C. Whittle, S. Tiwari, S. Yan, and J. Williams, "Emergency remote teaching environment: a conceptual framework for responsive online teaching in crises", Information and Learning Sciences, 2020.

[9] C. Hodges, S. Moore, B. Lockee, T. Trust, and A. Bond, "The difference between emergency remote teaching and online learning", Educause review, 27, pp. 1-12, 2020.

[10] Microsoft Teams [Online]. Available from: https://www.microsoft.com/en-us/microsoft-teams/group-chat-software 2022.07.31

[11] Zoom: Zoom Meetings & Chat [Online]. Available from: https://zoom.us/meetings 2022.07.31

[12] Manaba [Online]. Available from: https://manaba.jp/products/ 2022.07.31

[13] Microsoft Stream [Online]. Available from: https://www.microsoft.com/en-us/microsoft-365/microsoft-stream 2022.07.31

[14] Ben Willmott, "The Agile Paper Airplane Game". [Online]. Available from: https://www.ppm.academy/post/the-agile-paper-airplane-game 2022.07.31

Towards Measurable Motivation in Software Development

Niladri Saha
Tampere University
Tampere, Finland
bensous@gmail.com

Abdullah Israr
Tampere University
Tampere, Finland
abdullah.israr@tuni.fi

Outi Sievi-Korte
Tampere University
Tampere, Finland
outi.sievi-korte@tuni.fi

Fabian Fagerholm
Aalto University
Helsinki, Finland
fabian.fagerholm@aalto.fi

***Abstract*—Information Technology (IT) experts are feeling the strain of fast-paced, demanding work, and working measures for improved well-being are increasingly being established. One essential element of well-being is motivation. Motivation is critical in order to maintain smoothly working processes and quality in completed tasks. To detect and intercept situations where motivation begins to decrease, we need means to identify changes in motivation. To automatically detect such changes requires ways to measure motivation levels from data at hand. In this study, we present preliminary results towards defining measurable motivational factors. Our approach relies on emotional indicators of motivational change that can be detected automatically from software repositories. Our results show that the emotional content of commit comments and issue texts, extracted using sentiment analysis and emotion detection, is correlated to varying degrees with collaboration and risk metrics. We point to possibilities for future work on more sophisticated measures with more complex data.**

***Index Terms*—motivation, emotions, developer experience, data mining, software development.**

I. Introduction

Working life has undergone a bewildering change in recent years. Adoption of remote work and utilization of software tools for tasks that were previously handled manually or via face-to-face communication, continues to grow. Information Technology (IT) experts are increasingly feeling the pressure of fast-paced work, as 57% of technology company employees report burnout in the United States [1]. The situation could be remedied by ensuring processes and workflows take into account the human factors of software developers, particularly considering motivation. Motivated employees can handle stress better and are also more productive and less prone to errors [2].

On the one hand, motivation at work is tightly linked to tasks. Tasks should be well-mapped to the skills of an employee, while still offering meaningful challenge. Further, there should be the right amount of work given with regard to the time that can be spent for them [2]. Both the contents of the task (what kind of work there is to be done), and the process to complete the task (how the work should be done) impact motivation.

While there are many studies on how to improve software processes regarding prioritizing tasks in teams, handling communication, etc., so far there are few studies on how to incorporate human factors, and particularly motivation of developers as part of the process. Considering individuals on a personal level, emotions have been identified as one of the most central motivators of human behavior. There is strong evidence that experiencing and expressing positive emotions and moods enhances performance at individual, group, and organizational levels [3]. Motivation is altogether a multifaceted concept. There are extrinsic and intrinsic factors to consider, and different factors have non-trivial relationships. The importance of factors also varies between individuals.

Our long-term goal is to create a model of motivation that, when used with smart methods, can be applied as a tool to improve processes by including factors related to well-being at work. We strive to identify motivational factors in software development tasks that can be automatically extracted and measured from data available on the tasks. This kind of data modeling could enable quick reactions and interventions to correct workflows.

In this study, we take the first steps towards defining factors for this kind of motivational model. We mine data from open-source software repositories. We combine analyses on sentiments and emotions with metrics on software development tasks (complexity of the task, risk level and found collaboration). The preliminary results as revealed in Section IV imply that there are correlations between different task-related metrics and emotions identified from task-related data. While we are still far from a complete measurable model, the results are encouraging and spark discussions on possible research directions. This paper proceeds as follows. In Section II-A we will give background on the concepts of emotion and motivation and go through related work. In Section III we outline the utilized research process and define the metrics we use in the study. In Section IV we give our preliminary results based on collected data and statistical calculations. In Section V-A we reflect how the results can be interpreted considering known theories on emotion and discuss the limitations of the study. Finally, we conclude in Section VI.

II. Background and Related Work

A. Emotions and Motivation

Emotions are strong feelings "deriving from one's circumstances, mood, or relationships with others" [4]. They are responses to specific internal and external events [5]. Emotions include psychological and physiological processes, but defining emotion has proven difficult [6] and no final scientific consensus exists. Emotions are intertwined with mood, temperament, personality, disposition, and creativity [7]. Theories of basic emotions give classifications of discrete, measurable, and physiologically distinct emotions. A foundational example is Ekman's theory of basic emotions, which lists six emotions: anger, disgust, fear, happiness, sadness, and surprise [8]. Emotions may also be understood through a multi-dimensional analysis, which often gives rise to a two-factor model consisting of valence ("tone", positive – negative) and arousal ("intensity", passive – energized). These two are not a full explanation of the wide range of emotional experiences that humans can have, but they are theorized to map to an important emotional component called core affect [9].

Motivation is often defined as the explanation behind why people initiate, continue, or terminate a certain behavior at a particular time [10]. The stronger the motivational state, the more likely that it influences behavior. Content theories of motivation aim to describe what goals always or usually motivate people. For example, according to Herzberg's two-factor theory, certain workplace factors result in job satisfaction and are thus motivators, while hygiene factors are those that lead to dissatisfaction if absent, but do not produce satisfaction in themselves [11]. The two-factor theory has been the basis for other theories that consider motivation in the workplace, such as the Job Characteristics Theory, a theory of work design that seeks to enrich work by affecting motivational outcomes [12].

Emotion can be seen as a driving force behind motivation [13], and high or low motivation is often associated with specific emotions. Emotion is a crucial part of the motivational processes and can be used as an indicator of those processes.

B. Related work

Beecham et al. [14] found several motivating and de-motivating factors for software engineers. However, the study does not mention any technique to calculate them or what kind of data the factors could be based on.

Sharp et al. [15] developed an enhanced model for motivation by using the concepts of Beecham et al. [14] and several existing models, such as the Job Characteristics Model (Theory) [12]. The enhanced version considers individual characteristics in addition to other software engineering characteristics. The contextual factors here denote the work setting, i.e., the external environment like leadership, company's performance, and so on.

An empirical study on how the motivational model applies in practice has been conducted in Pakistan [16], where the Hofstede Cultural Dimension Model was taken into account to understand the results. Authors highlight the need to include culture when interpreting motivational factors.

Graziotin et al. [17] proposed an approach to find factors that create unhappiness among software developers. The factors listed for unhappiness can be considered as de-motivators, and matches with the de-motivating factors provided by Beecham et al. [14]. However, Graziotin et al. [17] did not provide a way to measure these factors either.

Ortu et al. [18] implemented an approach to store the issue details from issue tracking systems like Jira. This approach can be used to further extract details related to the issue that are relevant in motivation mining. While the study mentioned issue fixing time as one of the factors that affect emotion, as well as motivation of a developer, it did not show how it can be measured. Ortu et al. later added an emotional classification to the extracted data set [19]. However, the emotion is decided manually and there is no sentiment analysis in the approach. No detailed study has been made to elaborate the process of extracting motivational factors.

Utilizing techniques to mine software repositories, Mäntylä et al. [20] have studied how time pressure and productivity could be deduced. With similar data, Graziotin et al. [21] show that unhappiness is tied to low motivation and repetitive tasks, among other factors. While these studies link repository mining and motivation, they do not yet reveal how the nature of tasks affect motivation. Similarly to Ortu et al. [19], we have fetched issue, commit, and contribution details for each developer, but go further by also extracting different metrics from the issue and commit details. We have used the set of motivational and de-motivational factors as defined by Beecham et al. [14], and the approach of Sharp et al. [15] is further considered in understanding the outcome.

III. Research Process

The general problem we are trying to solve is *What task-related factors motivate software experts?* Since our first step to investigate this focuses on open-source software development, we are specifically looking into the following research questions (RQs):

- RQ1: What are the factors in software development tasks that impact the motivation of a developer?
- RQ2: What factors can be measured?
- RQ3: What kind of relationships are there between different factors?

The research process to answer these questions proceeded as follows. We perused the literature to learn about existing motivational studies on software development (background for RQ1). We listed found motivators and de-motivators and categorized them to measurable and non-measurable (initial step for RQ2). In the following, we will give details on how we collected data from open-source software repositories (Section III-A) and what metrics we developed for measuring motivational factors (based on literature and available data) (Section III-B).

A. Data collection

We used the PyGitHub library (supporting Python v3+) to extract data from GitHub. Issue details from 35 GitHub repositories were extracted, following the approach of Rath et al. [22]. A total of 26566 issue comments from closed issues were collected. We further collected 6520 commits from these closed issues. Out of these, we selected only those issues and commits where the *same developer* had both *commented* on the issue and *committed* the code, so that we could focus on the data provided by the software developer actually performing a certain task (committing the code that resolved the issue). We particularly wanted to focus on the developer performing the task in order to get a clear view of task-related motivational factors, which is our main interest.

As a result, our final dataset has 1069 records (issue and commit pairs), with data from 139 individual developers, ranging from 2015 to October 2021. Based on labels used in the repositories, issues are categorized into five main categories: Bug, Documentation, Enhancement, Feature and Others. In the category "Others", all type of issues that do not belong any of the four categories mentioned are considered. For sentiment analysis, we used TextBlob, and for identifying emotions from text, we used Text2Emotion.

B. Metrics for Motivation

Beecham et al. [14] list 21 motivators and 15 de-motivators that are particular for software engineers. We categorized these into measurable and non-measurable based on an estimation of whether we could calculate a numerical value for the factor. Factors that would have required information from organizational policies, personal skills, etc. were at this stage categorized as non-measurable. For the measurable motivators we examined what kind of data we were able to get from GitHub, and created a mapping between the motivators and available data. Ultimately, we were able to formulate metrics for three motivators, given in Table I. Figure 1 further illustrates what kind of data from issues and commits was used with which tools and metrics.

We recognize that categorizing the factors is problematic. Had we had access to organizational data, other factors could have been labeled as "measurable" as well. Further, as this is the first iteration, the suggested metrics are simple. For example, for collaboration we might envision more complicated formulae, taking into account past connections or collaboration across different projects. The limitations of data, metrics and scope are further discussed in Section V-C.

The defined metrics are based on literature. Lines Of Code (LOC) is commonly used to determine the size and the complexity of software. For example, Nystedt and Santos [23] and Tashtoush et al. [24] describe LOC as one of the approaches in complexity calculation of a software. In addition, we take into account the number of files involved in changes, demonstrating how contained (or not) the changes are to a specific part of code. Together, lines of code and number of files are combined for our complexity metric (1). We categorized complexity as high, if it is larger than the average complexity in the specific category of issues (Bug, Documentation, Enhancement, Feature or Others), and as low, if it is below average of the specific category.

Beecham et al. [14] list collaboration as one of the motivational factors that affects software engineers when they are working in a team projects. In our collaboration metric (2), we count as collaborators those who (in addition to the developer

TABLE I
METRICS FOR MOTIVATIONAL FACTORS.

Motivational factor	Related data	Formula
Technically challenging work (Complexity of tasks)	Number of files, number of files changed, number of lines changed	$Ci = nL * nF$ (1), Ci = Complexity of an issue at code level, nL = Number of changed lines (in commit), nF = Number of changed files (in commit)
Participation/ Involvement/ Working with others	Information on assignee, commenter, commit author	$CS = CL - ML$ (2), CS = Collaboration Score, CL = Number of collaborators, ML = Number of mentions
Risk/Risk related to project delivery time	Completion time of issues	R_i = High, if $Ct_i > Avg(Ct)$, R_i = Low, if $Ct_i < Avg(Ct)$ (3), R_i = Risk of an issue, Ct_i = Completion time of an issue

pushing the commit) are tagged to comments or marked as assignees, commenters or commit authors to an issue. We then subtract those who have only been mentioned, but show no active participation in the issue.

Finally, Raphael [25] names delivery time or completion time as one of the profound risks in any agile software development project. Based on this, we calculate risk (3) based on how much the completion time of an issue deviates from the average. If the completion time for an issue is greater than the average completion time for the same issue category, the risk is high, otherwise risk is low. We recognize that calculating risk in this hindsight fashion has its limits.

IV. PRELIMINARY RESULTS

In Tables II and IV, we present results concerning the complexity metric. Considering our categorization between high and low complexity, there were 116 high complexity issues and 950 low complexity issues. Note that for some commits the comment field is blank, thus the percentages do not sum to 100%, as no emotion could be detected for blank fields. Also for some issues (commits) complexity was zero, in which cases they were discarded. We can clearly see from Table II that there are distinct differences between the emotions expressed in issue comments (usually utilized discussing the task with others in the community) and commit comments (usually used to summarize the solution). While already 40.5% of all high complexity issues were found Happy, in commit comments the percentage went up to 66.4%. Yet, for low complexity issues, the portion of Happy comments was similar for both issue comments and commit comments. A distinct difference between issues and commit comments is also found in texts expressing Surprise – there are some of such in issues, but none in commits. Finally, looking at the distribution of emotions, Happy is clearly the dominant emotion for both high and low complexity tasks and both in issues and commits.

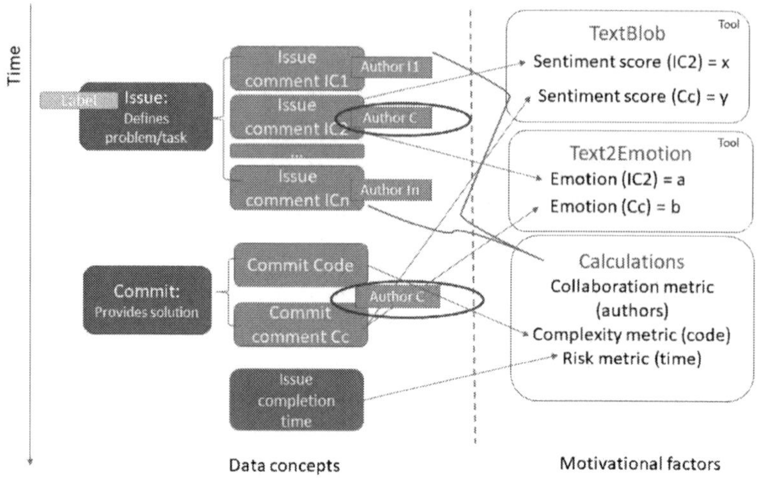

Fig. 1. Conceptual model of data collected for the study, analysis tools used to collect and process the data, and metrics extracted based on the raw data as indicators of motivational factors.

The second-most common emotion varies greatly. For issues, there is an equal amount of comments categorized as Sad or Fear for both high and low complexity issues. For low complexity issues, there is also a similar amount of issue comments labeled as Angry, while for high complexity issues Angry is very rarely found. For commit comments, on the other hand, Angry is clearly the second most commonly found emotion both for high and low complexity tasks, Fear and Sad being more seldom found.

Conducting a multinomial regression test for statistical significance showed that data source (issue or commit) was statistically significant in explaining the found emotion ($p = 0.00$), while level of complexity was not ($p = 0.065$).

In Table IV, we give the average complexity and completion time of issues by category. The used categories are gained by labels used in the mined projects. While four labels (Feature, Enhancement, Bug, Documentation) were consistently used in all repositories, other labels varied greatly, and have been combined under "Others". Here we can see that features have the highest complexity and highest completion time – though we should note the very low number of features (4). Bugs have the lowest complexity, and are on the lower end of used time to complete. Documentation may intuitively seem surprisingly complex, but this may be explained via systematic documentation involving small changes across multiple files.

In Table III, we summarize emotions found in high and low risk issues. In total we found 265 high risk issues and 804 low risk issue. The results are very similar to those in complexity, particularly regarding the differences between issues and commits. and the high percentage of Angry found in commits compared to issues. There are further similarities in how the percentage of "Happy" is much higher in high risk issues than commits made for high risk issues, while for low risk issues, the percentage of "Happy" comments is similar for issues and commits. However, contrary to complexity, conducting a multinomial regression test for statistical significance showed that both the data source (issue or commit) ($p = 0.00$) and the risk level ($p = 0.009$) were statistically significant in explaining the found emotion. Considering how similar the results intuitively appear, this prompts us to reconsider the method for categorization of complexity.

Finally, in Table V we have mapped collaboration values to emotions. Interestingly, issues and commit comments labeled as Happy have the lowest collaboration score on average, while highest collaboration scores are found on issues as Angry or Sad, and both issues and commits labeled as Fear.

V. Discussion

A. *Reflections*

In both issues and commits of both high and low complexity, Happy was the dominant emotion. This is consistent with prior research on software developer happiness [21]. As an emotional component of motivation, happiness could be both an outcome of successful goal attainment and an antecedent that increases the likelihood of purposeful action. It is not surprising that the Happy emotion appears frequently in the data: happy developers more likely create comments.

However, looking more closely at the data, more high-complexity commit comments were Happy than high-complexity issues, while for low complexity commits and issues, Happy comments were about the same. We speculate that this may be an outcome of goal attainment: when a developer completes a high-complexity task, their emotional state tends toward happiness and this is reflected in how the commit message turns out. In issues, happiness is not as strongly represented because the matter is still under discussion and the developer has not yet reached closure on the task. Similarly, low-complexity tasks do not result in a sense of achievement of the same magnitude as high-complexity tasks. That there were some occurrences of Surprise in issues but none in commits

TABLE II
EMOTIONS BY COMPLEXITY

Emotion	Source	Complexity category	Count	Percentage (per complexity category)
Happy	Issue	High	47	40.5%
		Low	458	48.2%
	Commit comment	High	77	66.4%
		Low	479	50.4%
Sad	Issue	High	27	23.3%
		Low	200	21%
	Commit comment	High	8	6.9%
		Low	89	9.3%
Surprise	Issue	High	13	11.2%
		Low	50	5.3%
	Commit comment	High	-	
		Low	-	
Fear	Issue	High	27	23.3%
		Low	220	23.2%
	Commit comment	High	4	3.4%
		Low	88	9.3%
Angry	Issue	High	2	1.7%
		Low	22	23.2%
	Commit comment	High	26	22.4%
		Low	265	27.9%

TABLE III
EMOTIONS CATEGORIZED BY RISK LEVEL

Emotion	Source	Risk level	Count	Percentage
Happy	Issue	High	131	49.4%
		Low	377	46.9%
	Commit comment	High	166	62.7%
		Low	391	48.6%
Sad	Issue	High	55	20.8%
		Low	172	21.4%
	Commit comment	High	9	3.4%
		Low	88	10.9%
Surprise	Issue	High	20	7.5%
		Low	43	5.3%
	Commit comment	High	-	
		Low	-	
Fear	Issue	High	54	20.4%
		Low	193	24.0%
	Commit comment	High	21	8.0%
		Low	73	9.1%
Angry	Issue	High	5	1.9%
		Low	19	2.4%
	Commit comment	High	67	25.3%
		Low	224	27.9%

TABLE IV
AVERAGE COMPLEXITY AND COMPLETION TIMES

Issue category	Count	Avg. complexity	Avg. completion time (hours)
Feature	4	204995	288
Enhancement	77	3642	216
Bug	114	1100	187
Documentation	288	24840	179
Others	556	6454	257

TABLE V
COLLABORATION

Emotion	Source	Count	Average collaboration score
Happy	Issue	508	1.274
	Commit comment	557	1.540
Sad	Issue	227	1.978
	Commit comment	97	1.701
Surprise	Issue	63	1.873
	Commit comment	-	
Fear	Issue	247	1.968
	Commit comment	94	1.915
Angry	Issue	24	1.958
	Commit comment	291	1.732

is probably a reflection of the ongoing nature of the former and closure in the latter.

The second-most common emotion varied greatly among high- and low-complexity issues and commit comments. The Angry emotion was the second-most common one for high- and low-complexity commit comments, while it was rarely found in high-complexity issue comments. This emotion may be related to getting stuck (commenting in issues) or feeling that work performed by oneself or others is inadequate (commenting in both issues and commits).

An Angry emotion is seen as moderate to high on the arousal dimension, and in terms of motivation may thus be a driver for action. Fear is also often seen as moderate to high on arousal, which is visible in somewhat higher occurrence in both high- and low-complexity issues. In commit comments, however, we did not see Fear nor Sad emotions. For Fear, this could be due to the valence dimension of the emotion: fear is not conducive to creativity and action, and is motivationally more likely to result in withdrawal or self-regulation. A similar explanation could be plausible in the case of Sad emotions, which is found more in issues and less in commits.

Beecham et al. [14] and Sharp et al. [15] list a number of external signs or outcomes showing the level of motivation among software engineers. These include retention, productivity, project delivery time, absenteeism, and project success. Whereas these signs are on the project and organizational levels, our findings address motivation on the individual level. Project and organizational indicators typically react to changes slowly or even completely after the fact, as in retention and project success. Motivation, measured via emotional indicators visible in actual work products or by-products is a more direct view into the individual and collaborative processes. They may also provide more direct means of understanding what it is about software engineers' work that is motivating and de-motivating and open paths toward acting upon motivational changes based on emotional expressions in work artifacts.

B. Addressing research questions

Looking into both the quantitative results as well as our reflections on them, we address our research questions.

RQ1: What are factors in software development tasks that impact the motivation of a developer? Examining the literature in the field revealed a number of extensive studies, listing both motivators and de-motivators for software engineers. Based on our quantitative data, there is (varying) correlation between identified measurable elements and the identified emotions in tasks. The risk of missing a deadline, i.e., the time it takes to complete a task, was shown to have statistical impact on the emotion found. While the level of complexity using our categorization between high and low complexity was not found significant, there were indications that a more fine-grained view of complexity could produce significant results.

RQ2: What factors can be measured? Utilizing data from GitHub and comparing it with the motivators and de-motivators found in literature, we have identified complexity of task, collaboration/teamwork, risk of delay, emotion and sentiment as measurable factors. More factors could be identified with more sophisticated data mining approaches or additional data sources.

RQ3: What kind of relationships are there between different factors? While our data prompts discussion on the relationship between different motivational factors, more work is required to properly understand them. We are currently performing a qualitative study to further understand and validate our quantitative findings, as well as experimenting with clustering algorithms to discover relationships between the factors.

C. Limitations

As we are presenting preliminary results, we acknowledge a number of limitations. First, we need more sophisticated methods to enhance the existing metrics. A particular concern is how the metrics can be either generalized or re-focused into other contexts where the primary work products are not code, but rather the manipulation of other kinds of artifacts.

Secondly, the question of transferability remains open . These results pertain to software developers in Open Source Software projects. To what extent they can be generalized to software engineers in other contexts, remains an open question.

Finally, the study results contain some uncertainty in attributing the detected emotions. We did not attempt to separate emotions attributed to the individual situation of each participant, to the task itself, to the tools used, or to the collaborative environment. We also could not distinguish the precise motivational role of each emotion expression. For instance, in the case of Anger, we did not separate between anger that increased emotion and resulted in action from anger as an expression after such an action (e.g., having fixed an issue, a person's commit message may express anger about the issue or its underlying reasons). However, it was not an aim of this study to reach that level of attribution; we aimed to examine associations between tasks and motivation-indicating emotions on a more general level.

VI. Conclusions

Our vision is to address a very complex, multi-faceted problem: identifying motivational factors in software development work and creating smart ways to intervene when motivation drops; and introducing more sensitivity to human factors into software processes and workflows. Our preliminary results are a stepping stone towards finding a measurable model of motivational factors. Our findings give positive indications that we can translate motivational factors into measurable metrics, and find statistically significant relationships between task-related metrics and experienced emotions. More work is needed to fine-tune metrics (more data, qualitative validation) and particularly to understand the causality between task and emotion (e.g., feelings impacting task duration or vice versa). Further work is also needed to have a larger dataset, enabling a broader statistical analysis, as well as complementing it with a qualitative study. We hope to inspire discussions and research openings in this direction by releasing the preliminary results on our vision. Some possible avenues would be to investigate how digitization or transferability of tasks affects the emotions of developers.

References

[1] K. McCarthy, "Close to 60 percent of surveyed tech workers are burnt out—credit karma tops the list for most employees suffering from burnout," 2018, retrieved: 06/2022. [Online]. Available: https://tinyurl.com/softwareburnout

[2] P. Hirvikoski, "Kokemuksia työhyvinvoinnista, (in engl: Experiences on well-being at work)," Master's thesis, Tampere University, 2011.

[3] S. G. Barsade and D. E. Gibson, "Why does affect matter in organizations?" *Academy of management perspectives*, vol. 21, pp. 36–59, 2007.

[4] O. U. Press, "Emotion," in *Lexico.com*, 2021, retrieved: 07/2022. [Online]. Available: https://www.lexico.com/definition/emotion

[5] D. L. Schacter, D. T. Gilbert, and D. M. Wegner, *Psychology: European Edition*, 3rd ed. New York: Worth, 2011.

[6] K. R. Scherer, "What are emotions? and how can they be measured?" *Social Science Information*, vol. 44, no. 4, pp. 695–729, 2005.

[7] J. R. Averill, "Individual differences in emotional creativity: Structure and correlates," *Journ. of Personality*, vol. 67, no. 2, pp. 331–371, 1999.

[8] M. N. Shiota, "Ekman's theory of basic emotions," in *The SAGE Encyclopedia of Theory in Psychology*, H. L. Miller, Ed. Thousand Oaks, CA: Sage Publications, 2016, pp. 249–250.

[9] J. A. Russell, "Core affect and the psychological construction of emotion." *Psychological review*, vol. 110, no. 1, pp. 145–172, 2003.

[10] B. Weiner, "Motivation: An overview," in *Encyclopedia of Psychology*, A. E. Kazdin, Ed. American Psychological Association, 2000.

[11] F. Herzberg, B. Mausner, and B. B. Snyderman, *The Motivation to Work*, 2nd ed. New York: Wiley, 1959.

[12] J. Hackman and G. R. Oldham, "Motivation through the design of work: test of a theory," *Organizational Behavior and Human Performance*, vol. 16, no. 2, pp. 250–279, 1976.

[13] S. J. C. Gaulin and D. H. McBurney, *Evolutionary Psychology*. Prentice Hall, 2003.

[14] S. Beecham, N. Baddoo, T. Hall, H. Robinson, and H. Sharp, "Motivation in software engineering: A systematic literature review," *Information and Software Technology*, vol. 50, pp. 860–878, 2008.

[15] H. Sharp, N. Baddoo, S. Beecham, T. Hall, and H. Robinson, "Models of motivation in software engineering," *Information and Software Technology*, vol. 51, pp. 219–233, 2009.

[16] I. Asghar and M. Usman, "Motivational and de-motivational factors for software engineers: An empirical investigation," in *11th Int. Conf. Frontiers of Information Technology*, 2013, pp. 66–71.

[17] D. Graziotin, X. Wang, and P. Abrahamsson, "Are happy developers more productive," in *Proc. Product-Focused Software Process Improvement*. Springer Berlin Heidelberg, 2013, pp. 50–64.

[18] M. Ortu, A. Murgia, G. Destefanis, P. Tonelli, T. Roberto, M. Marchesi, and B. Adams, "The emotional side of software developers in JIRA," in *13th Working Conf. on Mining Software Repositories*. ACM, 2016, pp. 480–483.

[19] G. Destefanis, M. Ortu, D. Bowes, M. Marchesi, and R. Tonelli, "On measuring affects of github issues' commenters," in *Proceedings of the 3rd International Workshop on Emotion Awareness in Software Engineering*, ser. SEmotion '18. ACM, 2018, pp. 14–19.

[20] M. Mäntylä, B. Adams, G. Destefanis, D. Graziotin, and M. Ortu, "Mining valence, arousal, and dominance: Possibilities for detecting burnout and productivity?" in *13th Int. Conf. on Mining Software Repositories*. ACM, 2016, pp. 247–258.

[21] D. Graziotin, F. Fagerholm, X. Wang, and P. Abrahamsson, "What happens when software developers are (un)happy," *Journal of Systems and Software*, vol. 140, pp. 32–47, 2018.

[22] M. Rath, P. Rempel, and P. Mäder, "The IlmSeven dataset," in *25th Int. Requirements Engineering Conf.*, 2017, pp. 516–519.

[23] S. Nystedt and C. Sandros, "Software complexity and project performance," Master's thesis, University of Gothenburg, 1999.

[24] M. A.-M. Yahya Tashtoush and B. Arkok, "The correlation among software complexity metrics with case study," *International Journal of Advanced Computer Research*, vol. 4, pp. 414–419, 2014.

[25] "Common risks in agile projects and how to deal with them," 2021, retrieved: 06/2022. [Online]. Available: https://www.gratasoftware.com/common-risks-agile-projects-deal/

How to Fill the Gap between Practice and Higher Education: Performing eduScrum with Real World Problems in Virtual Distance Teaching

Michael Neumann
Dpt. of Business Information Systems
Hochschule Hannover
Hannover, Germany
michael.neumann@hs-hannover.de

David Mötefindt
Software Development
AWIN AG
Hannover, Germany
david.moetefindt@awin.com

Lukas Linke
Customer Management Tech
Otto GmbH & Co KG.
Hamburg, Germany
lukas.linke@otto.de

Dirk Radtke
Agile Processes
Otto GmbH & Co KG.
Hamburg, Germany
dirk.radtke2@otto.de

Annika Mattstädt
Agile Processes
Otto GmbH & Co KG.
Hamburg, Germany
annika.mattstaedt@otto.de

Frederik Herzig
HR Management
Otto GmbH & Co KG.
Hamburg, Germany
frederik.herzig@otto.de

Patricia Regel
Advertising Services
Otto GmbH & Co KG.
Hamburg, Germany
patricia.regel@otto.de

***Abstract*—Social skills are essential for a successful understanding of agile methods in software development. Several studies highlight the opportunities and advantages of integrating real-world projects and problems while collaborating with companies into higher education using agile methods. This integration comes with several opportunities and advantages for both the students and the company. The students are able to interact with real-world software development teams, analyze and understand their challenges and identify possible measures to tackle them. However, the integration of real-world problems and companies is complex and may come with a high effort in terms of coordination and preparation of the course. The challenges related to the interaction and communication with students are increased by virtual distance teaching during the Covid-19 pandemic as direct contact with students is missing. Also, we do not know how problem-based learning in virtual distance teaching is valued by the students. This paper presents our adapted eduScrum approach and learning outcome of integrating experiments with real-world software development teams from two companies into a Master of Science course organized in virtual distance teaching. The evaluation shows that students value analyzing real-world problems using agile methods. They highlight the interaction with real-world software development teams. Also, the students appreciate the organization of the course using an iterative approach with eduScrum. Based on our findings, we present four recommendations for the integration of agile methods and real world problems into higher education in virtual distance teaching settings. The results of our paper contribute to the practitioner and researcher/lecturer community, as we provide valuable insights how to fill the gap between practice and higher education in virtual distance settings.**

***Index Terms*—Agile methods, agile education, eduscrum, distance learning, virtual distance teaching, problem based learning, Covid-19.**

I. Introduction

This paper describes the integration from real world problems provided by companies (clients) into the Master of Science course "Innovative Methods of Project Management" during the Covid-19 pandemic and related distance teaching activities. A central purpose of the course is to integrate challenges and problems from the real world. We prepared, organized and conducted the course with an adapted eduScrum method and integrated real world clients since the summer term in 2019.

Agile and hybrid methods are well-known approaches in software development for more than two decades [1]. The use of agile methods like Scrum is widely accepted in practice [2] and education [3]. Agile methods focus on social aspects like collaboration and communication [4]. Thus, (social) values and principles are of high importance in the field of agile software development. The widely use of agile methods in practice led to an increased integration into higher education over the years [5], [6]. Also, the combination of software processes with the integration of real world problems or project based approaches is often described by other authors (e.g., [7]–[10]). Agile methods were adapted for their use in educational settings by several lecturers (e.g., [11]–[16]). Especially, the focus on social aspects and teaching such skills is of high importance in higher education [17].

The Covid-19 pandemic and the switch to virtual distance teaching provides several challenges for lecturers and students in higher education (e.g., [18]–[20]). Especially, project related courses in lab settings may be affected from the switch, but also most of the courses, which comprises physical activities such as game based learning approaches were influenced (e.g., Lego Serious Play [21]). In 2019, we adapted the eduScrum method for higher educational settings in an onsite environment and integrated real world clients to the course [22]. Thus, the new situation also provides several challenges to us as our course organization set-up was initially designed for onsite teaching. This leads us to our two research questions:

- **RQ1:** How can we perform eduScrum integrating real world problems in higher education in a virtual distance teaching environment?
- **RQ2:** How do the students value the work with eduScrum in a virtual distance teaching environment?

This paper focuses on our adaptions during the Covid-19 pandemic and how we counteract the challenges of distance learning. However, we identified several upcoming challenges related to the new circumstances occurred due to the pandemic. We present four recommendations for other lecturers, which are interested to overcome specific challenges in nowadays higher education and integrate agile methods as well as real world problems to their courses.

The paper at hand is structured as follows: First, we describe the related work in Section II, followed by the course overview in Section III. We explain the data collection and give a brief overview of our results in Section IV. The results are discussed in Section V. Before the paper closes with a conclusion in Section VII, we present our recommendations for other lecturers in Section VI.

II. Related Work

To provide an overview of the literature related to the topic of our study, we searched for primary studies dealing with agile methods in higher educating using problem-based approaches in virtual distance classroom settings during the Covid-19 pandemic. The search was performed in two digital libraries (Google Scholar and Scopus) and focused on peer reviewed literature.

We identified five studies dealing with findings related to the Covid-19 indicated switch to distance teaching. Matthies et al. [18] discuss the impact of the switch to a remote teaching in their agile software engineering project course during the Covid-19 pandemic. The authors identified ten challenges concerning the distance teaching activities and present specific counter measurements. Most of these challenges are also described in practitioner contexts like decreased social exchange (e.g., [23], [24]) or less focus due to distractions [25]. Matthies et al. also identified 13 opportunities, which positively affected the teaching activities [18].

Stevanovic et al. analyzed the students perspective of virtual distance teaching during Covid-19 [26]. The survey results show that students lost focus in virtual distance settings. Also the motivation of the students is negatively affected, especially for students, which are used to onsite teaching. Iglesias-Pradas et al. point out that the ad hoc switch to virtual distance teaching during Covid-19 is not comparable to a prepared, permanent integration of virtual distance teaching in higher education [27]. The authors recommend drawing lessons from distance teaching during Covid-19 and transferring suitable concepts to the post-pandemic period.

Another paper, which deals with the Covid-19 related impact on teaching activities is presented by Siegel et al. in form of a workgroup report [20]. The authors describe how the teaching landscape may look like after the pandemic indicating the lessons learned from the past two years with Covid-19. However, the literature concerning the impact of distance learning, especially related to the field of software engineering and agile software development in particular is limited [28] and needs more attention.

Although we performed the literature search in two digital libraries, we could not identify peer-reviewed studies dealing with agile methods using problem-based approaches in higher education virtual classroom settings.

III. Course Overview

A. General Information of the Course

The course *Innovative Methods of Project Management* is organized annually during the summer term and integrated into the Master of Science program *Digital Transformation.* The master program is supervised by the Business Computing department of the University of Applied Sciences and Arts - Hochschule Hannover since winter term 2018/2019. A student group comprises 25 persons.

Each term is divided into different phases: lecture period (16 weeks), examination period (three weeks) and lecture-free period (seven weeks). The course is planned with total effort of 180 hours (68 hours in attendance, 112 hours self study). The 68 hours are planned as lecture units, as well as during the Covid-19 pandemic. Thus, the course is planned with four units á 45 minutes per week in an onsite setting.

In the course, students should gain an understanding and knowledge of new (innovative) methods and upcoming challenges of project management. The students should be able to select and perform specific systematic measures to counteract relevant challenges. An outline of the learning objectives is given in Table I.

TABLE I
LEARNING OBJECTIVES

Learning objectives
Understand the characteristics, challenges and opportunities of agile, plan-based and hybrid approaches in a software development context
Understand the challenges of intercultural project teams
Understand the challenges of (virtual) distributed international teams
Leadership and team coordination for different project sizes
Conflict management in projects
Presentation of status reports for selected stakeholder

The examination is split into a written paper and a presentation of the study results by each students team. 50 percent of the grade results from both types of examination.

Our course was initially designed for classroom teaching in person, as we are an onsite university. The global shift to virtual and distance learning due to Covid-19 affected also our university. Covid-19 reached Germany in February 2020. The summer term in 2020 started in March at our university. After two weeks of onsite teaching in March 2020, we switched to virtual distance teaching. Thus, the course was offered once in person (2019) and two times virtually in a distance learning (2020 and 2021).

B. Pre-pandemic Course Information

This subsection describes the course organization during the summer terms of 2019 and 2020 and aims to provide an understanding of our adapted eduScrum approach based on classroom teaching.

The eduScrum approach was developed by Willy Wijnands for organizing school lessons [29]. Wijnands et al. present their guidelines for the agile education method in the eduScrum guide [30]. The eduScrum guide describes specific practices, artifacts and roles, as well as a process model aiming to provide a common understanding how eduScrum may be performed in schools. However, the approach is not designed for higher education integrating real world problems and clients or stakeholders into the teaching activities. Thus, we decided to adapt the eduScrum method based on the theoretical knowledge of well-known agile methods such as Scrum with the aim to enable students to work with agile practices and gain practice-relevant experiences. We present the elements of our adapted eduScrum approach for higher eduction in Figure 1.

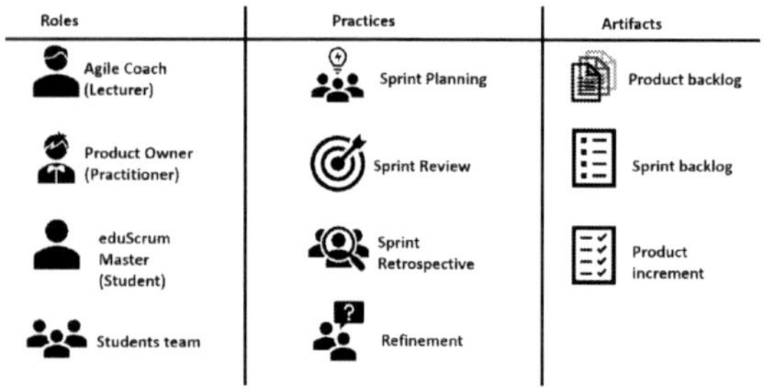

Fig. 1. Elements of the adapted eduScrum approach

Our adaptions affect the roles, practices (events) and artifacts of the eduScrum approach. In a first step, we added the role of an Agile Coach, which is taken by the lecturer. The Agile Coach is responsible for supporting the students related to upcoming questions related to the course organization or the underlying theoretical knowledge or challenges during the term. Furthermore, we changed the responsibilities of the Product Owner. The practitioner from a specific company takes this role and is responsible for preparing a product backlog, which comprises specific requirements for the students teams and keeping the backlog up to date. The role also supports the students teams related to content-related questions or challenges, e.g., providing project or company documentations such as guidelines. The students team is self-organized and thus, decides how to implement the specific requirements from the product backlog. The size of the team is restricted to three to seven students. Each students team choose one student, who takes the role of the eduScrum Master. This role is responsible for removing impediments during a sprint.

We organized the agile practices Sprint Planning, Review and Retrospective with respect to the eduScrum Guide. In terms of conducting respective practices such as the Retrospective the students team have the possibility to select specific micro practices (or techniques), such as the starfish model [31]. However, we added the refinement meeting to our adapted eduScrum approach, as we identified the need for integrating an agile practice which aims to provide the possibility for the students and product owners to collaborate directly concerning the quality of the product backlog. The refinement always takes place in the week between the sprint changes.

The artifacts are not described in the eduScrum guide. Thus, we decided to integrate necessary artifacts from Scrum [32], in order to integrate real world companies, which are used to work with artifacts, like product/sprint backlogs and increments. It provides the possibility for the students to discuss specific requirements documented in the backlogs and deal with challenges such as not done increments or negotiations with the product owner.

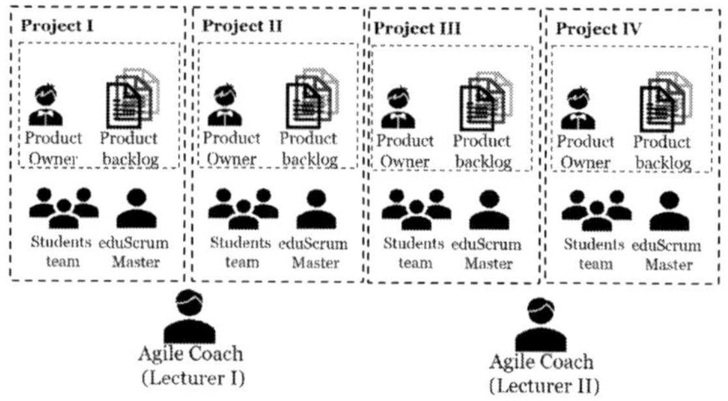

Fig. 2. Course organization in 2019 and 2020

Changes in the students team (e.g., new team assignments) are not planned in the term. The students should get a chance to learn the challenges and opportunities of a team development through the whole term and gain experience of such a process.

In 2019 and 2020, the course was prepared and performed by a teaching pair. Each agile coach was responsible for supporting two student teams (see Figure 2). We integrated four companies in the summer terms in both years. We selected the companies based on their project proposals related to the learning objectives of the course. All companies are part of our educational and research network and from certain industries like finance, retail or chemical. For instance, the companies proposed projects with the aim to identify success factors of an agile transition in the finance industry, or to analyze project management methods in use at an energy company in order to provide an approach for a tailored hybrid project management approach. All projects are based on real world problems and challenges.

We split the student group of 25 persons and assigned the students randomly to one of the four eduScrum student teams. Each student team had one associated product owner and project.

During the first lecture of the summer terms in 2019 and 2020, we held an introductory event in which we explained the module's organization, the examination requirements and repeated basic theory. Building on this, a kick-off meeting was held with the product owners in the second event. The kick-off meetings were already student team-specific events, so each product owner held the event with the respective student team. The aim of the kick-off meeting was to ensure a uniform understanding of the requirements and goals of the respective project and to be able to move on to the iterative organization in the form of sprints. In the third week of the term, the event was the first sprint planning. Starting this week, two-weekly sprints were planned and executed. In the week without a sprint planning, refinement meetings were held with the aim of discussing open questions or ambiguities. One week before the exam date (submission of the written exam and presentation of the results), the last sprint in the respective term ended.

C. Modified Course Organization due to Virtual Distance Teaching

This subsection describes the course organization during the summer term of 2021 and aims to provide an understanding of our corrections made due to the switch to virtual distance teaching during the Covid-19 pandemic.

Our experiences of 2019 and 2020 have shown that the preparation of the projects with several companies is extensive and complex. In addition, there is a risk when integrating several companies that the product owner cannot always guarantee high-quality support for the students, for example with regard to the quality of the requirements. Due to this challenge and an organizational change, which meant that only one lecturer was available for the summer term 2021, we decided to integrate fewer companies into the course with the same number of projects in order to decrease the organization and coordination workload.

Due to the effects of the Covid-19 pandemic on how agile software development teams work (e.g., [33], [34]), we have also decided to integrate companies whose teams having a high degree of maturity in terms of agile methods. We assumed that the challenges caused by virtual collaboration had increased and therefore wanted to integrate companies that have already successfully met these challenges in the first year of the pandemic aiming to provide the opportunity that our students benefit from these experiences. Thus, we sent inquiries to six companies from our network and provided them with comprehensive requirements such as the provision of several projects at the same time and dedicated support for each student team. We then held preliminary talks with four companies and ultimately selected two companies. The companies come from the e-commerce and online marketing sectors.

The preparation lay on both sides, the companies and university side. The preparation activities for the summer term 2021 started with initial discussions in November 2020 (see Figure 3. We discussed the specific project aims and fine-tuned the requirements in January and February 2021. The companies

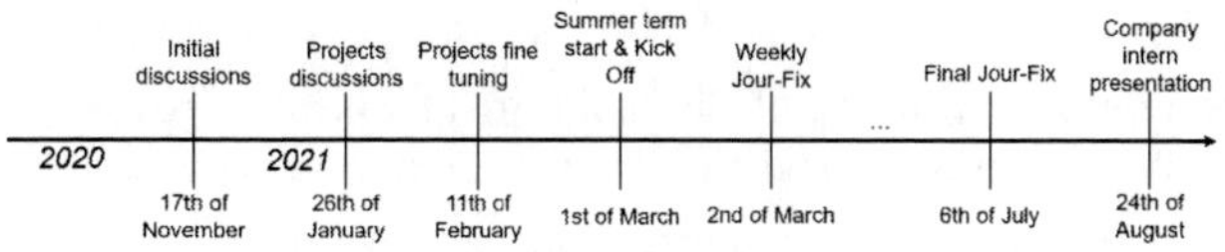

Fig. 3. Timeline summer term 2021

created internal accounts for the students in order to provide access on the company internal infrastructure. Furthermore, our colleagues at the companies discussed with agile software development teams their motivation to work with students on specific projects, challenges or conduct experiments together. Also, we discussed and clarified all research specific documentations such as non disclosure agreements and privacy policies. On university side we prepared the courses in our e-learning platform and the plan of the timeline throughout the summer term including the examination dates.

We divided the student group of 25 persons randomly into five eduScrum student teams and assigned a product owner and a project to each student team. A description of the projects is shown in Table II.

TABLE II
OVERVIEW OF THE PROJECTS IN SUMMER TERM 2021

Company identifier	Project goal
Company A	We want to understand how a 4-day workweek and a remote work setting influences the use of agile methods in software development
Company B	Analyze if a reduced workload leads to a higher quality of work. We assume that the teams outcome can be maintained with a reduced workload. What measures are there to reduce the workload? How is the quality of work rated?
Company B	What works conditions (e.g., room for maneuver; flexibility in terms of time and location; social resources) make "good work" possible. "Good work" means both the perspective of work quality and quantity, but also that people work in a mode that works in the long term and does not "wear out".
Company B	We want to analyze how personal autonomous gains and interaction losses in remote work settings are impacting the teams work.
Company B	We want to understand if and how self-direction and self-organization became more important and maybe a critical skill for work success during the remote work.

Concerning the eduScrum approach, we did several adaptions related to the switch to virtual distance teaching.

First, we decided in discussions with the companies that a high level of self-organization of the student teams may be a good idea but needs support from our sides. In order to be able to support the student teams, we defined the refinement meetings as obligatory. The student teams should prepare the meetings in terms of discussing requirements, providing insights on problems and challenges related to the team work.

Second, we wanted to increase the opportunities to provide feedback in order to support the self-optimization of the teams. Thus, the support of experienced practitioners from the company is necessary and we (lecturer and companies) decided that the product owners from the company should have at least five years of experiences working in agile software development. The student teams got the opportunity to perform retrospectives aiming to optimize the self-optimization through the term and discuss upcoming problems directly with professional support from the company and university side. The decision who (agile coach from university and/or product owner from company side) support the student teams lay by the students.

Third, the phenomena of video call fatigue and increased (mental) effort of meetings in remote work in practice is described in the literature (e.g., [23], [24]). Thus, we decided to conduct the team events with a timebox of 60 minutes and camera always on policy. The timebox support focusing on specific aspects, which need to be discussed or presented in the performed agile practices. The timebox was also defined for further meetings like workshops, besides the regular weekly schedule. Although we did not ask for the specific work environment and equipment of the students, all of them respected the camera always on policy and activated their cameras during our video calls. We did not had any major infrastructure related problems in terms of internet connection or hardware issues.

Fourth, besides all scheduled events and meetings, we offered support and availability to the students by several communication types (chat, email, phone and video calls) in order to provide as much support as possible during the term.

Finally, we prepared and performed a kick-off and introduction event at the first lecture. We used the event to explain the course organization, regulations according to the examination and the theoretical basis. Also, the product owners gave a brief overview of the company and the project aims. From the second lecture and during the term, we ran a two-week sprint rhythm. Thus, as in the 2019 and 2020 summer terms, a sprint planning and review was carried out every two weeks. The student teams and the product owner and agile coach were obligated to be present at the sprint planning dates. In the weeks without Sprint Change, optional Refinement Meetings were held. To ensure coordination with the companies, we have planned and carried out weekly jour-fix appointments. A project coordination group was set up at both companies, consisting of the product owners, the agile coach and stakeholders from the respective agile software development teams. The jour-fix events aimed to remove impediments, to synchronize the product coordination group and to prepare further measurements and tasks. The jour-fix events were conducted over the entire term. In addition to the examination presentations, the results were also presented in the companies. These took place after the summer term and did not influence the evaluation.

IV. Evaluation

In this section, we explain the used evaluation methods and give a brief overview of the results.

A. Evaluation Method

Usually, we conduct the evaluation data via an anonymized and analog survey at the end of each term. Due to the switch to virtual distance teaching the evaluation survey was transferred to a digitized version. We decided to conduct the evaluation data via the online survey two times, once during the term and the other one after the examination. The survey consists of eight closed questions using a likert scale of 5 (1 totally agree - 5 totally disagree). Mainly the closed questions ask for the quality of didactic. Also, two open questions are part of the survey. The students have the opportunity to name specific aspects that they liked or didn't like.

In addition to the data collection with the online survey, we used qualitative data collection. By participating in agile practices, eduScrum offers the opportunity to observe the work results and organization of the students regularly. There is also space for informal discussions with the students. The same applies to the weekly exchange with the product owners, in which we discussed our impressions of the student groups and their results. We documented the data collected anonymously in a Microsoft Excel file and compared it with the data from the online survey at the end of the term to validate it.

B. Results Overview

The first online survey was sent to the students on the 17th of May 2021. The students had 14 days to fill it out. 14 students (out of 25) took part in the first survey. The second survey was sent to the students on the 9th of August 2021. In the second version, they had 21 days to participate to the survey. Only six students (out of 24; one student de-registered) completed the second survey. The low response rate may have several reasons, e.g. the time as the survey was sent during the free lecture period. However, we notice a decreased rate of respondents in online survey compared before the Covid-19 pandemic and a physical survey.

The students used different tools during the term. Certain tools were selected by the companies (e.g., Atlassian Confluence, Atlassian Jira, MS Teams) or the university (Moodle). Others were selected by the student teams (like Google Docs or Trello). We give an overview of the tools in Table III.

V. Discussion

In this section, we will discuss the results of our evaluation data and answer the two research questions of our study.

We begin with our first research question: How can we perform eduScrum integrating real world problems in higher education?

We present our adapted eduScrum approach for higher education and the optimization adaptions for virtual distance teaching in Section III. The virtual distance teaching comes with several challenges in higher education. In particular, we noticed an increased effort of preparing and organizing

TABLE III
OVERVIEW OF THE TOOLS IN USE

Tool	Objective of use
Atlassion Confluence	Visualization of the sprint backlog
Atlassion Jira	Sharing and management of documents
Dropbox	Sharing and management of documents
Google Docs	Sharing and management of documents
Moodle	Learning platform
MS Excel	Documentation
MS Powerpoint	Results presentation
MS Teams	Team communication and coordination
MS Word	Documentation
Trello	Visualization of the sprint backlog
WhatsApp	Team communication and coordination

TABLE IV
AVERAGE SCORES ON THE COURSE CONTENT AND LECTURERS QUALITY

Survey item	Avg. score (1st survey)	Avg. score (2nd survey)
Overall, I rate the content of the course positive.	1.7	1
The course content was conveyed clearly.	2	1
The lecturer explains in a way that is easy to understand.	1.8	1
The students actively contributed to the success of the course.	1.6	1
There is a pleasant atmosphere between students and lecturers.	1.6	1
I was encouraged for independent thinking.	1.6	1
I had the opportunity to actively participate.	1.7	1

courses. Also the coaching and support of students take more time in such an environment. Also, we want to point especially to the situation when we are integrating external partners in our lectures. The coordination and collaboration with companies is complex and takes an increased effort. However, the switch to virtual distance teaching also provides several opportunities. We were able to integrate companies from other cities and areas of Germany to our course. This provides the opportunity to focus on specific social skills also in a distributed remote work environment. In addition, we have already collaborated with the selected companies on other research projects. Another important aspect was the existing experience in remote work settings, as the summer term in 2021 was already the third term in a virtual distance teaching environment during the Covid-19 pandemic. So everybody involved had experiences with distance teaching and learning or remote work. We also had the advantage that most of the students already knew each other, so effective team development could be carried out.

Interestingly, the students rate the course organization overall positive (1.7 and 1 in average scores; see Table IV). We assumed that the direct virtual lecture environment will be missed by the students and that the responsiveness of the lecturer will be decreased. Interestingly, the students value the visibility and quick response time from the lecturer and their product owners. For instance, one student mentioned in the survey: "*The commitment of the lecturer is great! The lecturer is always available and takes a lot of time for the group work*". The aspect of lecturer support for the student teams is also validated by several informal talks between the students and the lecturer as well as the product owners.

Also some improvement proposals were made by the students. The interaction and communication among the student teams could be improved. This could lead to a better transfer of learn effects from other teams. Following this idea, we recommend to implement a community of practice in which the eduScrum masters can be discuss their learning's to improve the collaboration among the specific teams. Another facet which is described negatively is the extensive project scope and thus, the needed effort to provide good results.

The second research question is defined as: How do the students value the work with eduScrum in a virtual distance teaching environment?

In general, the students enjoyed the organization with eduScrum. The survey data as well as our formal (during agile practices) and informal talks and discussions with the students show mostly positive feedback. Especially, the integration of practice related problems from real world companies and the work with software development teams were valued by the students. Also the research characteristic of the projects, especially conducting experiments with the software development teams were rated positively. For instance, a student commented in the survey: "*In this course, the practice-oriented character that is attributed to a university was lived... Just as you know it from agile software development and it can also be expected of Master's students, there was a high degree of self-organization and also personal responsibility... We had free ones Decision-making power when considering possible experiments, as long as they are scientifically sound and added value can be hoped for.*" Another student described the used eduScrum method in a virtual distance teaching environment as: "Excellent example of how an online event works".

However, we identified several improvement measures, especially concerning the forming phase of the teams at the beginning of the term. Also the transfer of theoretical knowledge could be improved in the future. Thus, we recommend to perform workshops with the whole course at the first two or three lectures. Also it could be helpful to implement specific team development measures per eduScrum students team, especially with the support from the already integrated practitioners from the companies.

VI. LESSONS LEARNED AND RECOMMENDATIONS

In this section, we present six specific recommendations for integrating agile methods into higher education in virtual distance settings. The recommendations are based on our experiences from the summer terms in 2020 and 2021.

a) Recommendation 1: Overcome the social distancing in virtual classroom settings: One major challenge in virtual classroom settings is social distancing between the lecturer and the class, as well between the students. This challenge may becoming a problem especially in didactic approaches with group based organizations through the term. Our experiences and the results of this paper show that the usage of an agile method and specific agile practices support us to overcome the social distancing. Due to the regular (weekly) coordination and the associated expectation on all sides (companies, lecturers, students) to produce results regularly and to put them up for discussion, the need arises in the student groups to work together on solutions in self-study. This circumstance leads to an increased focus among the students. In the last two summer terms we have not experienced a situation in which groups of students have not taken an examination. From our point of view, the students benefit from the organization of the course, since there is a likelihood of working in practice in the future and being confronted with social distances in remote work settings.

b) Recommendation 2: Increase the focus of students in virtual classroom settings: We also used strict timeboxes for agile practices in use aiming to support the students focus during the video calls. The timeboxes were 60 minutes for the weekly meetings per student team. This short timebox helping to minimize the risk of video call fatigue [18]. Thus, the defined weekly schedule increased the opportunity to perform the agile practices effective and leads to a better focus of the student teams. Similar effects are described by Matthies et al. [18]. If necessary, we have planned and carried out additional coordination and clarification appointments on other days of the week.

c) Recommendation 3: Impacting the motivation of students in virtual classroom settings through the term: A positive impact on motivation of students is of high relevance when organizing courses with problem based approaches. The relevance of the course topics, the course organization and the examination may motivate students performing good results and stay focused through a term. Several studies show that our didactic approach and the course organization support the motivation of students [7], [35]. However, the examination was planned within the examination period and we discussed internally several options to integrate part-examinations during the term. We decided to define four increments based on the content, which needs to be provided for the examination. The student teams had to present the increments during the term on specific dates, which we communicated in the first lecture. The increments support a goal-oriented learning for the students' exam and provides us the opportunity to investigate the students results. The student teams presented the increments in several ways using various tools and got directly feedback by the product owners and agile coach. Thus, we recommend a clear communication what is expected by university and company side through the term, which leads to a positive impact on students motivation.

d) Recommendation 4: Increase the opportunities to support the students in virtual distance teaching: Even if the use of agile methods is not an option for other lecturers, we would like to point out that a specific, targeted exchange with students brings advantages in virtual distance settings. Especially, when organizing a course in groups, we have found that questions were more often asked by the students and introverted students also participate more often. Interestingly, we cannot confirm these experiences for other modern didactic approaches such as flipped classroom with larger groups. We therefore recommend considering how the possibilities for specific support from lecturers can be optimized in virtual distance teaching. From our point of view, the offer to contact the IT professionals involved in the course is also supportive. Even if the social distance causes a loss of trust between teachers and students, the offer to contact other people (in our case from the companies) may be helpful in order to be able to increase the support. Based on our learning's, offering specific agile practices such as refinements and retrospective meetings help the students to counteract the decrease of feedback within the student teams and among the stakeholders. This may lead to an increased trust, especially between lecturers and students and thus, lead to the opportunity to support the students related to specific problems and challenges they have.

e) Recommendation 5: Increase the collaboration with companies and integrate real world problems into higher education: The integration of real world problems including the collaboration with companies may lead to a high effort of preparing and performing courses in higher education. However, several studies show that the problem based learning approach provide several positive effects on the students motivation and learning outcomes, especially when integrating real world problems and IT professionals (see Section II). From our point of view, it is helpful to strive for collaboration with several companies and to align it in the long term. The preparation and implementation of courses in higher education requires thorough preparation. This requires mutual trust and a corresponding commitment to agreements on both sides. We made a conscious decision to work with companies with whom we performed various research projects in the past. The regular and recurring collaboration inevitably leads to a trusting cooperation in which common goals can be pursued and so the companies can also benefit by having the opportunity, for example, to scientifically examine current challenges and problems. The strong practical relevance combined with scientific work is an advantage for the students. They have the opportunity to get insights from different contexts and have the opportunity to examine specific problems scientifically.

f) Recommendation 6: Engage the students for publishing their research: After completing the examination of the course, we gave all student groups the opportunity to strive for scientific publications based on the results gained from their work in the summer term. Four out of five groups took advantage of this opportunity. On the one hand, this shows us that the Master's students are interested in scientific work. The motivation of the participating students was always high. This is shown in particular by the fact that the publication processes of some papers continue to this day. One of the four papers has been already published [36]. Furthermore, two papers are currently in the review process (one at a conference, one at a journal). Another paper is in revision for a German-language journal. To prepare for writing the paper, we first held a workshop on scientific work and writing. This workshop was structured in the same way for all four student groups. On the basis of the workshop, we jointly defined specific measures to optimize the written examination, which were largely carried out by the students. We recommend other teachers, especially in master courses, to motivate students about science and to show them specific possibilities to share their results in the research community. Even if the publication does not work on the first try, the learning effect is given, for example for the master's thesis and other scientific projects in future.

VII. Conclusion and Future Work

The Covid-19 pandemic came with several challenges and advantages for teaching in higher educational settings. Many universities were not used to organize and perform distance learning courses before the pandemic.

This paper presents our learning's performing an adapted eduScrum approach for higher education in virtual distance teaching with integrated real world problems. We adapted eduScrum for the use in virtual distance teaching in a Master of Science course in the summer term 2021. Our results show that the students value the work with eduScrum and collaborating with companies aiming to analyze their real world challenges and problems. Also, the research focused characteristic of the projects is perceived positively by the students. From the lecturer and companies points of view, we recommend to switch the focus to more scientific grounds while using problem-based learning approaches in higher education. We saw valuable research results, which we could submit at conferences and journals. The first paper is already published, further papers are currently under review.

Based on our results we present four recommendations for other lecturers to integrate agile methods using a problem-based approach in virtual classroom settings (recommendations 1 to 4). Furthermore, we call to increase the collaboration with companies and set the focus on scientific grounds and motivating students for scientific activities (recommendations 5 and 6):

- Recommendation 1: Overcome the social distancing in virtual classroom settings
- Recommendation 2: Increase the focus of students in virtual classroom settings
- Recommendation 3: Impacting the motivation of students in virtual classroom settings during the term
- Recommendation 4: Increase the opportunities to support the students in virtual distance teaching
- Recommendation 5: Increase the collaboration with companies and integrate real world problems into higher education
- Recommendation 6: Engage the students for publishing their research

In the future, we are planning to put more focus on the research characteristic and aim to support the students in scientific activities. Also, we want to consolidate the cooperation with the companies for the long term and work on strategies how to establish collaborations also in undergraduate courses.

Appendices

The survey data is available at the academic cloud: https://sync.academiccloud.de/index.php/s/JIsGAOS6is5OlVs

Acknowledgment

First of all, we would like to thank our partners from practice, who put a lot of suggestions, ideas and effort into the preparation of the projects. A lot of effort was also put into the summer term regarding coordination and establishing contacts with the respective software development teams. Particularly noteworthy here is the effort at the operationally working agile software development teams, who were involved in the various research methods (experiments, semi-structured interviews, etc.) and always actively supported the students and projects. We also would like to thank the students for their engagement during the summer term and their willingness to take part in further events such as panel discussions and presentations of results at the companies.

References

[1] VersionOne and Collabnet, "15th annual state of agile survey report," 2021, (Last accessed: October 2022). [Online]. Available: https://www.stateofagile.com/

[2] M. Kuhrmann et al., "Hybrid software development approaches in practice: A european perspective," *IEEE Software*, vol. 36, no. 4, pp. 20–31, 2019.

[3] V. Mahnič, "Scrum in software engineering courses: an outline of the literature," *Global Journal of Engineering Education*, vol. 17, pp. 77–83, 2015.

[4] E. Whitworth and R. Biddle, "The social nature of agile teams," in *Agile 2007*, J. Eckstein, Ed. Los Alamitos, Calif.: IEEE Computer Soc, 2007, pp. 26–36.

[5] A. López-Alcarria, A. Olivares-Vicente, and F. Poza-Vilches, "A systematic review of the use of agile methodologies in education to foster sustainability competencies," *Sustainability*, vol. 11, no. 10, 2017.

[6] T. F. Otero, R. Barwaldt, L. O. Topin, S. V. Menezes, M. J. R. Torres, and A. L. de Castro Freitas, "Agile methodologies at an educational context: a systematic review," in *Proceedings of the 2020 IEEE Frontiers in Education Conference (FIE)*. IEEE, 2020, pp. 1–5.

[7] W. Brown, L. Zhang, D. K. Sharma, I. Dabipi, W. Zhu, Y. Jin, and D. Bagwell, "Engaging undergraduate engineering and aviation students to explore project based learning with regard to community impact using data analytics in higher education," in *Proceedings of the 2019 IEEE Frontiers in Education Conference (FIE)*, 2019, pp. 1–5.

[8] M. Gorlatova, J. Sarik, P. Kinget, I. Kymissis, and G. Zussman, "Project-based learning within a large-scale interdisciplinary research effort," in *Proceedings of the 18th Conference on Innovation and Technology in Computer Science Education*, ser. ITiCSE '13, 2013, p. 207–212.

[9] R. Wlodarski and A. Poniszewska-Maranda, "Applying a traditional software development process to drive projects in higher education," in *Proceedings of the 45th Euromicro Conference on Software Engineering and Advanced Applications (SEAA)*, 2019, pp. 309–316.

[10] M. Zarb, T. Young, and W. Ballew, "Integrating real-world clients in a project management module," in *Proceedings of the 2019 ACM Conference on Innovation and Technology in Computer Science Education*, ser. ITiCSE '19. New York, NY, USA: Association for Computing Machinery, 2019, p. 329–330.

[11] J. Dinis-Carvalho, S. Fernandes, and J. C. R. Filho, "Combining lean teaching and learning with eduscrum," *International Journal of Six Sigma and Competitive Advantage*, vol. 10, pp. 221–235, 2017.

[12] S. Hof, M. Kropp, and M. Landolt, "Use of gamification to teach agile values and collaboration: A multi-week scrum simulation project in an undergraduate software engineering course," ser. ITiCSE '17. New York, NY, USA: Association for Computing Machinery, 2017, p. 323–328.

[13] P. K. Linos, R. Rybarczyk, and N. Partenheimer, "Involving it professionals in scrum student teams: An empirical study on the impact of students' learning," in *Proceedings of the 2020 IEEE Frontiers in Education Conference (FIE)*, 2020, pp. 1–9.

[14] C. Matthies, T. Kowark, and M. Uflacker, "Teaching agile the agile way — employing self-organizing teams in a university software engineering course," in *2016 ASEE International Forum*. New Orleans, Louisiana: ASEE Conferences, June 2016, https://peer.asee.org/27259.

[15] C. Matthies, "Scrum2kanban: Integrating kanban and scrum in a university software engineering capstone course," in *Proceedings of the 2nd International Workshop on Software Engineering Education for Millennials*, ser. SEEM '18, 2018, p. 48–55.

[16] J. C. Metrôlho, F. R. Ribeiro, and P. Passão, "Teaching agile software engineering practices using scrum and a low-code development platform – a case study," in *Proceedings of the 15th Conference on Software Engineering Advances*, 2020, pp. 160–165.

[17] G. Lang, "Agile learning: Sprinting through the semester," *Information Systems Education Journal*, vol. 15, no. 3, pp. 14–21, 2017.

[18] C. Matthies, R. Teusner, and M. Perscheid, "Challenges (and opportunities!) of a remote agile software engineering project course during covid-19," in *Proceedings of the 55th Hawaii International Conference on System Sciences*, 2022, pp. 911–920.

[19] Y. Y. Ng and A. Przybyłek, "Instructor presence in video lectures: Preliminary findings from an online experiment," *IEEE Access*, vol. 9, pp. 36 485–36 499, 2021.

[20] A. A. Siegel et al., "Teaching through a global pandemic: Educational landscapes before, during and after covid-19," in *Proceedings of the 2021 Working Group Reports on Innovation and Technology in Computer Science Education*, ser. ITiCSE-WGR '21. New York, NY, USA: Association for Computing Machinery, 2022, p. 1–25.

[21] M. Paasivaara, V. Heikkilä, C. Lassenius, and T. Toivola, "Teaching students scrum using lego blocks," in *Companion Proceedings of the 36th International Conference on Software Engineering*, ser. ICSE Companion 2014, 2014, p. 382–391.

[22] M. Neumann and L. Baumann, "Agile methods in higher education: Adapting and using eduscrum with real world projects," in *Proceedings of the 2021 IEEE Frontiers in Education Conference (FIE)*, 2021, pp. 1–8.

[23] K. Marek, E. Winska, and W. Dabrowski, "The state of agile software development teams during the covid-19 pandemic," in *Proceedings of the 5th International Conference on Lean and Agile Software Development*. [S.l.]: Springer, 2021, vol. 408, pp. 24–39.

[24] M. Neumann, Y. Bogdanov, M. Lier, and L. Baumann, "The sars-cov-2 pandemic and agile methodologies in software development: A multiple case study in germany," in *Proceedings of the 5th International Conference on Lean and Agile Software Development*. [S.l.]: Springer, 2021, vol. 408, pp. 40–58.

[25] S. A. Butt, S. Misra, M. W. Anjum, and S. A. Hassan, "Agile project development issues during covid-19," in *Proceedings of the 5th International Conference on Lean and Agile Software Development*. [S.l.]: Springer, 2021, vol. 408, pp. 59–70.

[26] A. Stevanovic, R. Bozic, and S. Radovic, "Higher education studentsexperiences and opinion about distance learning during the covid-19 pandemic," *Journal of Computer Assisted Learning*, vol. 37, no. 6, pp. 1682–1693, 2021.

[27] S. Iglesias-Pradas, Hernandez-Garcia, J. Chaparro-Pelaez, and J. L. Prieto, "Emergency remote teaching and students' academic performance in higher education during the covid-19 pandemic: A case study." *Computers in human behavior*, vol. 119, 2021.

[28] M. Bond, S. Bedenlier, V. Marin, and M. Haendel, "Emergency remote teaching in higher education: mapping the first global online semester," *International Journal of Educational Technology in Higher Education*, vol. 18, no. 50, 2021.

[29] W. Wijnands and A. Stolze, "Transforming education with eduscrum," in *Agile and Lean Concepts for Teaching and Learning*, 2019, pp. 95–114.

[30] W. Wijnands et al., "The eduscrum guide," 2020, (Last accessed October 2022). [Online]. Available: https://www.eduscrum.nl/img/The_eduScrum_guide_English_2.pdf

[31] A. Przybyłek, M. Albecka, O. Springer, and W. Kowalski, "Game-based sprint retrospectives: multiple action research," *Empirical Software Engineering*, vol. 27, no. 1, 2022.

[32] K. Schwaber and J. Sutherland, "The scrum guide," 2021, (Last accessed: October 2022). [Online]. Available: https://www.scrumguides.org/scrum-guide.html

[33] M. Neumann and Y. Bogdanov, "The impact of covid 19 on agile software development: A systematic literature review," in *Proceedings of the 55th Hawaii International Conference on System Sciences*, 2022.

[34] N. Ozkan, O. Erdil, and M. Ş. Gök, "Agile teams working from home during the covid-19 pandemic: A literature review on new advantages and challenges," in *Proceedings of the 6th International Conference on Lean and Agile Software Development*. Springer International Publishing, 2022, pp. 38–60.

[35] V. Mahnič, "Teaching scrum through team-project work: Students' perceptions and teacher's observations," *International Journal of Engineering Education*, vol. 26, p. 96, 2010.

[36] J. Topp, J. H. Hille, M. Neumann, and D. Mötefindt, "How a 4-day work week and remote work affect agile software development teams," in *Proceedings of the 6th International Conference on Lean and Agile Software Development (LASD)*, Cham, 2022, pp. 61–77.

An Interactive Digital Twin for Visual Querying and Process Mining

Spyros Loizou
Department of Computer Engineering and Informatics
Cyprus University of Technology
Limassol, Cyprus
e-mail: spyros.loizou@cut.ac.cy

Andreas S. Andreou
Department of Computer Engineering and Informatics
Cyprus University of Technology
Limassol, Cyprus
e-mail: andreas.andreou@cut.ac.cy

Abstract — **Large volumes of structured, semi-structured and unstructured data are produced daily by industrial businesses which require analysis and processing with appropriate models and algorithms to obtain valuable knowledge. This paper introduces a framework for business technology that combines the notion of Digital Twins with Process Mining aiming at delivering a simple and efficient way to retrieve customized data and process it with the use of graphical techniques, the providing interactive visualization of process mining steps. More specifically, the proposed framework provides the ability to define different data sources and link these sources with a visual query generator which constructs, executes and depicts graphically the results of custom queries. The framework also includes sophisticated Artificial Intelligence / Machine Learning algorithms for data analysis, filtering and prediction. The framework is demonstrated through an interactive dashboard, which was implemented in Python to support a fully operational and visual process mining environment that facilitates decision making without the need of programming or data management skills.**

Keywords- Big Data; Digital Twin; Business Process Mining; Visual Querying; Visual Analytics.

I. INTRODUCTION

Nowadays, the new, most popular scientific trends worldwide are the Internet of things (IoT), big data, cloud computing and Artificial Intelligence (AI). All these technologies generate a large volume of data which may be structured, semi-structured and unstructured. Big data analysis models and algorithms are used to organize, analyze and mine raw data to obtain valuable knowledge. Data visualization represents data in some systematic form including attributes and variables for the unit of available information. Visualization of data allows users and businesses mash up data sources to create custom analytical views [1]. Data processing and visualization include data mining, data collection of various types, structured or unstructured, as well as their knowledge-based representation techniques to transform primary data to meaningful data.

A Digital Twin is a virtual representation of an object or system that spans its lifecycle, is updated from real-time data, and uses simulation, machine learning and reasoning to support decision-making. In addition, the digital twin can also make predictions about how an asset or process will evolve or behave in the future [2].

Process Mining is a technique relating the fields of data science and process management to support the analysis of operational processes based on event logs. The goal of process mining is to turn event data into insights and actions. Process mining techniques use event data to show what people, machines, and organizations are really doing. Process mining provides novel insights that can be used to identify the executional path taken by operational processes and address their performance and compliance problems.

The relevant open research challenge of this area is to investigate how Digital Twins may contribute to enhancing the applicability and efficiency of process models so as to prevent costly failures in physical objects or activities, and improve quality and productivity, by using advanced analytical, monitoring and predictive capabilities, test processes and services.

This paper proposes the integration of Process Mining with Digital Twins, which targets providing interactive visualization capabilities of data related process mining steps. In this context, a framework is described for defining the data sources, linking them to a visual query generator, and finally depicting graphically the results. The framework may also utilize sophisticated algorithms residing in its Artificial Intelligence / Machine Learning module, mostly for performing data analysis and prediction. This interactive approach essentially provides smart data processing (logs and events) and graphical visualization of the insights produced. The user environment is simple, self-explanatory and ergonomic, while its graphical form and usability allow non-expert users, that is, users without prior knowledge in the area of databases or process mining algorithms, to easily structure and run queries, execute steps for process mining modeling, and receive the result in a comprehensible, interactive form. These features make the proposed approach unique and quite appealing to personnel in industrial environments, such as production engineers and shift managers, who wish to be continuously informed about selected parts in a process cycle. A prototype tool has been developed as a proof of concept which provide the basic functionality described above. The tool is work in progress and enhanced.

The rest of the paper is structured as follows: Section 2 discusses related work and provides the technical background in the areas of Process Mining and Digital Twins. Section 3 presents the proposed framework and describes how Digital Twins are integrated with specific process mining phases. This is followed by a system demonstration in Section 4. Finally, Section 5 concludes the paper and highlights future work directions.

II. Technical Background/Related Work

This section provides a short description of the technical background behind Digital Twins, visualization platforms for data processing and process mining, and outlines related studies. To the best of our knowledge, there are no studies in the literature reporting the integration of graphical environments for interactive, visual smart data processing with process mining based on event logs.

A. Data Processing and Visualization

The area of smart data processing comprises the ability to clearly define, interoperate, openly share, access, transform, link, syndicate, and manage data. Under this perspective, it becomes crucial to have various knowledge-based metadata representation techniques to structure datasets, annotate them, link them with associated processes and software services, and deliver or syndicate information to recipients. Smart Data Processing Systems are used to include various topics to fully utilize the aforementioned capabilities, such as data ingestion, data aggregation of an enormous variety of structured, unstructured and semi-structured datasets, knowledge-based meta-data representation techniques for the conversion of raw into smart data, data privacy and protection, automated deployment, run-time software performance monitoring and dynamic configuration.

Data visualization is the graphical representation of information and data. By using visual elements like charts, graphs, and maps, data visualization tools provide an accessible way to see and understand trends, outliers, and patterns in data. In the world of Big Data, data visualization tools and technologies are the challenges tackled in different papers focusing on how to analyze massive amounts of information and make data-driven decisions. Visualization-based data discovery methods allow business users to mash up disparate data sources to create custom analytical views. Wang et al. [1] present new methods and advances of Big Data visualization through introducing conventional visualization methods and the extension of some of them for handling big data, discussing the challenges of big data visualization, and analyzing technology progress in big data visualization.

Steed et al. [3] describe and demonstrate a visual analytics system, called the Exploratory Data analysis ENvironment (EDEN), with specific application to the analysis of complex earth system simulation datasets. EDEN represents the type of interactive visual analysis tools that is necessary to transform data into insights, thereby improving critical comprehension of earth system processes.

B. Digital Twins

A Digital Twin (DT) is traditionally characterized by two-way interactions between the digital and the physical world. A DT offers error optimization to save money and time, reduces defects and manages the lifecycle of the Internet of things (IoT). A DT represents a powerful technology because it is able to stream, optimize and analyze data in the virtual and physical world. This paper utilizes the idea of DTs to graphically represent and interact with event data and process logs and applies this approach to industrial environments.

Several papers address the problem of monitoring real-time data and optimization of an industrial production line or product design. Vachalek et al. [4] describe a project which is a technological concept focusing on the continuous optimization of production processes, proactive maintenance, and continuous processing of process data. This project is essentially promoting the concept of Industry 4.0, while its basic goal is to support the existing production structures within the automotive industry and the most efficient use of resources by augmented production and planning strategies, such as DTs. Schluse et al. [5] introduce the concept of Experimental Digital Twins (EDTs) as a new structuring element for simulation-based systems engineering processes and their interdisciplinary and cross-domain simulation in Virtual Test Beds (VTBs). This enables comprehensive simulations on system level and allows for seamless connection between virtual and real worlds in hybrid scenarios. It also introduces new structures and processes to consistently use simulations in varying application scenarios through-out the life-cycle. Fuller et al. [6] present the challenges, applications, and enabling technologies for Artificial Intelligence, Internet of Things (IoT) and DTs. A review of publications relating to DTs is performed, producing a categorical review of recent papers which discusses a range of papers residing in different scientific areas and presents the current state of research, providing at the same time an assessment of the enabling technologies, challenges and open research issues for DTs.

C. Process Mining

Process mining is a technique designed to discover, monitor and improve real processes by extracting readily available knowledge from event logs stored in information systems. Process mining includes process discovery, that is, extracting process models from an event log file. Moreover, process mining techniques use different algorithms to extract and organize data and business flows, with the top 5 mining algorithms being Alpha Miner, Fuzzy miner, Heuristic miner, Inductive Miner and Genetic miner. Alpha Miner generates a Petri Net model in which all the transactions are visible, unique and correspond to the classified events.

A Petri net is a tuple $N = (P, T, F, W, m_0)$, where,

$P=\{p_1, p_2, \ldots, p_m\}$ is a finite set of places,
$T=\{t_1, t_2, \ldots, t_k\}$ is a finite set of transitions,
places P and transitions T are disjoint ($P \cap T = \emptyset$),
$F \subseteq (P \times T) \cup (T \times P)$ is the flow relation (arcs),
$W : ((P \times T) \cup (T \times P)) \rightarrow \{1, 2, \ldots\}$ is the arc weight mapping (where $W(f) = 0$ for all $f \notin F$, and $W(f) > 0$ for all $f \in F$), and $m_0 : P \rightarrow \{1, 2, \ldots\}$ is the initial marking representing the initial distribution of tokens.

The Heuristics Miner algorithm deals with activities expressed as time-based intervals. Burattin et al. [7] introduced a new definition of the direct succession relation based on time-based intervals. A single event is represented as an activity. Accorsi et al. [8] promote the topic of process mining and define a set of guiding principles and list important challenges, to guide for software developers, scientists, consultants, business managers, and end-users. The goal is to increase the maturity of process mining as a new tool to improve the (re)design, control, and support of operational business processes. Bozkaya et al. [9] propose a methodology to perform process diagnostics, based on process mining. Given an event log of an information system within an organization, process diagnostics gives a broad overview of the organization's process(es) within a short period of time.

Recent studies have explored the use of Digital Twins for process mining: Park et al. [10] proposed a digital twin interface model as a representation of an organization that reflects the current state of business processes. Using this representation, process analysts are able to define constraints and actions that are continuously monitored and triggered to improve business processes. Pan et al. [11] presented a data-driven Digital Twin framework integrated with Building Information Modeling (BIM), IoT, and data mining for advanced project management, which can facilitate data communication and exploration to better understand, predict, and optimize the physical construction operations.

None of the studies on coupling Digital Twins with process mining thus far has been concentrated on defining, linking and analyzing data used for process modelling or enhancement through approaches that alleviate the need for expert knowledge. This paper addresses this challenge and provides the means for a totally different user experience based on visual querying and process mining data-driven tasks, which is characterized by simplicity, self-explainability, ease of use and graphical ergonomics.

III. METHODOLOGY

The basic idea of using visual analytics is to represent the information in a graphical and meaningful visual manner, allowing the user to interact with the information, gain insight, and make better decisions. The visual representation of the information reduces complexity in cognitive work needed to perform certain tasks and derives insight from massive, dynamic, and often conflicting data by providing timely, defensible, and understandable assessments [12].

The main target of this paper is to combine Digital Twins and process mining in a unified graphical and interactive dashboard to deliver visual representation of business data and logs, which allows for the execution of visual queries and the launch of intelligent (Artificial Intelligence and Machine Learnings) algorithms. This target is realized through a framework that describes how to transform data into a Digital Twin visual representation and then use this representation to construct and execute customized visual queries for selected process data describing the business flow. In this respect, the framework is rather generic to be able to apply in every business and data context. Figure 1 depicts the architectural structure of this approach, which involves two distinct parts: (i) the mechanism for importing data sources residing in a database (tables, fields, relationships and semantics), as well as process mining related data in the form of log files and event streams; (ii) the interactive dashboard, which offers multiple functions for constructing and executing queries in a simple, visual manner, without requiring knowledge on databases or Structured Query Language (SQL), enhanced by a set of AI/ML modules (e.g. Neural Networks, Evolutionary Algorithm and Fuzzy Logic) that provide data cleaning and/or prediction, and recommendations. The framework is generic in the sense that it does not pose strict development restrictions on the data importing mechanisms (e.g., format, files, data models, etc.) or to the mechanisms for performing visual processing of the data. Therefore, the proposed architecture essentially converts process mining into an interactive procedure that utilizes Digital Twins to visualize data and processes retrieved from logs and files stored in a database. This involves interacting with all information present in logs (activities, resources, cost, time performance, etc.) which may now be represented graphically, depicting all data connections and relations, as well as the hierarchical flow of data that is followed within the business.

Furthermore, the framework couples AI and machine learning algorithms that are stored in its smart engine. These algorithms may be trained and executed in the background to enable smart data processing, including filtering and cleaning (e.g., removing or modifying data that is incorrect, incomplete, irrelevant, duplicated, or improperly formatted as it may hinder the process or provide inaccurate results), prediction and predictive analytics, classification, etc. Using visual task execution (querying and machine learning) in the background enables users that will use these steps to obtain the desired results without the need of programming skills or prior knowledge on intelligent algorithms. The smart engine is able to host as many intelligent algorithms as desired, while the process for adding them into the engine is simple and straightforward, following the principles of ML-Ops [13]. Currently, the smart engine is under development comprising several implementations of neural networks for prediction and recommendations.

A dedicated software tool was developed to demonstrate the proposed framework, which was built in Python, mainly using pm4py, pandas and Streamlit libraries. Pm4py was the main instrument for implementing well-known process mining tasks and algorithms. Streamlit, which is an open-source framework that creates applications for data science and machine learning in a short time, was utilized to support the development of an interactive, flexible and user-friendly dashboard. Finally, pandas, which is a dedicated library that offers data structures and operations for manipulating tables and time series, was responsible for managing all data from databases and events from log files. Lastly, Unity was the environment used to produce playful, aesthetically correct and user-friendly graphics for the presentation and interactive use of the dashboard. Unity [14] is a cross-platform game engine, which is primarily used to develop video games and simulations for computers, consoles and mobile devices.

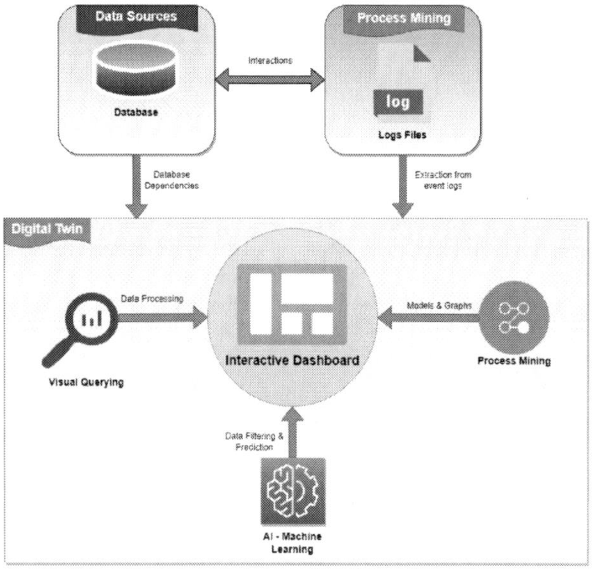

Figure 1. Architecture of the proposed framework for visual and interactive process mining.

IV. SYSTEM DEMONSTRATION

The supporting software system is currently under development and its current form supports two process discovery algorithms, namely the Directly Follows Graph and the Heuristic Miner.

Figure 2 illustrates the Directly Follows Graph which is constructed using process mining logs that depict the average time for each process event. In this graph, each node represents an activity, and the arcs describe the relationships between various activities.

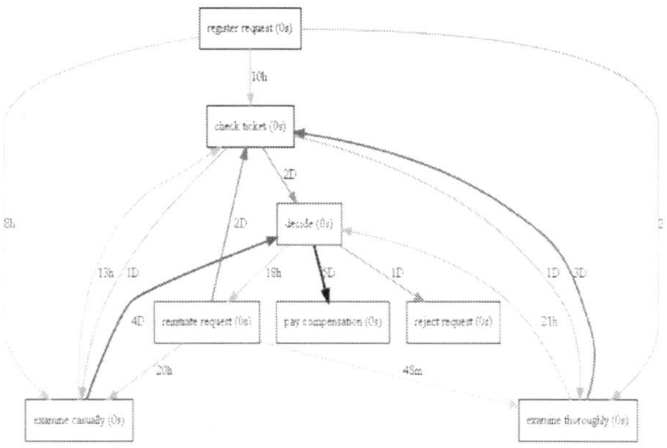

Figure 2. Directly Follows Graph based on average time.

Figure 3 presents the Heuristic Miner that is considered an improvement of the Alpha Miner algorithm and acts on the Directly Follows Graph. It provides a way to handle noise and to find common constructs. The output of the algorithm is a Heuristics Net, an object that contains both the activities and the relationships between them.

The interactive dashboard developed offers the ability to graphically analyze large volumes of information and facilitate data-driven decision making. A demonstration workflow of this graphical dashboard is provided as follows:

In step 1, the user is able to select the tables they wish to process from a pool of data available (Figure 4). This is performed by dragging and dropping in the central part of the screen called workspace or canvas, any table from the list appearing on the right.

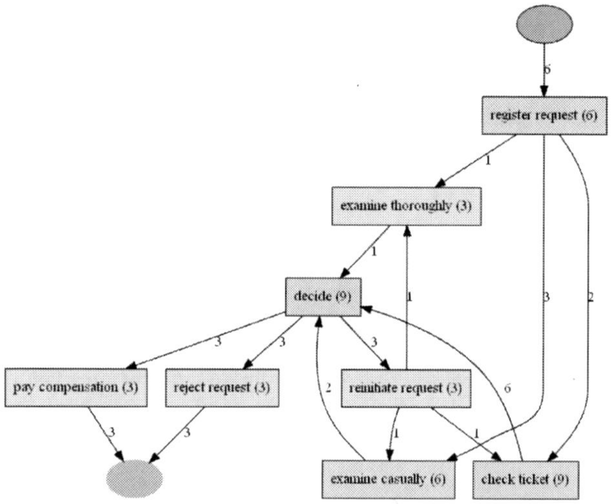

Figure 3. Heuristic Miner.

When tables are inserted into the workspace, any existing relationships are automatically depicted, showing the links between fields. The user may also select a field and reveal any links to other tables and the corresponding attributes. The dashboard supports the importing of disparate data sources in its pool of tables, allowing users to mash up different information to create custom analytical views.

Subsequently in Step 2, the user selects the fields they want to work with and defines the type of processing they wish to perform. To do so, they select an action from a toolbar at the bottom center of the screen (Figure 5), which dictates how a field is to be processed, (e.g., defines a threshold value or logical condition – Figure 6). In essence, the user constructs a query without the need of prior knowledge on SQL statements or semantics. They just define the action that needs to be executed and the system runs it and visualizes the results.

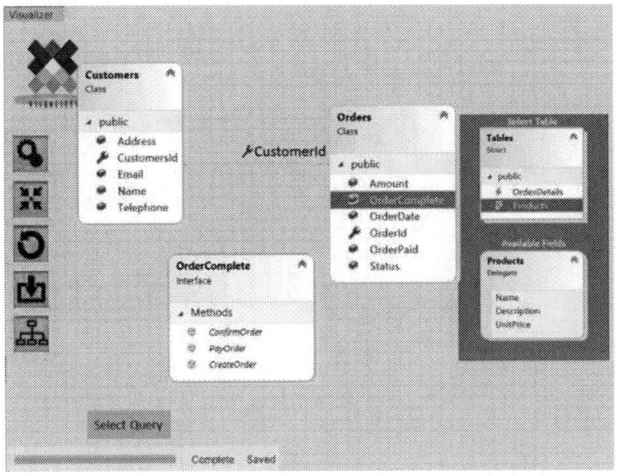

Figure 4. Selection of tables and attributes of interest.

The results are presented in various tabular and graphical forms (Figure 7). Each presentation form is interactive, as the user can point and click on a certain part of the visual information and be redirected to another part which relates new data from existing ones, such as flattening of data in process mining terms [8] or offers a different visual representation (e.g., from tabular form to a pie chart).

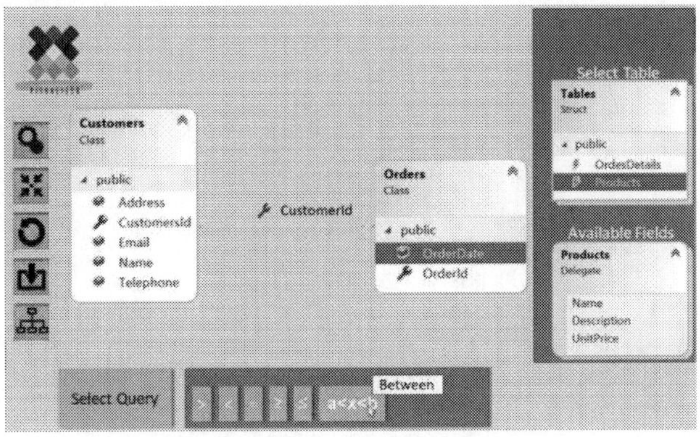

Figure 5. Selection of logical and arithmetic operators

This short presentation of the proposed framework demonstrates its usefulness and applicability. The user is able to utilize its functionality and depict graphically selected data values, connections and relations, as well as construct and execute queries in a simple, visual and interactive way. In addition, she may produce models presenting the hierarchical flow of data that is followed within the business, the sequence and dependencies of events within a business process, etc.

All this data manipulation and business process graphical information is produced requiring from users little or no prior experience and knowledge on either databases and SQL queries, or process mining and process models, thus making the framework suitable for practical use in real environments by workers that specialize in other tasks, such as manufacturing and production.

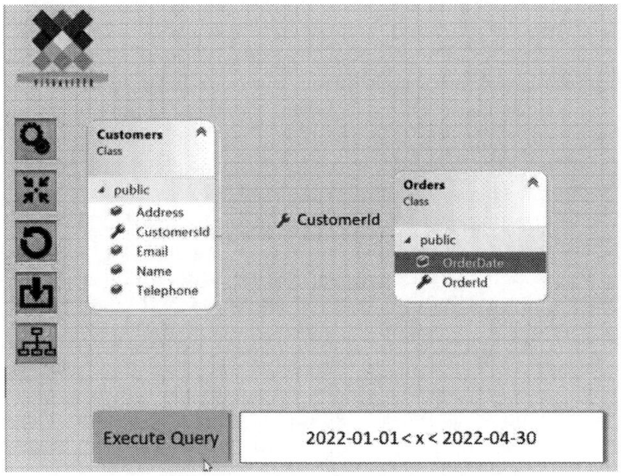

Figure 6. Creation and execution of a visual query.

Figure 7. Results obtained from a visual query.

V. CONCLUSIONS

The area of Big Data Visualization and Analytics is in great need for efficient and simple ways to retrieve customized data mainly with the use of graphical techniques. This paper addressed the challenge of providing a framework which provides the ability to define data sources in the form of tables, attributes and relationships, and then process and analyze this data based on the concept of visual querying. More specifically, the framework builds upon the notions of Digital Twins to provide smart data processing and data analytics, and especially targets at bridging graphical methods with algorithms and activities from the area of process mining. Overall, this approach provides a fully operational and interactive environment in which meaningful business process data is depicted graphically to clients/organizations, and functional decision making, and predictive analytics are supported.

The combination of Digital Twins and Business Process Mining offers an interactive visual representation of business data and logs. Process data is first transformed into parts of a DT and then specific functionality is provided that gives the ability to the user to create and execute customized queries of the data and the business flow and visualize results in a graphical and interactive form. Digital twins investigate in depth the relationships between the data mainly with a graphical technique. Algorithms are made available to users who will use standard steps to obtain the desired results without the need of programming skills.

Future work will concentrate on the following: (i) Data management will be enhanced with the use of Data Lakes in which sorted and cleaned data will be hosted, thus ensuring the highest quality of data is fed into the AI/ML algorithms; (ii) Further expansion of the interactive dashboard with inclusion of more sophisticated visualization features supporting predictive analytics; and, (iii) Enhancement of the visualization component with interactive capabilities that will suggest business flow corrections to achieve better process results.

ACKNOWLEDGMENT

This paper is part of the outcomes of the CSA Twinning project DESTINI. This project has received funding from the European Union's Horizon 2020 research and innovation programme under grant agreement No 945357.

REFERENCES

[1] L. Wang, G. Wang, and C. A. Alexander, "Big Data and Visualization: Methods, Challenges and Technology Progress," *Digit. Technol.*, vol. 1, no. 1, pp. 33–38, 2015, doi: 10.12691/dt-1-1-7.

[2] A. Rasheed, O. San, and T. Kvamsdal, "Digital twin: Values, challenges and enablers from a modeling perspective," *IEEE Access*, vol. 8, pp. 21980–22012, 2020, doi: 10.1109/ACCESS.2020.2970143.

[3] C. A. Steed *et al.*, "Big data visual analytics for exploratory earth system simulation analysis," *Comput. Geosci.*, vol. 61, pp. 71–82, 2013, doi: 10.1016/j.cageo.2013.07.025.

[4] J. Vachalek, L. Bartalsky, O. Rovny, D. Sismisova, M. Morhac, and M. Loksik, "The digital twin of an industrial production line within the industry 4.0 concept," *Proc. 2017 21st Int. Conf. Process Control. PC 2017*, pp. 258–262, 2017, doi: 10.1109/PC.2017.7976223.

[5] M. Schluse, M. Priggemeyer, L. Atorf, and J. Rossmann, "Experimentable Digital Twins-Streamlining Simulation-Based Systems Engineering for Industry 4.0," *IEEE Trans. Ind. Informatics*, vol. 14, no. 4, pp. 1722–1731, 2018, doi: 10.1109/TII.2018.2804917.

[6] A. Fuller, Z. Fan, C. Day, and C. Barlow, "Digital Twin: Enabling Technologies, Challenges and Open Research," *IEEE Access*, vol. 8, pp. 108952–108971, 2020, doi: 10.1109/ACCESS.2020.2998358.

[7] A. Burattin, *Process mining techniques in business environments: Theoretical aspects, algorithms, techniques and open challenges in process mining*, vol. 207. 2015.

[8] R. Accorsi, M. Ullrich, and W. M. P. Van Der Aalst, *Process mining*, vol. 35, no. 5. 2012.

[9] M. Bozkaya, J. Gabriels, and J. M. Van Der Werf, "Process diagnostics: A method based on process mining," *Proc. - Int. Conf. Information, Process. Knowl. Manag. eKNOW 2009*, no. 2, pp. 22–27, 2009, doi: 10.1109/eKNOW.2009.29.

[10] G. Park and W. M. P. Van Der Aalst, "Realizing A Digital Twin of An Organization Using Action-oriented Process Mining," *Proc. - 2021 3rd Int. Conf. Process Mining, ICPM 2021*, pp. 104–111, 2021, doi: 10.1109/ICPM53251.2021.9576846.

[11] Y. Pan and L. Zhang, "A BIM-data mining integrated digital twin framework for advanced project management," *Autom. Constr.*, vol. 124, no. July 2020, p. 103564, 2021, doi: 10.1016/j.autcon.2021.103564.

[12] C. Mehrotra, N. Chitransh, and A. Singh, "Scope and challenges of visual analytics: A survey," *Proceeding - IEEE Int. Conf. Comput. Commun. Autom. ICCCA 2017*, vol. 2017-Janua, no. 4404, pp. 1229–1234, 2017, doi: 10.1109/CCAA.2017.8229987.

[13] S. Makinen, H. Skogstrom, E. Laaksonen, and T. Mikkonen, "Who needs MLOps: What data scientists seek to accomplish and how can MLOps help?," *Proc. - 2021 IEEE/ACM 1st Work. AI Eng. - Softw. Eng. AI, WAIN 2021*, pp. 109–112, 2021, doi: 10.1109/WAIN52551.2021.00024.

[14] Unity, [online] https://unity.com/, [accessed Oct. 2022]

A Case Study on Combining Model-based Testing and Constraint Programming for Path Coverage

M. Carmen de Castro-Cabrera
Department of Computer Science
University of Cádiz
Cádiz, Spain
email:maricarmen.decastro@uca.es

Antonio García-Dominguez
Department of Computer Science
University of York
York, United Kingdom
email:a.garcia-dominguez@york.ac.uk

Inmaculada Medina-Bulo
Department of Computer Science
University of Cádiz
Cádiz, Spain
email:inmaculada.medina@uca.es

***Abstract*—In the context of advances in software testing, this paper is related to the generation of test suites and black box testing. Test coverage is a popular technique to evaluate test quality: a test suite that can exercise a large part of the paths in a program will provide a high confidence that the program will work as expected. One way to obtain test suites with high path coverage is through model-based testing, and specifically using a diagram, which represents the various states in the program and their possible transitions. Using model-based testing, it is possible to obtain a set of paths that achieves a set of coverage criteria. Constraint programming approaches can then be used to turn each path into a test case with its program inputs and oracle, by solving the input and output constraints collected along the path. In this paper, we present a case study on this combination of techniques, by developing a state diagram that represents a popular piece of software, and using it to derive a set of test cases that achieve path coverage through constraint programming. Specifically, two tools have been used: GraphWalker (to obtain a set of paths through the program) and MiniZinc (to obtain test inputs by solving the constraints along the paths). We have obtained good results on the `cat` GNU Coreutils utility, especially in terms of ease of understanding the logic of the software through the GraphWalker diagram and its visual execution, as well as the agility in obtaining the restrictions to be solved to achieve path coverage.**

Index Terms*—*Keywords–Model-based Testing; Path Coverage; Constraint Programming; GraphWalker; MiniZinc.

I. Introduction

Model-Based Testing (MBT) is one of the most frequently used techniques in software testing, because it can represent the program in a schematic and simplified way, abstracting from the implementation details or the language used. As defined in [15]: "Model-based testing is an efficient and adaptable method of testing software by creating a model describing the behavior of the system under test". In addition, it is easier to check the coverage criteria on the program model. This technique is used at different levels of software testing, especially in system testing, and with a broad range of levels of automation with various tools [1] [10]. One of the tools is GraphWalker (GW) [11], which provides graphical model design and execution capabilities. On the other hand, in order to test a software, it is useful to have a set of test cases that meet some coverage criteria. To achieve this coverage, it is usual during test case generation to establish some restrictions on the inputs and expected outputs of the program. In order to solve the constraints needed to follow a specific path and identify the expected outputs, one option is to use Constraint Programming (CP). In [8], CP is described as "The basic idea in constraint programming is that the user states the constraints and a general purpose constraint solver is used to solve them. Constraints are just relations, and a Constraint Satisfaction Problem (CSP) states which relations should hold among the given decision variables". Like MBT, CP has tools to implement the constraint models: Kjellerstrand surveyed the available tools in [9].

In this paper, MiniZinc (MZ) [6] will be used to implement the constraint models of the paths obtained with GW. A combination of both techniques has the advantage of automating the testing process, simplifying the visual understanding of the logic of the program to be tested, the execution of the model itself, and the generation of a test suite that meets certain path coverage criteria [12]. We propose an example of using both techniques for the `cat` utility.

This paper is organized as follows: Section II introduces the proposal and the concepts of the techniques used, Section III develops the `cat` case study, explaining the tools used and the process followed to obtain the model and the set of test cases. Section IV summarizes related work and finally, Section V presents conclusions and future work.

II. Proposal

This section describes in a generic way the process followed to generate test cases suites with path coverage, starting from a model of the program under test, and then CP to implement the constraints of the paths to cover. We have based this only on the execution and specification of the program (without accessing the source code). The starting point is to create a model of the software's behaviour, such as a Finite State Machine (FSM). The FSM can *transition* from one state to another in response to some inputs. In this paper, states are represented by nodes (or vertices) and transitions by edges. The proposed combination follows these steps:

1) **Model-Based Testing**: create a model of the program behaviour as a finite state machine, by defining and labeling states and transitions; add input and output

constraints for each transition expressed by propositional logic; run the model with a given path generator and coverage criteria (e.g., full edge coverage and random search), achieving a set of paths that fulfil that coverage as output of this step.

2) **Constraint Programming**: from the paths generated previously, collect the input constraints, mapping to implement as CP models covering the paths; execute the implemented models to obtain the test suite; run the program to be tested with the test suite obtained in the previous step, using the output constraints from the relevant path as the test oracle.

A. *Formalisation of input and output conditions as a CSP*

This paper considers the example given as a CSP (Constraint Satisfaction Problem) by declaring constraints on the problem area (the space of possible solutions) and consequently finding solutions that satisfy all the constraints. In order to formally represent the input and output conditions included in the GW model diagram, the notation of a CSP proposed by Barber et al. in [7] will be followed. The focus in this paper is on problems with finite domains, which consist of a finite set of variables, a finite domain of values for each variable and a set of constraints that limit the possible values that these variables can take in their domain. The resolution of a CSP, as usual with representation systems, consists of two phases:

1) Modelling the problem as a constraint satisfaction problem (CSP).
2) Processing the constraints by means of search algorithms: this step in our approach is achieved by MiniZinc and the solvers integrated in it.

Definition 1. A constraint satisfaction problem (CSP) is an ordered triple (X, D, C) where:

- X is a set of n variables $x_1, ..., x_n$.
- $D = \langle D_1, ..., D_n \rangle$ is a vector of domains (D_i is the domain containing all the possible values that the variable x_i can take).
- C is a finite set of constraints. Each constraint is defined on a set of k variables by means of a predicate that restricts the values that the variables can take.

Definition 2. An assignment of variables, (x, a), is a variable-value pair representing the assignment of the value a to the variable x. An assignment of a set of variables is a tuple of ordered pairs, $((x_1, a_1), ..., (x_i, a_i))$, where each ordered pair (x_i, a_i) assigns the value a_i to the variable x_i.

Definition 3. A solution to a CSP is an assignment of values to all variables such that all constraints are satisfied. So, a solution is a tuple containing all the variables of the problem.

Specifically for our example `cat` utility, X is represented by the variable x, D represents all the possible values of the variable x, according to the defined domain (strings), and C is formed by all the propositions applicable to the variables and which establish restrictions on their values (e.g.,: $is\_word(x)$ belongs to C; it is true when x is a string that contains alphabet characters). Table I shows the notation to express our CSP logic propositions in GW and their mappings to MZ.

III. Case Study

To show our approach, the GNU Coreutils `cat` tool has been selected [4]. Its manual page [5] shows that it takes a number of optional flags, followed by zero or more file paths, and it will be used as reference material to design a set of black-box tests. Based on the options, inputs and outputs when executing `cat`, we will draw the diagram of the program model. The rest of this section will explain how the steps in Section II will be applied to `cat`.

A. *GraphWalker diagram*

GW is an open-source MBT tool [11] available in three versions: web-based, console-based, and Eclipse plugin.

From a model, GW will generate a walk through it. A model has a start element, a generator that determines how the next step in the path is chosen, and an associated stop condition that tells GW when to finish its execution. This is formulated through an expression such as `random(edge_coverage(100))`, which represents a random walk aiming for 100% edge coverage. GW models can contain arbitrary JavaScript-based code for the *actions* and *guards* of their transitions. A transition will only activate and will execute its action if its guard evaluates to a true value. For example, in `cat`, a guard would be, if the `-b` option overrides the `-n` option, in order to execute the `-n` option, it must be checked that the `-b` option has not been previously executed. This is carried out by checking whether the output condition of option `-b` is already in the condition list of the path.

1) Modeling `cat` in GW: Figure 1 shows the GW model for `cat`. Three states have been considered: an initial state (`init`), a state that includes the options (`options`) and an exit status (`exit`). There is an empty (epsilon) transition from `init` to `options` that represents the start of the inputs for the test case, an `end_of_args` transition from `options` to `exit` that marks the end of the list of arguments, and a `loop` transition that returns to `init`, signalling the start of the next test case. The `loop` transition is needed to allow a single execution of GW to produce multiple tests that all together meet the required coverage criteria: without it, only one test case would be generated. There is a transition for each of the `cat` input arguments (`-b`, `-E`, `-n`, `-s`, `-T`, `-v`, `input`), that loop back to the same `options` state, allowing multiple options and inputs to be accumulated. In addition to these options, other options appear in the manual such as `-A`,

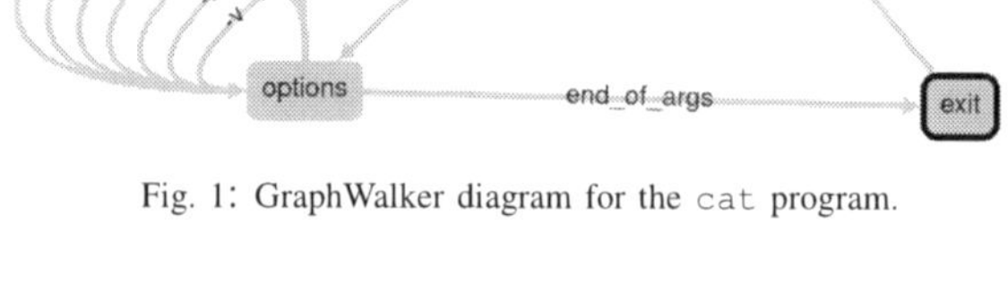

Fig. 1: GraphWalker diagram for the `cat` program.

TABLE I: MAPPING INTERMEDIATE CODE TO MINIZINC CONSTRAINT.

Proposition	MiniZinc constraint
$input\_string(x)$	`var x: string;`
$contains(x, s)$	`str_contains(x, s);`
$is\_word(x)$	`str_len(x) > 0; str_alphabet(x, \abcd...");`
$is\_nonprinting(x)$	`var x: string of {"\n","\b"," "}; str_len(x) > 0; str_alphabet(x, "\n\b...");`
$x > 0$	`var x: int; x > 0;`
$output\_string(x)$	`var x: string;`

`-e` or `-t`, but they have been simplified for clarity and because they are shorthand combinations of the previous ones.

2) Adding the input and output constraints of each transition in propositional logic language: For each of the `cat` options, input and output restrictions were modelled through transition guards and actions. These guards and actions were defined so that valid combinations of options are tested, and unnecessary repetitions of options are avoided to keep the length of the list of arguments within a readable size. For each option's transition, a guard is used to ensure that it is not already included in the path, and an action records the additional constraints for the current path. Input and output constraints in the GW model are expressed as conjunction of propositions. For example, for the option `-E`, which displays $ character at end of each line, the action records the input condition that is $input\_string(s) \wedge contains(s, "\backslash n")$, meaning that must have at least two lines (with an end line character), in order to observe its effect on lines in the output. The added output condition is $output\_string(o) \wedge contains("\$", o)$.

3) Validating the GW model through execution: GW was given the expression `random(edge_coverage(100) && reached_vertex(exit))` to generate a walk over the graph: a random walk that achieves full edge coverage and reaches the `exit` state. The model was then run and visited elements were colored: by the end of the execution, the entire diagram had been colored. Furthermore, by running the model in the GW CLI (GraphWalker Command-Line Interface), we obtain a set of paths that will result in a set of test cases that meets the coverage conditions.

B. Constraint programming with MiniZinc

MiniZinc is an open source constraint modeling language. It can be used to model constraint satisfaction problems and high-level, solver-independent optimization problems. The default distribution of MiniZinc includes a graphical interface for ease of use, as well as examples [6]. The data file is separate from the model file. Both are translated to obtain a FlatZinc model, which depends on the specific solver used. A MiniZinc model consists of a set of variables and parameter declarations, followed by a set of constraints. Given that `cat` is a text-centric program, we used MiniZinc with the G-Strings solver, a variant of the Gecode solver which can solve constraints over strings [13] [14].

1) Implementing each path's input constraints as CP models in MZ: A base template for all constraint models in `cat` was created, containing the variables and generic constraints that needed to be met for all paths. This was followed by a set of constraint model fragment for each option of `cat` achieved from GW output and mapping to MZ language, as shown in Table I. For instance, Listing 1 shows the model for the input constraints when using both `-T` and `-E` as options.

```
%%% GENERIC INPUT VARIABLES (all options)
var string of {"a","b"..."z",":","/",".","\n","\b","␣","\t"}:
    input_string;
%%% CONDITIONS – INPUT CONSTRAINTS
constraint str_len(input_string) > 0; % must not be empty
%%% –T option input constraint: must have TAB
constraint str_contains(input_string, "\t");
%%% –E option input constraint: must have linebreak
constraint str_contains(input_string, "\n");

solve satisfy;
```

Listing 1: Excerpt of MiniZinc model for running `cat` with -T and -E.

2) Running the implemented model in MZ to obtain the test cases of the defined set: The MZ models can then be solved from the command line, using `mzn-gstrings modelName.mzn`. The execution of the model in Listing 1 can be redirected to a file (e.g., a text file named `InputTEoptions.txt`) as a test case of the previously obtained suite with GW. It will generate a test case to check the execution of `cat` with the options `-TE`. Therefore, it must have at least one tab character and two lines (an end-of-line character).

C. Test `cat` against the obtained test cases

The output file of the previous execution (InputTEoptions.txt) is the input to execute `cat` with the indicated options: `cat -TE InputTEoptions.txt`. The output conditions specified in the GW diagram model (step 1) provide an oracle to check whether the execution of `cat` with the corresponding options and the file containing the input information generated by MZ is met. Continuing with the example above, the output conditions were $output\_string(x) \wedge contains("\backslash t", x) \wedge contains("\$", x)$. It has been verified that the inputs are indeed generated correctly by meeting the input constraints for the combined options of each path. It is important to note that our configuration of GW produces random walks, and therefore each execution may produce a different set of tests that achieves the same coverage criteria. The following results are from a specific execution of GW, using the command-line version to execute the JSON file produced by the web-based modeling tool (GW Studio). The execution produced input and output conditions for 5 test cases, which were then solved with MiniZinc to generate the specific inputs to be used. Table II shows the characteristics of the test cases. Four combined MZ models have been implemented to

TABLE II: RESULTS OF `cat` TEST SUITE EXECUTION, INCLUDING LINE COVERAGE OVER ITS 281 LINES

Test suite	Options	Cumulative line coverage (%)
Tc_1	-E ,-s	38.79
Tc_2	(none)	38.79
Tc_3	-s ,-b	43.71
Tc_4	-E ,-T ,-n, -b, -s	46.62
Tc_5	-E ,-T, -v ,-b ,-s	51.25

generate the inputs for each of these test cases (https://nube.uca.es/index.php/s/Z3lHZFAueE6FV4G) (Tc_2 represents when no option has been applied). Afterwards, `cat` has been run applying the options and inputs generated by the combined MZ models, obtaining the expected results. The constraints on the outputs have been checked manually. In addition, to find out the percentage of executed code, we have also used the source code coverage analysis and profiling tool, `gcov` (https://gcc.gnu.org/onlinedocs/gcc/Gcov.html), which generates accurate counts of the number of times each statement in a program is executed and annotates the source code to add instrumentation. Over 281 executed lines of source code, every test case has executed the cumulative percentage indicated in the Table II. We can observe that when these test cases are run consecutively, the tc_1 covers 38.79% of the lines executed; there is no difference in coverage between the tc_1 and tc_2, since no options are included in the cat run. From the tc_1 to the tc_3, line coverage increases by 4.92 points, by simply substituting option -E for option -b, reaching 43.71% of lines covered. Nevertheless, between the tc_3 and tc_4 case, despite the inclusion of two more options, the percentage of line coverage only increases 2.91 points over the previous one. Finally, it is interesting to note that between the tc_4 and tc_5 cases, the coverage increases up to 4.63 points, having the same number of options as the previous case, simply substituting option -n by option -v, reaching a cumulative percentage, total for all the test cases of 51.25.

IV. RELATED WORK

In [3], Sun et al. propose a constraint-based model-driven testing approach for web services. They extend the Web Services Description Language (WSDL) to include constraints related to web services behavior and make an empirical study with 3 real-life applications. Although it is a complete study, it is specific to web services, unlike our proposal, which aims to be more generic.

Vishal et al. [16] applied MBT using Spec Explorer to the Image Detection Subsystem responsible for generation, detection and translation of X-rays to images. They developed their own tool that interfaces Spec Explorer with a constraint solver to generate specific test data for the model. They used a small constraint solver called ZogSolve, limited and without recent updates compared to MiniZinc which contains a graphical interface and supports numerous constraint solvers and is updated frequently. Furthermore, Spec Explorer is proprietary software, unlike GraphWalker which is open source.

RESTest [2] is a framework for automated black-box testing of RESTful APIs (representational state transfer application programming interface). Among its main features, RESTest supports the specification and automated analysis of dependencies between parameters, allowing the use of constraint solvers for the automated generation of valid test cases. Similar to our proposal, it is based on tests for black box environments, where the code is not accessible. In this case, open source software tools are used, such as IDLReasoner. Given an the OpenAPI Specification (OAS) and a set of IDL dependencies (e.g., using IDL4OAS), the tool translates them into a CSP expressed in MiniZinc. Afterwards, they analyze the result of CSP, to find out whether an API call satisfies all dependencies between parameters. Therefore, CSP is used for the same purpose as in [16] to manage the dependencies between parameters. However, unlike the work presented here, MBT is used as a technique to obtain the system model, but visual representations such as those of GW are not used.

Overall, unlike other approaches, our proposal has the advantage of using two open source and frequently updated tools. In addition, the proposal aims to be more general, both in applications and in the domains in which it is applied.

Although a simple case study of the proposed technique has been presented for didactic purposes, we believe that it is possible to apply this technique to other more complex systems, as long as they can be represented in GraphWalker as a finite state transition machine and the input conditions can be represented as a set of constraints for a constraint solver system. For constraint implementation and execution, we have chosen MiniZinc, because of the advantages discussed in Section III, but it is possible to use other tools containing constraint solvers. Moreover, there may be other model representation software tools similar to GraphWalker that can be used to represent the model. It should be ensured that they are also capable of running such a model and that they are configurable in terms of path coverage.

V. CONCLUSION

It has been proposed to use the combined MBT and CP techniques to generate a test cases suite that meets the path coverage criteria. The process has been developed through a case study of a widely known utility, `cat`, using GraphWalker to represent the state model and execute it visually. GraphWalker has produced a set of paths providing sets of input constraints to be solved through CP using the MiniZinc tool to generate the test cases covering the paths. Finally, the results have been checked by running `cat` with the corresponding options and the generated inputs, while measuring test coverage with gcov. Therefore, we conclude that the combination of both techniques and the presented tools is a promising approach to facilitate software testing, making the process more readable by representing and running the model in a visual way. As future work, we intend to test this process with other larger programs and in other contexts, and introduce more formalisation and automation on the constraints.

ACKNOWLEDGMENTS

This work was partially funded by the Spanish Ministry of Science and Innovation and the European Regional Development Fund (ERDF) (projects RTI2018-093608-BC33 and RED2018-102472-T).

REFERENCES

[1] A. C. Dias Neto, R. Subramanyan, M. Vieira, and G. H. Travassos, "A Survey on Model-Based Testing Approaches: A Systematic Review". In: Proceedings of ASE 2007. pp. 31–36. ACM, NY, USA, 2007. https://doi.org/10.1145/1353673.1353681

[2] A. Martin-Lopez, S. Segura, and A. Ruiz-Cortés, "RESTest: Black-Box Constraint-Based Testing of RESTful Web APIs". In: Service-Oriented Computing. pp. 459–475. Springer International Publishing, Cham, 2020

[3] C. Sun, M. Li, J. Jia, and J. Han, "Constraint-based model-driven testing of web services for behavior conformance". In: International Conference on Service-Oriented Computing. pp. 543–559. Springer, 2018

[4] D. MacKenzie et al., "GNU Coreutils". Free Software Foundation, Inc, 1994-2022

[5] D. MacKenzie et al., "GNU Coreutils 9.1". Free Software Foundation, Inc, 1994-2022, https://www.gnu.org/software/coreutils/manual/html_node/cat-invocation.html, [Retrieved: July 2022]

[6] Data61 research network, CSIRO, "MiniZinc". https://www.minizinc.org/index.html, 2015, [Retrieved: July 2022]

[7] F. Barber and M. Salido, "Introducción a la programación de restricciones". [In English: "Introduction to constraint programming"]. Inteligencia Artificial, Revista Iberoamericana de Inteligencia Artificial vol. 7, pp. 13–30, 01 2003

[8] F. Rossi, P. van Beek, and T. Walsh, "Chapter 4 Constraint programming". In: Handbook of Knowledge Representation, Foundations of Artificial Intelligence, vol. 3, pp. 181–211. Elsevier, 2008. https://doi.org/10.1016/S1574-6526(07)03004-0

[9] H. Kjellerstrand, "Comparison of CP systems — and counting". In: SweConsNet Workshop 2012, 2012, [Retrieved: July 2022]

[10] M. Bernardino, E. M. Rodrigues, A. F. Zorzo, and L. Marchezan, "Systematic mapping study on MBT: tools and models". IET Software vol. 11, pp. 141–155, 2017

[11] N. Olsson and K. Karl, "GraphWalker, an open-source model-based testing tool". https://graphwalker.github.io/, [Retrieved: July 2022]

[12] P. Ammann and J. Offutt, "Introduction to software testing". Cambridge University Press, New York, 2nd edn., 2016

[13] R. Amadini et al., "Minizinc with strings". In: Logic-Based Program Synthesis and Transformation, pp. 59–75. Lecture Notes in Computer Science, Springer, 2017. https://doi.org/10.1007/9783319631394_4

[14] R. Amadini, G. Gange, P.J. Stuckey, and G. Tack, "GStrings Gecode with (dashed) string variables". https://github.com/ramadini/gecode, 2019, [Retrieved: July 2022]

[15] S. Rosaria and H. Robinson, "Applying models in your testing process". Information and Software Technology vol. 42, pp. 815–824, 2000. https://doi.org/https://doi.org/10.1016/S0950-5849(00)00125-7

[16] V. Vishal, M. Kovacioglu, R. Kherazi, and M. R. Mousavi, "Integrating Model-Based and Constraint-Based Testing Using SpecExplorer". In: IEEE 23rd International Symposium on Software Reliability Engineering Workshops. pp. 219–224, 2012. https://doi.org/10.1109/ISSREW.2012.88

Automated Testing: Testing Top 10 OWASP Vulnerabilities of Government Web Applications in Bangladesh

Azaz Ahamed
Computer Science & Engineering
Independent University, Bangladesh
2120637@iub.edu.bd

Nafiz Sadman
Silicon Orchard Ltd.
Bangladesh
nafiz@siliconorchard.com

Touseef Aziz Khan
Computer Science & Engineering
Independent University, Bangladesh
2120638@iub.edu.bd

Mahfuz Ibne Hannan
Computer Science & Engineering
Independent University, Bangladesh
2120635@iub.edu.bd

Farzana Sadia
Dept. of Software Engineering
Daffodil International University, Bangladesh
sadia_swe@diu.edu.bd

Mahady Hasan
Computer Science & Engineering
Independent University, Bangladesh
mahady@iub.edu.bd

***Abstract*—With an increase in the popularity of the Internet, there is also a rise in the number of security threats and vulnerabilities. The Open Web Application Security Project (OWASP) is an online community-driven project that provides a set of 10 most crucial security vulnerabilities to monitor and mitigate to have safer Internet connectivity. Automated software testing provides invaluable insights into the current situation regarding OWASP Top 10 2017 vulnerabilities for Web applications from the five sectors of the Bangladesh Government. In this research, comprehensive testing has been carried out using BurpSuite, ZAP and Netsparker to see recurring vulnerabilities among the sections of Web applications. We draw data-driven comparisons between these tools and evaluate them against Web applications from respective sectors and the results are presented accordingly. We found the Services and the Transportation sectors to be most vulnerable.**

***Index Terms*—Software Testing; Automated Testing; OWASP; Web Vulnerability; Testing Tools**

I. INTRODUCTION

With the advancement and adoption of Web technology, more and more government services are provided by online Web applications these days. Sophisticated online portals are visited by thousands of citizens every day as they become more and more reliant on their convenience. Naturally, Web applications like these store sensitive user information. With such adoption, comes great concern for security to protect the data and privacy of the users of such platforms [1]. Newer and more sophisticated attacks need to be monitored around the clock due to the advancements in Web technology [2].

Current issues remain where Web applications like these are not properly or regularly tested for OWASP (Open Web Application Security Project) vulnerabilities as seen in test results disseminated in later sections of this paper. Our purpose is to understand how the selected government Web applications from different sectors fare against the testing tools.

According to a news article [3], approximately 147–200 Bangladeshi entities, including government agencies, were exploited during April 2021. Before this, according to another article in 2019 [4], 3 private banks were targeted and exploited to steal almost $3 million. In 2016 in a similar type of heist, the hackers stole approximately $81 million from Bangladesh Bank's federal reserve. These are only a handful of the reported attacks.

This paper provides a selection of three automated vulnerability testing tools to find the OWASP Top 10 2017 vulnerabilities [5], [6]. The tools used in this research were: Netsparker, BurpSuite, and ZAP. The main motivations for selecting these three tools were the availability of existing security research [7], OWASP compliant threat detection features, reporting, and documentation of usage. According to past research, they are fast and reliable, especially when tested against known vulnerabilities [8]. The different sectors of government Web applications that were tested using the tools are Services, Telecommunication, Welfare, Health, and Transportation. Each test was run three times on the same Web application using the same tool. This methodology was adapted to mitigate any inconsistencies and establish a measurement of correctness for each testing tool. The results were averaged to come to a consistent comparison between the sectors, and testing tools were carefully compared for consistency. Common vulnerabilities among the Web applications are pointed out and different sectors are compared against one another based on how secure they are.

In this paper, we intend to:

- Explore the three popular OWASP compliant testing tools and their effectiveness in finding and recording OWASP's top 10 vulnerabilities.
- Test live Bangladesh Government Web applications, find their vulnerabilities and draw a comparison between them.

Our target is to find answers to the following questions:

- What is the current status of Bangladesh's sensitive Government Websites in terms of vulnerabilities?
- Which testing tools used in this research can best detect the most vulnerabilities of the Bangladeshi Government Websites?
- What do these vulnerabilities tell us about the Websites?

The organization of the paper is as follows: In Section 2, we present a brief technical background on OWASP and its list of top 10 vulnerabilities. In Section 3, we look into different literature reviews. We present our research methodology in Section 4 and discuss the results in Section 5. Finally, we conclude our research and future scope in Section 6.

II. TECHNICAL BACKGROUND

In this section, we briefly introduce OWASP. It is a non-profit, community-driven project whose primary aim is to study contemporary vulnerabilities in modern Web applications. The foundation present a set of standards for identifying the severity of the vulnerabilities, their possible causes, and their mitigation plans.

Table I summarizes the Top 10 OWASP 2017 Vulnerabilities with their acronyms. Throughout this paper, we will use these acronyms to denote corresponding vulnerabilities.

TABLE I
SUMMARY OF TOP 10 OWASP 2017

Vulnerabilities	Description	Denotations
A1:2017	Injection	A1
A2:2017	Broken Authentication	A2
A3:2017	Sensitive Data Exposure	A3
A4:2017	XML External Entities (XXE)	A4
A5:2017	Broken Access Control	A5
A6:2017	Security Misconfiguration	A6
A7:2017	Cross-Site Scripting (XSS)	A7
A8:2017	Insecure Deserialization	A8
A9:2017	Using Components with Known Vulnerabilities	A9
A10:2017	Insufficient Logging & Monitoring	A10

The OWASP Top 10 is a list of the ten most important and common vulnerabilities that may be found in most Web applications. The popularity of the Top 10 list enabled its adoption as a standard in many vulnerability testing tools. In Table 1, we can see the list of the OWASP Top 10 vulnerabilities and their denotations. All the tools used in this research adhere to the Top 10 classes of OWASP to report found vulnerabilities. BurpSuite, Netsparker, and ZAP are all OWASP compliant. They provide rich reports which accurately identify vulnerabilities according to the OWASP Top 10 classification. After finding the class of a vulnerability, we can refer to the OWASP Website to get a better understanding of its severity and possible mitigation ideas.

III. LITERATURE REVIEW

Deployed Websites often come with several vulnerability issues. These vulnerabilities have been extensively studied and systematically categorized into vulnerability standards. Batch-Nutman [5] studied the most frequent Web application vulnerabilities that can help firms better secure their data from such threats. The research aimed to help users and developers be better equipped to deal with the most common attacks and design strategies to avoid future attacks on their Web apps. The author tested 10 vulnerabilities listed in OWASP (Open Web Application Security Project) Top 10 [9] designed and developed a secure Web application by following the guidelines of the OWASP. The paper focused on the mitigation of Web application vulnerabilities through configuration changes, coding, and patch application. SQL injection, broken authentication, sensitive data exposure, broken access control, and XML external entities are among the OWASP top ten vulnerabilities. The Web application's security has been tested and proven to have a defense mechanism in place for the aforementioned vulnerabilities. There are several Web application vulnerability testing works [10]–[12]. Yulianton et al. [13] proposed a framework to detect Web application vulnerabilities using a combination of Dynamic Taint Analysis, Static Taint Analysis, and Black-box testing. The research showed that the combination of Dynamic and Static Taint Analysis fed to Black-box testing as metadata yielded greater accuracy and fewer false positives of vulnerabilities. The aforementioned research gives us the potential attacks on Websites and potential mitigations. However, the importance of testing during the development period is emphasized by Rangau et al. [14], who explained the emergence of DevSecOps [15] and how it has come to be important due to fast-paced deployment and a lack of proper security documentation. Afterward, they introduced tools like ZAP, JMeter, Selenium, etc., to implement dynamic testing for Web applications in CI/CD pipelines. Interestingly, the authors in [16] initially expressed concern regarding manual testing how many resource it requires, and the complications it introduces. Later the advantages of the Automated Testing tools are explored and the findings indicate to 68-75% increase in efficiency when it comes to time and effort in testing.

In this research, we test the effectiveness of three different testing tools namely Netsparker, BurpSuite, and ZAP on Bangladeshi Government Service Websites based on OWASP Top 10 2017 Web vulnerabilities. Comparative analysis of testing tools [1], [6], [17]–[19] focused on determining the efficiency of load testing and detection of several Web attacks, studying pen testing on several Web applications, and how network information is gathered using various tools about Websites to find the possibility of cyberattacks. Anantharaman et al. [8] discussed OWASP A09:2017 (i.e., Using Components with Known Vulnerabilities) and pointed out several ways software can be component-based vulnerable proof by having updated technological stacks and secure SSL. They have also noted some standard developer and tester practices and tools like BurpSuite that can help prevent vulnerabilities.

Various scanners have also been compared to check which type of scanners can detect the maximum vulnerabilities. [20] presented a systematic comparison between ZAP and Arachni testing tools across four vulnerabilities (SQL injection, XSS, CMDI, and LDAP). The authors used OWASP and WAVSEP as benchmarks. The authors conclude that ZAP outperformed Arachini and recommended that OWASP be used as standard benchmarking to evaluate testing results. [21] presented a comparative study of 8 Web vulnerability scanners (Acunetix, HP WebInspect, IBM AppScan, OWASP ZAP, SNLS-VK, Arachni, Vega, and Iron WASP) and tested on WebGoat and Damn Vulnerable Web Application (DVWA) which have pre-built vulnerabilities. Precision, recall, Youden index, OWASP Web benchmark evaluation (WBE), and the Web application security scanner evaluation criteria (WASSEC) were used to evaluate the performances of the tools. The authors concluded that all of the testing tools require improvement in terms of code coverage, detection rate, and reducing the number of false positives. Karangle et al. [22] compared modern security scanning tools, such as Uniscan and ZAP tools for testing vulnerabilities in Web applications through experimentation on 20 Websites. The paper goes into detail about penetration testing using these tools and how the Website URL's information is gathered to find the possibility of cyberattacks. Ultimately, they found that the ZAP tool performed faster than Uniscan, but Uniscan performed a deeper vulnerability analysis.

The scope of our research involves comparing the effectiveness of the three tools in terms of capturing the vulnerabilities listed in OWASP Top 10 2017 on the Bangladeshi Government Web services. Setiawan et al. [23] performed vulnerability analysis for government website applications and carried out using the Interactive Application Security Testing (IAST) approach. The study used three tools, namely Jenkins, API ZAP, and SonarQube. Moniruzzaman et al. [24] performed a systemized combination of black box and white box testing to detect vulnerabilities of different Bangladeshi Government and popular Websites using most of the common testing tools. They have found out that about 64% of the selected Websites are at risk of vulnerabilities. However, we also explicitly point out in our study the consistencies and inconsistencies in these tools.

IV. RESEARCH METHODOLOGY

To ensure proper documentation of vulnerabilities reported by each tool for each Website, an individual tool was run three times on each Website to give a proper baseline. The following data was collected from every test run:

- Number of runs (number of test runs on the same Website using the same tool).
- Time taken to complete the test (in minutes).
- Counts of vulnerabilities found for severities: Low, Medium, and High.
- Total number of vulnerabilities.

Multiple tests were run this way to understand the consistency of vulnerability reporting for each tool for a particular Website. Running multiple tests also helped to understand the UI/UX of the individual tools, which essentially gave us a way to judge their usability, accessibility, and applicability for finding OWASP Top 10 vulnerabilities.

Another goal was to determine how the government Web applications compare to each other in terms of vulnerabilities and determine if there is a correlation between the popularity of a Website and the number of vulnerabilities found there. For this, five government Web applications from different sectors were thoroughly tested with the testing tools for OWASP Top 10 vulnerabilities. The sectors are:

- Services
- Transportation
- Welfare
- Healthcare
- Telecommunications

After collecting the data found through testing, all the vulnerabilities were cross-matched with their corresponding OWASP vulnerabilities category and presented in a graphical format. There, we see the severity of the vulnerabilities: vulnerabilities found in sectors by tool and overall vulnerabilities found in different sectors.

Figure 1 represents our methodology workflow.

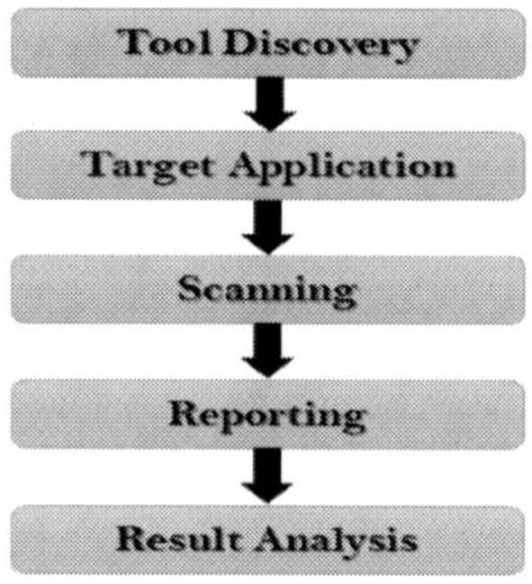

Fig. 1. Workflow of our methodology.

We can break down the process into 5 steps.

1) **Tool Discovery**: In this initial phase, the tools we selected were the most popular among their class for OWASP, as they had many resources and documentation and also, according to [7].
2) **Target Application**: In the target application phase, we chose some government Web applications that were used by citizens of the country and narrowed it down to the top 5 government Web applications.
3) **Scanning**: Several activities are carried out during this phase to perform vulnerability scanning. The vulnerability scan's goal is to identify a list of vulnerabilities in the test target. This study uses three tools: Netsparker, BurpSuite, and ZAP.
4) **Reporting**: During this phase, the tester/developer will document the possible results generated by the three tools throughout the vulnerability assessment process.
5) **Result Analysis**: In this final phase, the tester/developer analyzes the discovered vulnerability under the OWASP Top Ten 2017.

[24] tested several Bangladeshi Government Websites, but the vulnerability was mapped with Common Vulnerabilities and Exposures (CVE) and the test category was limited to 5 vulnerabilities. In this study, we covered major Bangladeshi Government Websites and presented an overview of vulnerabilities as per OWASP Top 10 2017 in the selected sites.

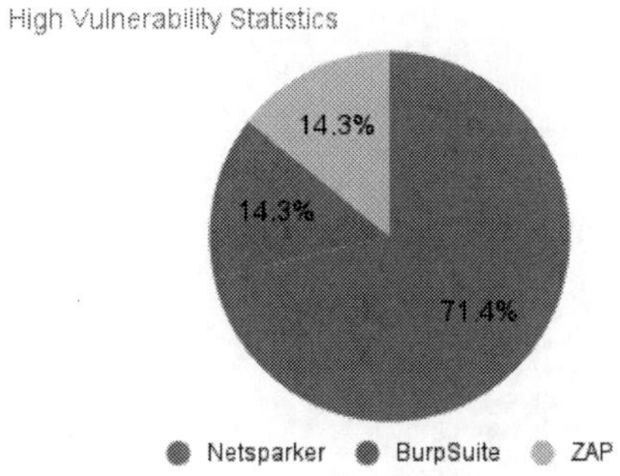

(a) High Vulnerability

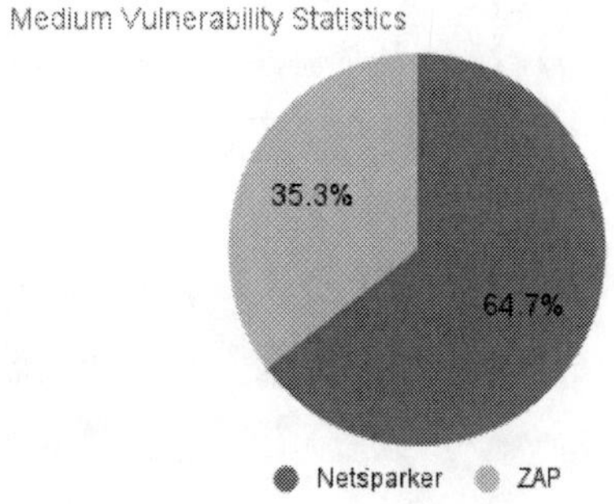

(b) Medium Vulnerability

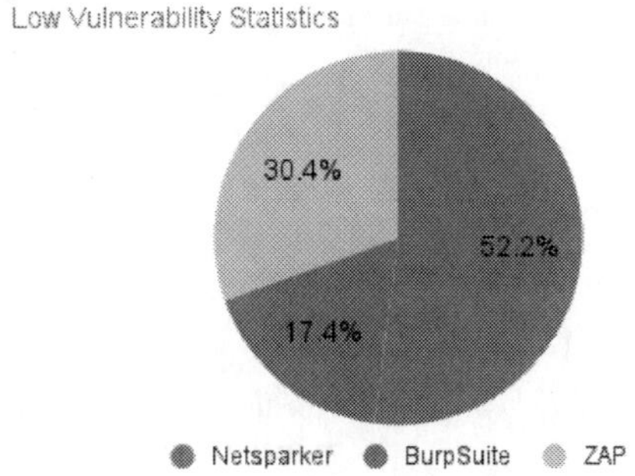

(c) Low Vulnerability

Fig. 2. Vulnerability statistics of each of the testing tools on our targeted Websites.

Our classification of High, Medium and Low vulnerabilities was aided by the OWASP Risk Factor (RF) table documented by [25]. Here, the top 10 vulnerability classes are given a Risk Factor score based on exploitability, security weakness detectability, and their technical impact on business. We have classified severity based on RF scores in the following manner:

- **LOW** *if* $4 \leq RF < 5$
- **MEDIUM** *if* $5 \leq RF < 7$
- **HIGH** *if* $RF \geq 7$

As all the testing tools report the classes of OWASP vulnerabilities, they are directly comparable to the RF scores and their corresponding severity classes.

Using the 2017 OWASP standard may seem like a limitation of this research when OWASP has announced 2021 standards. All the tools used to test vulnerabilities in this research have the option to generate reports for OWASP Top 10 2017. Therefore, we have selected OWASP 2017 as it is compatible with all the tools and the results can be compared consistently. OWASP 2021 classifications are not yet fully integrated with most vulnerability assessment tools on the market.

V. RESULT ANALYSIS

In this section, we dive deep into our findings in this research. We believe that the collected data gives us an accurate picture of the security and testing aspects of Government Web applications that deal with millions of sensitive user data every day.

If we take Figure 2 into account, we can observe that Netsparker can record the highest number of threats compared to BurpSuite and ZAP. According to the findings in Figure 2a, Netsparker records 5 times more high vulnerability threats than BurpSuite and ZAP. From Figure 2b, we can also observe that BurpSuite did not detect any Medium level threats which indicate that BurpSuite might not have enough features to test parameters when compared to Netsparker or ZAP. In Figure 2c, we can conclude that Netsparker had recorded the highest number of low vulnerability threats followed by ZAP then BurpSuite.

In Figure 3, we can see a breakdown of vulnerabilities and their severity for each sector of Web applications. OWASP vulnerabilities found by all the tools are aggregated for each sector of Web applications and classified into severity categories, as discussed earlier, based on RF scores. As we can see from the graph, Transportation and Services have the highest numbers of high-severity vulnerabilities. The high-severity vulnerabilities in Transportation and Service Web applications may result in the following scenarios:

1) *A1 - Injection*: Where unauthorized users can gain access to sensitive data to discover personal National Identity or License Information with malicious intent.

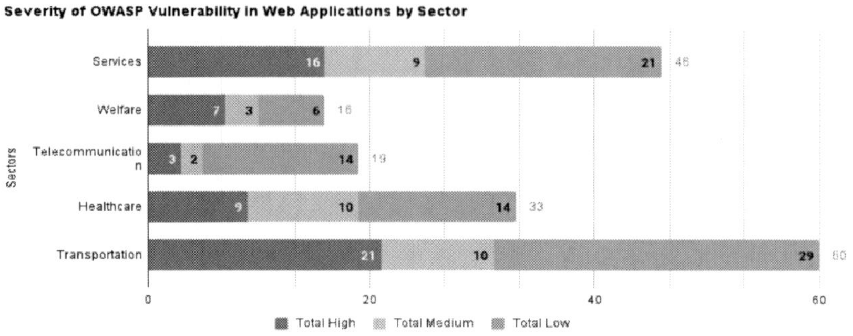

Fig. 3. Severity of OWASP Vulnerability in Web Applications by Sector.

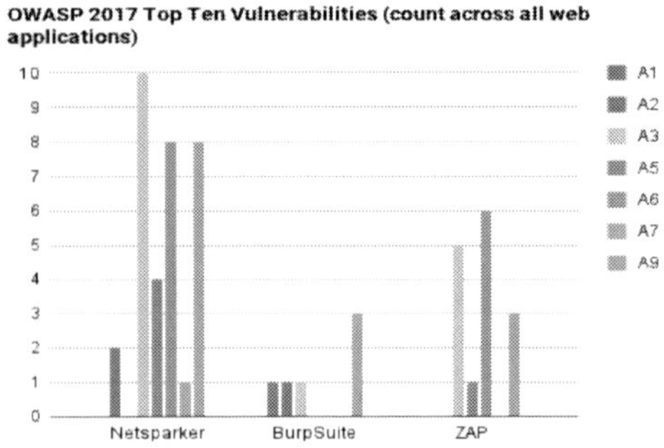

Fig. 4. OWASP 2017 Top 10 Vulnerabilities (Count across all Web applications).

2) *A2 - Broken Authentication*: Where attackers can use brute force to potentially gain access to make unauthorized changes to user identity information or forge official documents.
3) *A3 - Sensitive Data Exposure* Attackers exploit weak public/private key generation to gain access to data in transit using man-in-the-middle attacks to steal user details for illegal promotional material.
4) *A4 - XML External Entities* Older XML may enable uploading of hostile XML code through Uniform Resource Identifier (URI) network requests. This may allow remote code execution and possible denial-of-service attacks. This may result in system service downtime, causing very difficult circumstances.

Consequently, if we take a look at the medium/high-severity vulnerabilities in Healthcare, the following attack scenarios might also be true:

1) *A5 - Broken Access Control*: Where unauthorized users can make changes without any required permission. Here, the medical information of a user can be altered to make fake prescriptions to purchase unauthorized drugs.
2) *A7 - Cross Site Scripting*: Here, attackers can directly manipulate a user's browser to alter information using their credentials with remote code execution. This might result in false reports of ailments and also theft of user credentials.

These scenarios hold for the other sectors of Web applications. Low-severity vulnerabilities are not actively threatening, but may be exploitable in niche cases. Web applications from the Telecommunication sector had the lowest number of high/medium-severity vulnerabilities. We have an assumption that it may be more secure as the sector relies almost entirely on current technology and practices. Surprisingly, Welfare reported the lowest number of vulnerabilities in general, though it had a higher number of high-severity vulnerabilities than the Telecommunication sector. We think this may be due to smaller and relatively newer Web applications built with current tools and practices, whereas the applications in the Telecommunication sector were relatively mature.

According to Figure 4, we can observe that Netsparker detected the most vulnerabilities among the three tools, while ZAP was second and BurpSuite detected the least amount. It must also be noted that even though Netsparker and ZAP have similar results, Netsparker found more vulnerabilities such as A1 and A7, which ZAP did not detect. ZAP also failed to scan Welfare and Telecommunication Web applications, whereas Netsparker managed to scan all the Web applications. BurpSuite failed to scan the Transportation Web application after running for a long time. This indicates that ZAP and BurpSuite only executed surface-level scanning, while Netsparker did much deeper vulnerability analysis while scanning the Web applications. However, BurpSuite detected A2, which neither Netsparker nor ZAP were able to detect. If we observe the time taken by the testing tools to scan each Web application, ZAP is the fastest among all the tools, while BurpSuite comes in second and Netsparker takes the longest overall.

Across three runs for each Website with each testing tool, the test run with the highest number of classified vulnerabilities is kept. In this Figure 4, we can see the total number of OWASP Top 10 vulnerability classes found with each testing tool across all the tested applications.

Figure 5 illustrates the vulnerabilities discovered in various sectors. According to the chart, A6 (Security Misconfiguration) appears to be the most common vulnerability, closely

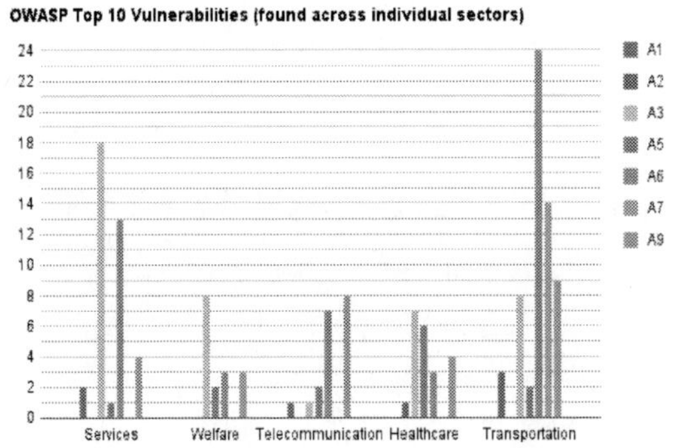

Fig. 5. OWASP 2017 Top 10 Vulnerabilities (Found across individual sectors).

followed by A3 (Sensitive Data Exposure) and A9 (Using Components With Known Vulnerabilities). According to the remediation provided in [5], we can resolve these issues for all of the vulnerabilities. Based on our targeted applications, we can see that Transportation is the most vulnerable, followed by Services.

Transportation plays a major role in the daily lives of citizens. According to Bangladesh Transport Data [26], there are approximately 4.5 million registered vehicles in Bangladesh as of June 2020. Based on this relevant data, we can conclude that there are approximately 4.5 million users of these applications whose information is at high risk. The second most dangerous application we discovered was Services, which includes business information, citizen information, banking services, etc. Bangladesh's current population is 164.7 million as of 2020, with some of them directly or indirectly using services whose data are at risk. Vulnerabilities in healthcare are much lower than what we found in Transportation and Service sectors. Telecommunications and Welfare have the lowest number of vulnerabilities. According to our findings, Severity can manifest itself in a variety of ways, such as A3, SSL (Secure Sockets Layer) certificates about to expire, session cookies not marked as secured, and weak ciphers enabled, and so on. For A6, it could be an insecure framework or a DB (database) user with administrative privileges, among other things. In A9, it typically deals with Apache, Tomcat, Bootstrap, JQuery, OpenSSL, PHP, Nginx, and other versions. These are some of the most common threats discovered in our research that developers may have overlooked. This has a domino effect, putting sensitive information at risk, such as registered holders' data, etc.

From the vulnerability results we discovered in this research, we can see that government Web applications in Bangladesh suffer from important security oversights. Most of the vulnerabilities arise from common software development pitfalls such as:

- Not writing maintainable code
- Not writing reusable code
- Not writing unit or integration tests
- Not maintaining up-to-date documentation of the project
- Not updating software packages used in software development

These are some of the steps that help catch 99% of the security issues or bugs in Software Development.

It is positively alarming to discover a high number of high-severity vulnerabilities in 3 out of 5 selected sectors of government Web applications. We hypothesize that this is due to the current state of maturity in technology in Bangladesh. More in-depth analysis and studies are required to validate this hypothesis, and we believe this to be an interesting arena for future research.

VI. CONCLUSIONS

In this research, we have compiled, compared, and contrasted the data collected to see how effectively BurpSuite, Netsparker and Zap record OWASP Top 10 vulnerabilities and report them. We have also seen OWASP vulnerabilities across all tested applications and common vulnerabilities and referred to their remediation possibilities.

The driving purpose of this study was to understand OWASP vulnerabilities and their impact on the sectors of Government Web applications in Bangladesh. Our target was to run as many tests using as many tools as possible to find consistent results of vulnerabilities. Additionally, during this research, we understood and learned how automated testing tools work. Though only three testing tools are used, in the future we intend to expand the list and draw a comparison between many other popular tools. In future research, we would like to find if specific tools are better for a specific type of Website e.g., Lighthouse [27] for Progressive Web Applications).

All the tests done in this paper are exclusively black box testing with a specified scan policy. This is due to not having direct access to source code to perform any static analysis. We believe that a combination of both black box and static analysis white box testing will provide better and deeper insight. Yulianton et al. [13] For now, black-box testing only provides us with information about what and how many vulnerabilities are there, but the crux of the issue might arise from the more apt question, "Why are the vulnerabilities there in the first place?"

Our next task is to broaden the scope of Websites used for testing vulnerabilities and use the latest OWASP Top 10 2021 guidelines. Along with black-box testing, we also look forward to adding white-box and grey-box testing. Having more insights can provide solutions toward better software development methodologies with strict adherence to testing guidelines.

REFERENCES

[1] L. F. de Lima, M. C. Horstmann, D. N. Neto, A. R. Grégio, F. Silva, and L. M. Peres, "On the challenges of automated testing of web vulnerabilities," in *2020 IEEE 29th International Conference on Enabling Technologies: Infrastructure for Collaborative Enterprises (WETICE)*. IEEE, 2020, pp. 203–206.

[2] A. Sołtysik-Piorunkiewicz and M. Krysiak, "The cyber threats analysis for web applications security in industry 4.0," in *Towards Industry 4.0—Current Challenges in Information Systems*. Springer, 2020, pp. 127–141.

[3] S. Rahman, "Latest cyber attack hit at least 147 bangladeshi entities," 2021. [Online]. Available: shorturl.at/qrz36

[4] S. Rehman, "Three banks hit by cyberattacks," 2016. [Online]. Available: https://www.thedailystar.net/frontpage/news/three-banks-hit-cyberattacks-1760629

[5] M. Bach-Nutman, "Understanding the top 10 owasp vulnerabilities," *arXiv preprint arXiv:2012.09960*, 2020.

[6] R. S. Devi and M. M. Kumar, "Testing for security weakness of web applications using ethical hacking," in *2020 4th International Conference on Trends in Electronics and Informatics (ICOEI)(48184)*. IEEE, 2020, pp. 354–361.

[7] F. Ö. Sönmez and B. G. Kiliç, "Holistic web application security visualization for multi-project and multi-phase dynamic application security test results," *IEEE Access*, vol. 9, pp. 25 858–25 884, 2021.

[8] N. Anantharaman and B. Wukkadada, "Identifying the usage of known vulnerabilities components based on owasp a9," in *2020 International Conference on Emerging Smart Computing and Informatics (ESCI)*. IEEE, 2020, pp. 88–91.

[9] S. K. Lala, A. Kumar, and T. Subbulakshmi, "Secure web development using owasp guidelines," in *2021 5th International Conference on Intelligent Computing and Control Systems (ICICCS)*. IEEE, 2021, pp. 323–332.

[10] D. Omeiza and J. Owusu-Tweneboah, "Web security investigation through penetration tests: A case study of an educational institution portal," *arXiv preprint arXiv:1811.01388*, 2018.

[11] N. Abdinurova, M. Galiyev, and A. Aitkulov, "Owasp vulnerabilities scanning of a private university websites," *Suleyman Demirel University Bulletin: Natural and Technical Sciences*, 2021.

[12] F. Holík and S. Neradova, "Vulnerabilities of modern web applications," in *2017 40th International Convention on Information and Communication Technology, Electronics and Microelectronics (MIPRO)*. IEEE, 2017, pp. 1256–1261.

[13] H. Yulianton, A. Trisetyarso, W. Suparta, B. S. Abbas, and C. H. Kang, "Web application vulnerability detection using taint analysis and black-box testing," in *IOP Conference Series: Materials Science and Engineering*, vol. 879, no. 1. IOP Publishing, 2020, p. 012031.

[14] T. Rangnau, R. v. Buijtenen, F. Fransen, and F. Turkmen, "Continuous security testing: A case study on integrating dynamic security testing tools in ci/cd pipelines," in *2020 IEEE 24th International Enterprise Distributed Object Computing Conference (EDOC)*. IEEE, 2020, pp. 145–154.

[15] "What is devsecops?" Apr 2018. [Online]. Available: https://www.redhat.com/en/topics/devops/what-is-devsecops

[16] M. Hanna, A. E. Aboutabl, and M.-S. M. Mostafa, "Automated software testing framework for web applications," *International Journal of Applied Engineering Research*, vol. 13, no. 11, pp. 9758–9767, 2018.

[17] R. Abbas, Z. Sultan, and S. N. Bhatti, "Comparative analysis of automated load testing tools: Apache jmeter, microsoft visual studio (tfs), loadrunner, siege," in *2017 International Conference on Communication Technologies (ComTech)*. IEEE, 2017, pp. 39–44.

[18] S. Tyagi and K. Kumar, "Evaluation of static web vulnerability analysis tools," in *2018 Fifth International Conference on Parallel, Distributed and Grid Computing (PDGC)*. IEEE, 2018, pp. 1–6.

[19] D. Dagar and A. Gupta, "A comparison of vulnerability assessment tools owasp 2.7. 0 & pentest on demo web application," *CPJ Global Review A National Journal of Chanderprabhu Jain College of Higher Studies*, pp. 46–50.

[20] B. Mburano and W. Si, "Evaluation of web vulnerability scanners based on owasp benchmark," in *2018 26th International Conference on Systems Engineering (ICSEng)*. IEEE, 2018, pp. 1–6.

[21] R. Amankwah, J. Chen, P. K. Kudjo, and D. Towey, "An empirical comparison of commercial and open-source web vulnerability scanners," *Software: Practice and Experience*, vol. 50, no. 9, pp. 1842–1857, 2020.

[22] N. Karangle, A. K. Mishra, and D. A. Khan, "Comparison of nikto and uniscan for measuring url vulnerability," in *2019 10th International Conference on Computing, Communication and Networking Technologies (ICCCNT)*. IEEE, 2019, pp. 1–6.

[23] H. Setiawan, L. E. Erlangga, and I. Baskoro, "Vulnerability analysis using the interactive application security testing (iast) approach for government x website applications," in *2020 3rd International Conference on Information and Communications Technology (ICOIACT)*. IEEE, 2020, pp. 471–475.

[24] M. Moniruzzaman, F. Chowdhury, and M. S. Ferdous, "Measuring vulnerabilities of bangladeshi websites," in *2019 International Conference on Electrical, Computer and Communication Engineering (ECCE)*. IEEE, 2019, pp. 1–7.

[25] A. van der Stock, B. Glas, N. Smithline, and T. Gigler, "Owasp top 10 2017: The ten most critical web application security risks," *OWASP Foundation*, p. 23, 2017.

[26] A. M. A. Obaida, "Number of motor vehicles," Aug 2022. [Online]. Available: http://dsce.edu.bd/db/Number_of_Motor_Vehicles

[27] "Overview - lighthouse," May 2022. [Online]. Available: https://developer.chrome.com/docs/lighthouse/overview/

Cloud Maturity Framework

A Guideline to Assess and Modernize Cloud Computing Applications and Workloads

Carlos Diego Cavalcanti Pereira
CESAR – Recife Center for Advanced Studies and Systems
Recife, Brazil
e-mail: cdcp@cesar.org.br

Carlos Alberto Costa Filho
Valcann - Cloud Intelligence
Recife, Brazil
e-mail: calberto@valcann.com.br

Felipe Silva Ferraz
CESAR – Recife Center for Advanced Studies and Systems
Recife, Brazil
e-mail: fsf@cesar.org.br

Abstract—**Organizations tend to implement and maintain their architecture in the cloud the same way they operate on premises, wasting the opportunity to use the benefits of cloud computing. Although the literature proposes several prescriptive models on how to modernize cloud architectures, these models are invariably too generic and do not indicate the current maturity level of the cloud architecture, nor do they technically specify what actions should be taken. This paper focuses on the proposal of a Cloud Maturity Framework to help organizations understand their current maturity level regarding the best modern practices of cloud computing architecture, by applying a set of practices on how to elicit its current maturity level and, implement and manage improvements.**

Keywords- cloud computing; application modernization; cloud modernization.

I. INTRODUCTION

Cloud computing migration projects tend to apply strategies during the migration process so that the fewest possible changes to the architecture are made in order to minimize the already natural frictions that any process of change applies [1]. In this sense, organizations keep their architectures in the cloud the same way they operated when on premises, wasting the opportunity to use the benefits of cloud computing and modern cloud architectures [2]. Cloud native or modern cloud architecture is a software approach of building, deploying, and managing modern applications in cloud computing environments [3]. Modern companies want to build highly scalable, flexible, and resilient applications that they can update quickly to meet customer demands [3]. Amazon Web Services, a leading cloud computing company, states that when carrying out modernization projects, enterprises can reduce payback periods to 6 months and reduce Total Cost of Ownership (TCO) by 64% [4]. Although the literature proposes several prescriptive models on how to modernize cloud architectures, those models are invariably too generic, focusing more on describing what to do rather than how to do it. They also do not indicate the current maturity level of the cloud architecture, nor do they technically specify how improvements should be implemented [5]. To address those opportunities, the present work proposes a maturity model for cloud computing architectures, covering a set of practices and processes on: how to assess a cloud workload summary and examine its components, how to establish a maturity baseline and a roadmap to cloud modernization, and how to deploy improvements and manage change processes.

The rest of the paper is structured as follows. In Section 2, we present the concept of maturity models. In Section 3, we present the Cloud Maturity Framework, covering the general model, workload layers, the modernization process and maturity classification. In Section 4, we discuss advances in cloud maturity models and proposed future work related to how to modernize cloud architectures. Finally, in Section 5, we present our conclusions.

II. MATURITY MODELS

A maturity model is an approach in which the effectiveness of a process or a general architecture is assessed to understand its current level in reference to a classification range [6]. Applying maturity models has become a common practice in computer science, especially in software engineering. So much that the literature presents a specification of a meta model for creating maturity models like the ISO 33001 standard [7]. Implementing a maturity model helps evaluate the achievement of process quality characteristics and the application of the results to the conduct of improvements.

Regarding cloud maturity evaluation, several models propose different approaches on how to evaluate the current state of cloud adoption, such as OACA Cloud Maturity Model [8]. Even the industry also provides several different approaches: AWS Well-Architected Framework [9], AWS Cloud Adoption Framework [10], Azure Well-Architected Framework [11], among others. Although those frameworks help to identify the level of adoption from a governance and processes perspective, they do not focus on a technical level and on how broad is the application of more modern cloud technologies, such as the use of containers, functions as services, event-driven architectures, among other implementations. That is, there is the opportunity to delve into how to classify the level of sophistication of a workload in the cloud, as well as the path to be followed to make it even more modern.

III. CLOUD MATURITY FRAMEWORK

The proposal of Cloud Maturity Framework intends to help organizations understand their current maturity level regarding the best practices of modern cloud computing architecture. It states that organizations should first list their high-value assets and analyze how they could benefit from improved scalability, security, and performance. The framework helps organizations understand how modernization can benefit business operations.

Cloud Maturity Framework goes beyond just defining generic goals of improvement processes and good architecture. It consists of a specific analysis in which it is possible to explore breadth and maturity of the cloud computing stack, integrating various related areas, and clarify the means to achieve a higher maturity in modern cloud architecture.

A. General Model

The Cloud Maturity Framework establishes a predefined structure as presented on Figure 1: a) Workload Layers; b) Modernization process; and c) Maturity classification.

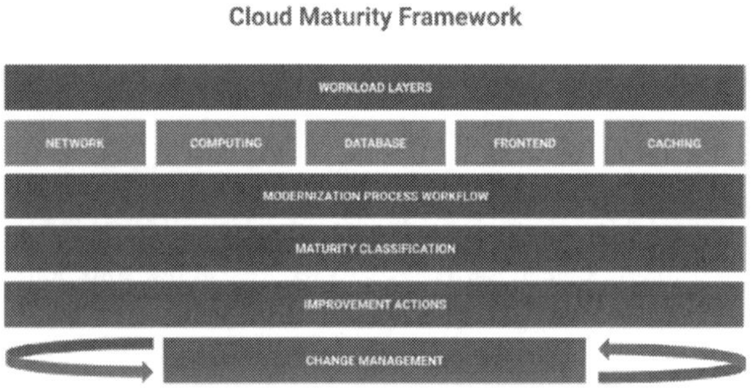

Figure 1. Cloud Maturity Framework

B. Workload Layers

One of the challenges when evaluating a cloud workload is to understand its blueprint and implications regarding integration between components [12]. Cloud computing provides access to large pools of distributed components - such as computing (servers, containers, functions as services) - for building high-quality applications [13].

Architectural patterns cover the architectural principles found in most cloud-native applications to enable the cloud application properties [14]. Service-based cloud architecture patterns target settings which components a workload may have [15]. Although the literature predicts different types of component categories, monolithic and distributed computing architectures, they usually consider the partitioning of their structure in contexts that involve: computing, data and communication [16]. In this sense, In order to ensure that these common components categories are covered in the maturity model, the framework proposes five categories of cloud components:

a) **Network Layer**: Foundation of cloud communications and networking. It establishes a set of network connections, access control lists, routing policies, and the application's boundaries.
b) **Computing Layer**: Usually related to the use of application components, such as virtual machines, containers, functions as services and others. Evaluating this layer helps to understand how it implements computing best practices.
c) **Database Layer**: The data tier, also known as the database layer, is where all of the information about user data and transactions are kept. It basically contains any data that has to be stored. The data is delivered to the computing layer for logic processing and then for rendering to the user.
d) **Front-end Layer**: Front-end layer is related to components at the edge of the application's architecture, such as Content Delivery Networks (CDN) and Object Storage.
e) **Caching Layer**: Components that process a time-consuming request, generally in memory, so that the requests can be handled faster. Caching components manage the data in memory rather than loading it directly from a database, network, or a storage volume.

C. Modernization Process

Cloud modernization is becoming more essential for migrating to public clouds [17]. Transitioning from monolithic, tightly connected architectures to modern distributed and serverless services requires a mix of high-demand technologies and expertise.

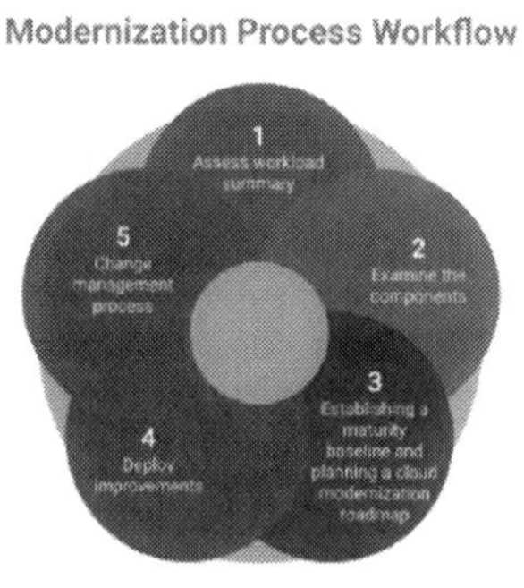

Figure 2. Modernization Process

Cloud Maturity Framework dictates that to perform a cloud modernization process - as presented on Figure 2 - a set of steps should be performed:

a) **Assess workload summary** - To understand the workload, the first step is to assess it and make an inventory of all components. This will make it possible to identify each component in the architecture and how it relates to each of the workload layers.

b) **Examine the components** - From the results of resource inventory, the next step will be to establish the general summary of the architecture. The purpose is to build, customize, and share detailed architecture insights of the workload based on live data retrieved from Cloud provider Application Programming Interface (APIs). The outcomes expected from this examination are architecture diagrams, query cost and usage reports (CURs), and resource classification from a functional perspective.

c) **Establishing a maturity baseline and planning a cloud modernization roadmap** - Architecture, design, and technology stack directly influence the modernization approach [12]. While it depends on the organization's desired goal, the path taken may depend on various archetypes. Achieving a simplified architecture, for example, requires a change in thinking, especially when considering options for new systems and integrations [6]. A detailed understanding of the current state of the legacy system, comparing current and future architecture, will help identify gaps and changes needed to be successfully modernized. Each workload layer will be evaluated from a maturity perspective. As the organization identifies its current maturity level, it will be possible to define which path they want to take, from simply moving one or a few levels up or even achieving excellence going forward to the higher possible maturity level.

d) **Deploy improvements** - After understanding the maturity level for each workload layer, it will be possible to define the gaps as adherent to a modern cloud application and infrastructure approach. More than simply applying changes and improvement directly to cloud provider console or CLI, for the Cloud Maturity Framework it is essential to apply infrastructure as code as a common practice because it is the essential characteristics of modern and cloud native infrastructure [3], as presented in Figure 3.

```
Resources:

 RemoveIngressRuleRole:
   Type: AWS::IAM::Role
   Properties:
     RoleName: RemoveIngressRule
     AssumeRolePolicyDocument:
       Statement:
         - Effect: Allow
           Principal:
             Service: lambda.amazonaws.com
           Action: sts:AssumeRole
     Policies:
       - PolicyName: RemoveIngressRulePolicy
         PolicyDocument:
           Version: "2012-10-17"
           Statement:
             - Effect: Allow
               Action: ['ec2:DescribeSecurityGroupRules',
'ec2:DescribeSecurityGroups', 'ec2:RevokeSecurityGroupIngress']
               Resource: '*'

 RemoveIngressRuleFunction:
   Type: AWS::Lambda::Function
   Properties:
     FunctionName: RemoveIngressRule
     Role: !GetAtt RemoveIngressRuleRole.Arn
     Runtime: python3.9
     Handler: index.lambda_handler
     Timeout: 60
     Code:
       ZipFile: |
         import json
         import boto3

         def lambda_handler(event, context):
             client = boto3.client('ec2')
             security_groups = client.describe_security_groups(
                 Filters=[
                     {
                         'Name' : 'ip-permission.cidr',
                         'Values': ['0.0.0.0/0']
                     }
                 ]
             )

             for security_group in security_groups["SecurityGroups"]:
                 security_group_rules =
client.describe_security_group_rules(
                                             Filters=[
                                                 {
                                                     'Name' : 'group-
id',
                                                     'Values':
[security_group["GroupId"]]
                                                 }
                                             ]
                                         )
                 for security_group_rule in
security_group_rules["SecurityGroupRules"]:
                     if("CidrIpv4" in security_group_rule.keys() and
security_group_rule["CidrIpv4"] == "0.0.0.0/0"):
                         client.revoke_security_group_ingress(
                             GroupId=security_group_rule["GroupId"],

SecurityGroupRuleIds=[security_group_rule["SecurityGroupRuleId"]]
                         )
             return {
                 'statusCode': 200,
                 'body': json.dumps('Hello from Lambda!')
             }
```

Figure 3. AWS Cloudformation improvement script to remove "Public open ports to virtual machine instances", level 1 maturity criteria for Computing Layer

e) **Change management process** - Cloud IT change management processes facilitate changes to IT systems in order to minimize risks to the production environment while adhering to policies, audit, and risk controls [18]. All tests, validations, approvals, and rejections must be documented as part of the pipeline deployment.

D. Maturity Classification

The maturity classification serves to analyze the maturity level of the organization's cloud computing practices and architecture [19]. Each of the five layers previously presented are evaluated from the perspective of specific maturity criteria. Each one of the layers have a set of criteria that should be validated, classified, and have an improvement directly related to it. Table 1 presents an example of maturity criterias of Computing Layer.

After being evaluated, the organization will have a classification score, as presented in Figure 4, which shows the roadmap that the organization will take to be more adherent to what is called modern architecture in the cloud [3].

1	2	3	4	5
MATURITY LEVEL CLASSIFICATION				

Figure 4. Maturity Level Classification

TABLE 1. MATURITY LEVEL CLASSIFICATION FOR COMPUTING LAYER

LAYER	MATURITY LEVEL	MATURITY CRITERIA
COMPUTING LAYER	MATURITY LEVEL 1	- Auto scaling disabled for virtual machine instances; - Load Balancer disabled for virtual machine instances; - Missing snapshots for block storage volumes; - Unencrypted block storage volumes; - Public open ports to virtual machine instances.
	MATURITY LEVEL 2	- Public accessible serverless function; - Block storage snapshots with public access; - Public virtual machine images; - Virtual machine instances without automation for status check failure; - Serverless functions environment variables without encryption enabled.
	MATURITY LEVEL 3	- Underutilized (<10%) container cluster; - Underutilized (< 30% capacity on average for last week) of virtual machine instances; - Automation for status check failure on virtual machines; - Out of date virtual machine images; - Pending scheduled maintenance events on virtual machines.
	MATURITY LEVEL 4	- Virtual machines are right sized; - Block storage is encrypted by default; - Block storage lifecycle management is enabled for backup; - Block storage volumes not attached to virtual machines; - Logging and alarms are configured.
	MATURITY LEVEL 5	- Virtual machine have termination protection; - Load Balancers placed in multiple availability zones; - There is no unused EIP; - Virtual machine images are private; - All resources are tagged.

IV. Towards Cloud Maturity And Future Works

A successful cloud modernization strategy starts with the business need in mind, having a tight connection to technical practices and tools [17]. As the journey to the cloud gathers pace, organizations have been looking for what is their current cloud maturity landscape so that they can accelerate cloud modernization [20].

As cloud computing has a natural entropy as a technological and incipient field, this research will continue to develop on Cloud Maturity Framework. Some initiatives were already mapped and are part of the development of the framework:

- Applying the framework in cloud modernization projects in different industries and collecting data on the implementation process, as well identifying benefits and challenges.
- Benchmarking the framework with other cloud modernization approaches.
- Open source the framework, so it can be used by both academia and industry, especially to continue the development of maturity criteria as well as developing and automating improvements for those criteria elicited.

V. Conclusions

Cloud modernization is both a technical and organizational goal, so it is important to develop well-defined strategies to ensure that both occur [12]. Both literature and industry had proposed different approaches to help organizations modernize their cloud workloads. Those approaches focus on defining what should be done to modernize, focusing on governance and processes perspective, but do not guide how to do it or what is the technical roadmap to be taken towards a modern cloud architecture, especially on a technical level.

As presented in this research, to define a roadmap it is essential to understand the current baseline and where the project is starting. Understanding the workload's current state enables the knowledge about the environment and the overall impact of the changes at different layers of the architecture. Cloud Maturity Framework addresses those challenges previously presented by defining a three part structure: a) Workload Layers; b) Modernization process; and c) Maturity classification. Moreover, the framework proposes a detailed set of maturity criteria and correlates it to technical improvements that, once applied, can overcome the architecture violations previously found in the target workload [21].

REFERENCES

[1] P. Jamshidi, A. Ahmad, and C. Pahl, "Cloud Migration Research: A Systematic Review," *IEEE Trans. Cloud Comput.*, vol. 1, no. 2, pp. 142–157, 2013, doi: 10.1109/TCC.2013.10.

[2] S. Bhardwaj, L. Jain, and S. Jain, "Cloud Computing : a Study of Infrastructure As a Service (Iaas)," *Int. J. Eng.*, vol. 2, no. 1, pp. 60–63, 2010.

[3] J. Garrison and K. Nova, *Cloud Native Infrastructure*. O'Reilly Media, Inc., 2017. [Online]. Available: https://www.oreilly.com/library/view/cloud-native-infrastructure/9781491984291/

[4] Amazon Web Services, "Modernize Your Applications, Drive Growth and Reduce TCO." https://aws.amazon.com/pt/enterprise/modernization/ (accessed Jun. 10, 2022).

[5] L. Wang *et al.*, "Cloud computing: A perspective study," *New Gener. Comput.*, vol. 28, no. 2, pp. 137–146, 2010, doi: 10.1007/s00354-008-0081-5.

[6] W. S. Humphrey, "Characterizing the software process: a maturity framework," *IEEE Softw.*, vol. 5, no. 2, pp. 73–79, 1988, doi: 10.1109/52.2014.

[7] International Organization for Standardization, "ISO/IEC 33001:2015 - Information technology — Process assessment — Concepts and terminology." ISO/IEC, 2015. Accessed: Sep. 10, 2022. [Online]. Available: https://www.iso.org/standard/54175.html

[8] M. Williams, R. Skipp, T. Scott, M. Estes, and W. Dupley, "OACA Cloud Maturity Model v4.0," Jun. 2018.

[9] "AWS Well-Architected Framework." Amazon Web Services. Accessed: Sep. 10, 2022. [Online]. Available: https://aws.amazon.com/pt/architecture/well-architected/

[10] "AWS Cloud Adoption Framework." Amazon Web Services. Accessed: Sep. 10, 2022. [Online]. Available: https://aws.amazon.com/pt/professional-services/CAF/

[11] "Azure Well-Architected Framework." Microsoft. Accessed: Sep. 10, 2022. [Online]. Available: https://learn.microsoft.com/en-us/azure/architecture/framework

[12] W. Lloyd *et al.*, "The cloud services Innovation platform - Enabling service-based environmental modeling using infrastructure-as-a-service cloud computing," *IEMSs 2012 - Manag. Resour. Ltd. Planet Proc. 6th Bienn. Meet. Int. Environ. Model. Softw. Soc.*, pp. 1208–1215, 2012.

[13] Y. Zhang, Z. Zheng, and M. R. Lyu, "Real-Time Performance Prediction for Cloud Components," in *2012 IEEE 15th International Symposium on Object/Component/Service-Oriented Real-Time Distributed Computing Workshops*, 2012, pp. 106–111. doi: 10.1109/ISORCW.2012.29.

[14] C. Fehling, F. Leymann, R. Retter, W. Schupeck, and P. Arbitter, "Cloud Application Architecture Patterns," in *Cloud Computing Patterns: Fundamentals to Design, Build, and Manage Cloud Applications*, Vienna: Springer Vienna, 2014, pp. 151–238. doi: 10.1007/978-3-7091-1568-8_4.

[15] P. Jamshidi, C. Pahl, S. Chinenyeze, and X. Liu, "Cloud Migration Patterns: A Multi-cloud Service Architecture Perspective," in *Service-Oriented Computing - ICSOC 2014 Workshops*, Cham, 2015, pp. 6–19.

[16] M. Richards and N. Ford, *Fundamentals of Software Architecture*. O'Reilly Media, Inc., 2020.

[17] G. Reese, *Cloud Application Architectures: Building Applications and Infrastructure in the Cloud*. O'Reilly Media, Inc., 2009.

[18] Amazon Web Services, "Implement change management process for cloud." Amazon Web Services, Jun. 2020. Accessed: Sep. 10, 2022. [Online]. Available: https://docs.aws.amazon.com/wellarchitected/latest/financial-services-industry-lens/implement-change-management-process-for-cloud.html

[19] CMMI Institute, "Capability Maturity Model Integration." ISACA, Mar. 2019. Accessed: Sep. 10, 2022. [Online]. Available: https://cmmiinstitute.com/cmmi

[20] V. Thumma, "Strategy for modernizing applications in the AWS Cloud." Amazon Web Services, Dec. 2020. Accessed: Jun. 10, 2022. [Online]. Available: https://docs.aws.amazon.com/prescriptive-guidance/latest/strategy-modernizing-applications/welcome.html

[21] N. J. Gunther, *Guerilla Capacity Planning: A Tactical Approach to Planning for Highly Scalable Applications and Services*, 1st ed. Springer Publishing Company, Incorporated, 2010.

Deriving Service-Oriented Dynamic Product Lines Knowledge from Informal User-Requirements: AI Based Approach

Najla Maalaoui
National School of Computer Sciences
RIADI Lab
Manouba University, Tunisia
email: najla.maalaoui@ensi-uma.tn

Raoudha Beltaifa
National School of Computer Sciences
RIADI Lab
Manouba University, Tunisia
email: raoudha.beltaifa@ensi.rnu.tn

Lamia Labed Jilani
National School of Computer Sciences
RIADI Lab
Manouba University, Tunisia
email: lamia.Labed@isg.rnu.tn

***Abstract*—A Service-Oriented Dynamic Software Product Line (SO-DSPL) is a family of service-oriented systems sharing a set of common features. Hence, they are automatically activated and deactivated depending on the running situation. Such product lines are designed to support their self-adaptation to new contexts and requirements. Particularly, user requirements can be analyzed and enriched thanks to the existing of the SO-DSPL ontology that we previously built. This will facilitate the configuration of a derived service from the family of services, corresponding both to the desired requirement and a specific context. As we know, a user requirement can be ambiguous, vague and incomplete, which motivate the need for the extraction of the hidden knowledge. Our challenge is to use artificial intelligence techniques to automatically extract new SO-DSPL knowledge from textual user requirements and derive appropriate services of the service line for the user. In this paper, our approach is based on Natural Language Processing (NLP) learning techniques, a rule engine and a reasoner. This process permits to better understand the user requirements, to predict other information about the requirements and to derive an appropriate service (software application as a combination of several services) in the SO-DSPL application engineering phase. We use the Smart Home product line and a dataset of textual user requirements to evaluate our proposal. Notes that when we say product, we mean an application based on service compositions.**

Index Terms*—*Service-Oriented Dynamic Software Product Lines; Ontology; User requirements; Natural language processing.

I. Introduction

The demand of customized service-based systems is constantly increasing from day to day. This requires tailoring and adapting a software system according to the specific customer needs. Faced with this challenge, Service Oriented Architecture (SOA) provides a promising mean for supporting continuously changing customers' needs, context and expectations, as more sophisticated software systems are connected to the Internet. However, developing reusable and dynamically reconfigurable service-based systems tailored to meet different customers' needs and contexts becomes a main challenge. To address this issue, the reuse approach has been suggested as one of the pioneer solutions. The Service Oriented Dynamic Software Product Line (SO-DSPL) technique has already been adopted as one of the most promising techniques for reuse. This framework is addressed by combining SOA with Dynamic Software Product Lines Engineering (DSPLE);

A SO-DSPL [15] is known as a family of service-oriented systems sharing a set of common features. Other than the common ones, as in Product Line Engineering, there is also a set of variable features. These features are managed according to the needs of a specific market segment and/or environment and are automatically activated and deactivated according to the running situation. SO-DSPLs support their self-adaptation to new context and requirements.

In order to get customized software, users can use their own language and their own knowledge to express freely their request. In that case, providers may not understand the client's requirements. But, such an understanding is essential to provide better products and services to consumers. Overall, facilitating the understanding between providers and customers requires a knowledge representation of customer's requirements. In a previous work [14], we are interested in SO-DSPL knowledge. In this work, we were studied the semantic relationship between the SO-DSPL knwolegde and their usability by DSPL activities. To unify the studies knowledge, we have proposed an ontology named "OntoSO-DSPL" that is developed in a modular way. OntoSO-DSPL has four modules (sub-ontologies) defined as: user context sub-ontology, service sub-ontology, DSPL sub-ontology and adaptation sub-ontology where each sub ontology is interested in covering a particular dimension. Based on this work, we have concluded that the user requirements knowledge play an important role in SPL activities, as well they influence derived SPL product. Thus, in SPLE, it is necessary to identify, document and maintain user requirements to be used by SPL activities. Therefore, there is a great need for an intelligent system able to represent, understand and interpret the user requirements from the textual request targeting a specific product in the SO-DSPL framework.

To tackle these challenges and facilitate the understanding of user requirements, a knowledge representation of the requirements is needed. For this purpose, we propose in this paper an approach that enables the interpretation of the user requirements through his/her textual request and transforms it to a formal representation (requirements structure) that will be later used by SPL activities such as, product derivation, user satisfaction analysis, product adaptation, etc.

The remainder of this paper is structured as follows. Section 2 introduces SO-DSPL engineering with a brief overview. In

Section 3, we motivate our contribution with the help of an example. In Section 4, we present the related works. Section 5 exposes our proposed approach and Section 6 presents an illustrative case. In Section 7, we evaluate our proposed approach. Finally, the last section concludes the paper and deals with future works.

II. Service Oriented Dynamic Software Product-line Engineering

Software Product-line engineering is a paradigm within software engineering, used to define and derive sets of similar products from reusable assets [15].The development life cycle of a product line encompasses two main processes: domain engineering and application engineering [15].While domain engineering focuses on establishing a reuse platform, application engineering is concerned with the effective reuse of assets across multiple products. Feature modeling is the main activity to represent and manage product line requirements as reusable assets by allowing users to derive customized product configurations [15]. Product configuration refers to the decision-making process of selecting an optimal set of features from the product line that comply with the feature model constraints and fulfill the product's requirements. A common visual representation for a feature model is a feature diagram. The feature diagram defines common features found in all products of the product line, known as mandatory features, and variable features that introduce variability within the product line, referred to as optional and alternative features. In addition, feature diagrams often contain cross-tree constraints: a feature can include or exclude other features by using requires or excludes constraints, respectively.

Dynamic Software Product Lines (DSPLs) provide configuration options to adjust a software system at runtime to deal with changes in the users' context [14] and Service-oriented dynamic software product lines (SO-DSPL) represent a class of DSPLs that are built on services and Service-Oriented Architectures (SOAs) [13]. Figure 1 shows a part of the smart home feature model.

III. Running Example

Performing service derivation by manual configuration and adaptation can generate inconsistency. In addition, it is difficult in the context of SO-DSPL due to the important number of features, constraints, contexts, adaptation rules and web services. Thus, describing requirements and their changes in a textual format facilitates configuration, however, it requires an automated knowledge extraction process that understand and manage user requirements, their changes and their impact on the current configuration in order to generate a corresponding configuration or adapting an existing one. To illustrate the challenges faces when configuring/ adapting based on textual requirements, we introduce a smart home system for home automation as an example of an SO-DSPL. The smart home consists of smart devices equipped with sensors and web service based actuators interconnected through a software system, which aims to automate a connected home. The smart home SO-DSPL aims to develop customized smart home products for its customers. Its customers can be an external client or a developer that needs to derive or adapt product. Based on the description of the smart home options, customers express their requests in natural language. As an example, the following request is given by a customer to express the important functionalities that must be covered by the derived product in order to satisfy his/her needs.

Req1: *In the morning, I am very lazy so I think that my smart home shall have voice command feature to operate activities from bathrooms which accelerates my morning routines. Because my children Lora and Alex are always doing something stupid, my home shall have a vacuum cleaner to clean my home floors when anything spills. Sometimes, I am very tired since I work all the day, so I prefer that the smart delivery of my home may be able to order delivery food by simple voice command.*

Requirement "Req1" is very vague and its description does not directly include the smart homes features, which makes matching more difficult. Thus, it must be processed to : 1) better present the needs, 2) predict features relative to the described requirements in order to derive the desired customer product, 3) to reuse fragments of requirements and/or to adapt previous product requirements to new ones. As a result, "Core requirements" are extracted.

A core requirements have the following structure:

<feature>+ <obligationdegree>? <goal>+ <item >* <condition>*

Where :

– * : *denotes a zero repetition to an infinite number of times repetitions.*

– + : *denotes repetition once or more number of times.*

– ? :*denotes a repetition zero or one time.*

– — :*denotes a disjunction (it signifies OR).*

– ! : *denotes a negation*

Feature is the system or the feature denoted by the requirement, obligation degree, which denotes the importance of the action that must be performed by the system or the feature, goal, which denotes the objective that must be attended by the feature/system, item, which denotes the entities affected by the goal that can be also a feature or all the system, and condition, which denotes self-adaptation triggering constraint in most cases. The condition is presented by a subject, action and additional parameters denoted by entities.

From the request "Req1", we can extract three core requirements presented in Table I: From the extracted core requirements, we derive two abstract partial products based on the DSPL associated to the feature model of Figure 1. We note that the feature "Smart delivery" is considered as an optional feature because its associated obligation degree indicates "should", which generate this two abstract partial products:

AbstractPartialProduct1 = Voice command, vacuum cleaner, smart delivery

AbstractPartialProduct2 = Voice command, vacuum cleaner

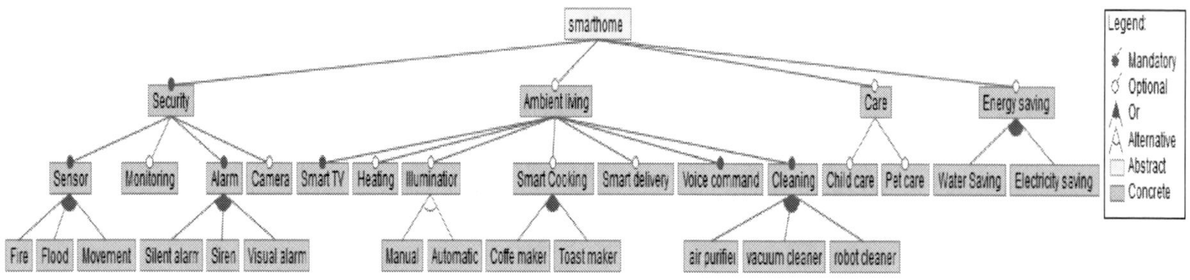

Figure. 1. Smart home SO-DSPL

TABLE I
EXTRACTED THREE CORE REQUIREMENTS

Elements	Core requirement1	Core requirement2	Core requirement3
feature	voice command	vacuum cleaner	smart delivery
obligation degree	must		should
goal	operate	clean	order
item	activities from bathrooms	floors	food
condition		when anything spills	voice command

However, the extracted partial products are note completed since the user has been restrictive in his choices. Thus, partial products are then enriched by other recommended features to satisfy the customer, with respect to SO-DSPL constraint. Then, the extracted features are then mapped to the correspond smart home features (sensors, actuators and web services) to derive the partial smart home product and activate the corresponding services at instant t.

Product1 = [Sensor, Fire, Alarm, Visual alarm, Smart TV, Voice command, cleaning, vacuum cleaner, smart delivery, air purify, Care, child care]
Product2 = [Sensor, Fire, Alarm, Visual alarm, Smart TV, Voice command, cleaning, vacuum cleaner, vacuum cleaner, air purify]
Product3 = [Sensor, Fire, Flood, Alarm, Siren, Smart TV, Voice command, cleaning, vacuum cleaner, robot cleaner, smart delivery, air purify]

Then, the extracted features are then mapped to the correspondent smart home features (sensors(denoted by S) and web services (denoted by WS) that trigger actuators) to derive the partial smart home product and activate the corresponding services at instant t.

SO-Product1 = [Fire WS35, S_fire, S_Movement, Visual alarm WS10, Smart TV WS13, S_voice,Voice command WS1101, vacuum cleaner WS125, smart delivery WS22, air purify WS45, child care WS234]
SO-Product2 = [S_fire, Fire WS35, S_Movement, Visual alarm WS10, Smart TV WS13,S_voice, Voice command WS1101, vacuum cleaner WS125,S_Dirt_detect, air purify WS136]
SO-Product3 = [Fire WS35, S_fire, S_Movement, S_flood, Flood WS321, Alarm WS1, Siren WS132, Smart TV WS13, S_voice, Voice command WS110, vacuum cleaner WS125, robot cleaner WS127, smart delivery WS22, S_Dirt_detect, air purify WS136]

To achieve this goal, features, obligation degree, goals, items and conditions of the three core requirements are used. The selection of the features mentioned in the core requirements in a product and their deselection in another one, are managed by the obligation degree of the core requirement. For example, if the obligation degree associated to the feature is "should" then the feature is optional, while if it is equals to "must" then the feature is mandatory. Then, based on the partial features selection, the rest of the features will be selected based on the feature model of the SO- DSPL and the contextual elements that influence it. Then, web services, sensors and actuators are associated with the selected features and then selected and so the service composition of the product is derived. This process is performed in first step by using an ontology populated by the extracted core requirements components (feature, obligation degree, goal, item, condition). The populated ontology includes a set of axioms and rules that: 1) allow in one hand the derivation of the product's service composition, and 2) the selection/ deselection of features based on the constraints of the feature model, and the constraints of contextual elements that influence the products derivation and adaptation (such as, user context, weather, etc.). For example, in the context where the user is a father, the created ontology axioms/rules recommend the feature "child care" in the product because child existence in the home is deduced. Recall that our aim is to automatically derive such knowledge based on core requirements from given requests and conceptualize them in an ontology to be used to infer new knowledge and used by different SO-DSPL activities, such as contextual product recommendation, derivation and adaptation.

IV. Related works

Requirements management in software reuse paradigms is supported by NLP in numerous tasks. There is an important set of well known techniques, used throughout the entire computer science field for these purposes, from which we can name Part Of Speech tagging [16] (POS), Name Entity Recognition (NER) [16], chunking [17]and types dependencies [18]. In the literature, we can find several proposals that try to combine different requirement engineering tasks with NLP tools. Some papers aim towards automatic or assisted generation of models (such as UML model) [1], [2], [3] and [21], some others try to extract requirements from free text documents [4], [4] and [6], in other cases authors look to improve and extend requirements documents [7] and [8] and some even try to use NLP to manage reusable software artifacts and requirements documents [9], [10] and [11]. For instance, In [25], the authors propose an approach to the interpretation, organization, and management of textual requirements through the use of application-specific ontologies and natural language processing.

Particularly, in SPLE, few works [6], [5], [12] are interested in requirement management using NLP tools. Thus, each requirements source varies from proposal to proposal, using as input software requirements in requirements specifications or extracted, for example, from public software project descriptions and even user opinions from download sites. Following, these requirements are pre-analized and semantically pre-processed with the objective of finding common features between them. Found features are later analyzed to detect which one of them can be represented as a feature model.

In [6], the authors propose a natural language processing approach based on contrastive analysis to identify commonalities and variabilities from the brochures of a group of vendors. In [12], the authors propose a semi-automated approach to extract features for reuse of Natural Language requirements. This approach uses the techniques from IR Information Retrieval and NLP. Latent Semantic Analysis with Singular Value Decomposition has been used to find similar review documents. This is followed by applying various clustering algorithms to cluster similar review documents. In [5], the authors present a semi-automatic approach for feature identification in the existing specifications. This is done by lexical analysis methods. Arias et al. have proposed a Framework for Managing Requirements of Software Product Lines in [13]. The proposed approach aims to define a working framework that allows structuring reusable artifacts of a software product line and retrieving them when new requirements arise. The proposal is composed of five steps, starting from elicited requirements to be pre-processed and divided into elemental pieces. Then, pre-processed requirements are semantically expanded and used to retrieve software artifacts. Then, the final product is a list of reusable software artifacts.

Based on the studied works, we conclude that requirements are used as input to be managed and to extract feature models. However, the success of requirements-based approaches is related to their relevance,the knowledge that they conceptualize and their ability to derive other relevant knowledge. Thus, the activity of requirement recognition to derive knowledge is very important. Such a user expresses his requirements with different forms in order to be satisfied by a product.To tackle this challenge, we propose in this work a framework for Core requirement Recognition from user requirement and their use to infer relevant knowledge to derive service-oriented product. The extracted core requirements are used then to populate the part of user context sub-ontology [14]in order to exploit the relationship between the requirements and other SO-DSPL concepts to infer new relevant knowledge.

V. Proposed framework for SO-DSPL Knowledge Extraction

In previous works we have defined an ontology for SO-DSPL [14] named "OntoSO-DSPL" that provides a knowledge capitalization in SO-DSPL framework by structuring, unifying, reasoning, disseminating SO-DSPL data and to be used in SO-DSPL activities such as services recommendation and selection, dynamic adaptation, runtime variability management and SO-DSPL context reasoning. Thus, the ontology should harmonize the SO-DSPL terminology and help engineers, configurators, and researchers to configure products, build and propose approaches that address the SO-DSPL's activities. In addition, our proposed ontology includes swrl rules that are responsible for inferring new knowledge and providing new facts through its reasoning capabilities. In this work, we used a fragment of the proposed ontology which includes concepts, data objects, data properties impacted by the user requirement knowledge, that we present by Figure 2. The knowledge extraction starts by the derivation of core requirements from textual user requirements. The obtained result is used by the reasoner engine to infer new knowledge and derive SO-DSPL products. As Figure 3 shows, the SO-DSPL knowledge extraction process is composed of three steps: 1) Requirements pre treatment and token extraction 2) Mapping of the extracted token and the core requirements elements by linguistic rules and core requirements derivation, 3) SO-DSPL ontology population and knowledge inferring. As we have mentioned in section 3, we define a core requirement as a product requirement that have the Following pattern:
CoreReq= <feature>+ <obligationdegree>? <goal>+ <item >* <condition>*

Our input is a product request represented as an informal text. The process of recognition and extraction of core requirements from this text involves three modules as shown in Figure3. The first module is an initialization one. It consists of request parsing and analyzing where grammatical information

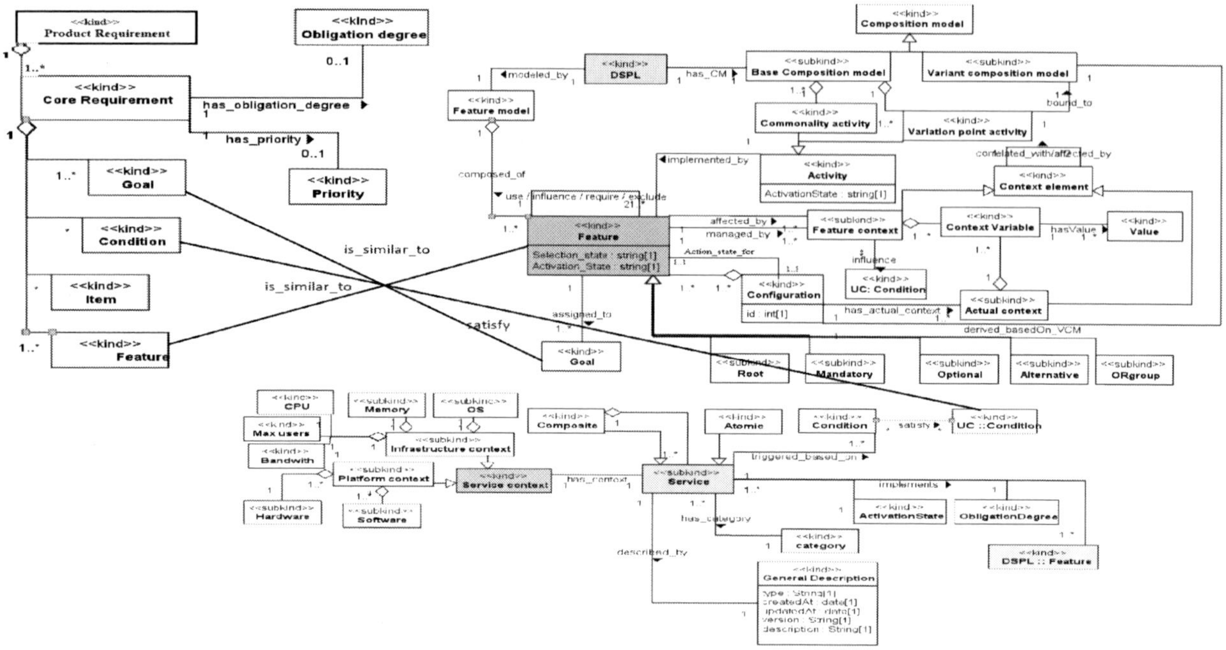

Figure. 2. OntoSO-DSPL meta-model

(ie part of speech (POS) [16]) and syntax information (ie type dependencies) [18]) are generated for each sentence) with the appropriate tokens. Many parsers, such as Stanford parsers and parsers in NLTK(Natural Language Toolkit),have been developed to recognize sentences and determine their corresponding parse trees. Based on the experimental evaluation performed in [14], the Stanford analyzer (which has also been integrated into NLTK) can perform better than various existing analyzers. We used Stanford Parser in this module to analyze the user requirements. We note that we can extract more than one core requirement from a product request.

The second module consists in the mapping between the pretreated sentence results and the core requirement by identifying the corresponding element to each requirement token. In the last module, the core requirement is automatically derived in accordance with the core requirement template. Notes that it can be a simple core requirement or a combination of several ones as previously shown in the running example.

A. Pre-treatment phase

We start with request segmentation with a tokenization and lemmatization process for morphological and syntactic analysis. A tokenization is the result of parsing a document down to its atomic elements named tokens. To this end, each token is labeled with PoS as a noun, verb, adverb, etc. Their dependencies are then analyzed. These two activities are performed using two natural language processing methods that are part of speech (PoS) and dependency analysis. The result is then passed in a " Phrase chunking " phase, which consists in segmenting and separating a sentence into its sub-constituents, such as noun, verb, and prepositional phrases.

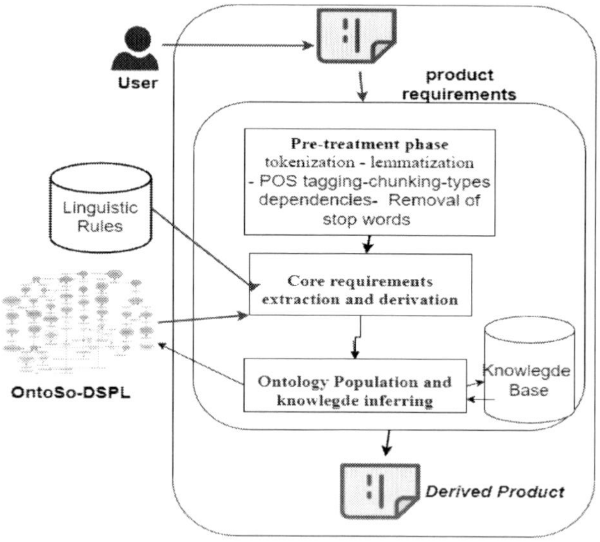

Figure. 3. SO-DSPL Knowledge Extraction Framework architecture

We built a few filter rules based on POS tagging to extract the appropriate content from the client's request. This is accomplished by creating a shallow parser. The latter parses the first step's tagged output chunk by chunk and word by word, applying filter rules to extract relevant content based on the chunk tag and the grammatical category (verb, singular noun, etc.) of the words that make up the chunk.

We maintain just Noun Chunks (NC), Verb Complex (VC), specifically those composed of infinitive verbs, ADJeCtive chunks (ADJC) and Prepositional Chunk (PC)(starting by the preposition IN followed by a Proper Noun NP). This stage produced a list of relevant components, each of which is made up of one or more words. After that, stop words (the most common words in a language and based on the analysis of the dataset) were removed from these chunks. This final step was again accomplished through the use of a filter rule, but this time by extracting the common terms from each chunk and preserving them as relevant components.

B. Core requirements extraction and derivation

To associate each token of the chunks results to its accorded Core requirement form element, we have compiled a list of linguistic rules that cover the most possible cases. Each rule refers to: 1) the grammatical category of the token (the used "PoS" are presented in Table II), 2) its linguistic environment that is the series of units that precede and follow it and 3) its typed dependencies with the other tokens. By applying the suitable rule for the token, we can associate it with the corresponding core requirement element and then, a textual core requirement will be derived based on its corresponding pattern. Moreover, a certainty factor is assigned to each rule serving later as a degree of membership to the core requirement element attributed with the rule.

1) Core requirements extraction linguistic rules: In this step, we split each component derived from the first module into semantically coherent tokens. Secondly, we apply linguistic rules according to the grammar category of each token. By applying the appropriate rule for the token, we can link it to the corresponding element of the core requirement form. We present some of these rules in Table II.

To describe these rules, we use a set of tags which represent the Part of Speech (PoS) of a token with the combination of dependency types as shown in II. Each rule consists of an antecedent and types dependencies that must be true to execute the rule. The antecedent concerns the grammatical category of the token (PoS) and its linguistic environment (the PoS of the token in question is in bold in the Table II), that is, the series of units that precede and follow the token. The type dependencies denote dependencies between the running token (mentioned t1) and another token (mentioned t2) (a conjunction of one or more conditional statements) and a consequent (a conclusion that can be made if the conditions in the antecedent hold true). Based on our running example, we have the user requirement: "My sensor should detect movement". The chunk "My sensor" is composed of the token PRP for personal pronoun "My" and the token NN for the noun "sensor". They are followed by a modal verb "MD", and a verb "VB". Thus, by applying rule R1 from Table II, we conclude that the token "sensor"is a feature.

2) Core requirement rule's Certainty Factor : The challenge of understanding natural language writings may be fraught with uncertainty. As a result, we need to be able to deal with ambiguous reasoning. A more accurate representation of knowledge needs to assign a weight to each rule. This weight can be interpreted as an evaluation measure of a rule of its correctness and pertinence.

Inspired by the Shortliffe's research [19], where the relation between the antecedents and the consequent of the rule is measured by a certainty factor which is associated with each rule, we propose to automatically compute this factor. It represents uncertainty.

Its value is greater when there is a close relation between the antecedents and the consequent. Thus, a factor CF is assigned to a rule. To calculate such weights, we conducted an empirical study of the set of linguistic rules on a dataset of users requirements [20]. It consists in running our system on the dataset and preserving the history of application of each rule for all the examples in test. Then, we calculate the measures of belief and disbelief, defined by experts, for each rule with (1) and 2 respectively:

$$MB(Ri) = \frac{NCA}{NA} \tag{1}$$

with NCA:he number of correct applications of the rule Ri NA:total number of applications of the rule Ri

$$MD(Ri) = \frac{NWA}{NA} \tag{2}$$

with NWA : the number of wrong applications of the rule Ri

$$MB(Ri) + MD(Ri) = 1 \tag{3}$$

MB(Ri) means that the rule Ri leads to a correct classification: the token can really be considered as an instance of a core requirement element, if not, we are talking about MD (Ri) (see (3)). The rules that are responsible only for a small number of correct classification can be deleted from the rule base because they are covering the exceptions in the dataset. An expert can specify a percentage value that has to be reached by each rule to remain in the rule base.

To select the relevant rules, we have fixed a minimum threshold of belief in the truth of a rule at 30 % (CF=0.3) based on methods proposed by Michael Hannon in [24]. Thus, we have trying different thresholds in the interval of [0.2 .. 0.5] to fix the threshold that maximize the precision and the recall of our proposed approach. Therefore, all the rules with a CF below this threshold are deleted because they deal with particular cases and helps to improve the error rate of the system.

After deleting uninteresting rules, we now have a set of linguistic rules each of which encompass an evaluation weight leading to deriving a textual core requirement and core requirement's concepts of the user context ontology by tokens extracted from a user's requirement. The majority of CF values of the remaining rules such indicated in Table II, do not exceed the 94% value. This is due to the fact that we deal with vague text input by clients.

TABLE II
AN EXTRACT OF LINGUISTIC RULES AND THEIR CF MEANS CERTAINTY FACTOR

Rule	Principal Pos	Dependency type antecedent	Grammar antecedent	Description	CF
R1	NN	Nsubj(t2, t1)	$(PRP?$|JJ*)| $(DT?$|JJ*) NN(MD|VB| CC)	If the token t1 is a noun (NN), it has a dependency nsubj with a verb (t2) and the antecedent is true then the t1 is a feature	0.93
R2	NN	Conj(t1,t2)	$(CC$|,) $(PRP?$|JJ*)| $(DT?$|JJ*) NN(MD|VB)	If the token t1 is a noun (NN), it has a dependency Conj with a verb (t2) and antecedent is true then the t1 is a feature	0.91
R3	VB	Nsubj(t1,t2)	MD?TO? VB|VBN	If the token t1 is a verb (VB|VBN), it has a dependency nsubj with a noun (NN) the antecedent is true then t1 is a goal	0.9
R4	VB	Nsubj(t1,t2)	MD? TO? VB|VBN |VBP RP	If the token t1 is a verb (VB|VBN |VBP), it have a dependency nsubj with a noun (NN), it is by a token t2 having the type "RP" and the antecedent is true then the concatenation of t1 and t2 is a goal	0.92
R5	MD	Aux(t2,t1)	MD VB	If the token t1 is a modal Verb (MD),its followed by a verb, it has an aux dependency with a verb the antecedent is true then t1 is an obligation degree	0.94
R6	(NN|NNS)	Obj(t2,t1)	VB($PRP?$|JJ*)| ($DT?$|JJ*)NN	If the token t1 is a noun (NN), it is included in a NP chunk,it has an obj dependency with a verb the and antecedent is true then t1 is an item	0.92
R7	NN	Nsubj(t2, t1)	$(PRP?$|JJ*)| $(DT?$|JJ*)NN (MD?) $(VB?$|VBZ)VBN (IN)	If the token t1 is a noun (NN), it has a dependency nsubj with a verb (t2) and the antecedent is true then the t1 is an Item	0.3
R8	(PRP|NN |NNS)	Nsubj(t1,t2)	IN $(PRP?$|JJ*)| $(DT?$|JJ*) PRP|NN|NNS $(VB$|CC)	If the token t1 is a noun or a possessive pronoun (PRP),it is proceeded by an "IN" that is equals to if/ when/where, it has a Nsubj dependency with a verb and the antecedent is true then t1 is a Subject of a condition	0.89
R9	(VB|VPB |VBZ)	mark(t1,t2)	$VB?$|VPB $RP?$|VBZ RB	If the token t1 is a verb, it has a mark dependency with a preposition (IN) and the antecedent is true then t1 is an action of a condition	0.92
R10	(NN|NNS)	advmod(t2,1) obj (t2, t1) obl(t2, t1)	(VB|VPB $RP?$|VBZ RB) DT? JJS? JJ* NP? NN|NNS	If the token t1 is a noun, is preceded at the position p-i by "IN" that is equals to if/ when/where, it has a advmod, obj and obl dependency with a verb then t1 is an entity of a condition	0.82

C. Ontology Population and Knowledge inferring

We intend, in this step, to populate the ontology with the new core requirements instance and derive new knowledge based on the extracted core requirements and knowledge that already exists to conceptualize the running SO-DSPL. As input of this step, we have the list of core requirements components extracted in the previous step to create the core requirement. In the first step, core requirement's concepts are instantiated. Then, with the given input, we start by creating a relationship between the CoreRequirement instance and the ObligationDegree instance. Next, we create instances of Composition relationship between CoreRequirement instance and Goal instances, between CoreRequirement instance and feature instances, between CoreRequirement instance and item instances and between CoreRequirement instance and Condition instances, as many as there are instances in Goals,items, features and condition.

We note that users can express their desired options(i.e. feature) by different terms that are different from the terms used to express DSPL features, thus, for the mapping between the two terms we use similarity to identify the associated DSPL feature (For example vacuum cleaner can be named robot cleaner or Aspirateur Vacuum Cleaner). As well, since core requirement's condition presents the situation to trigger the goal, matching core requirement's condition and the service condition aims to select the WS that satisfy the user core requirement. Thus, we calculate similarity between core requiment's condition and WS condition; if the similarity result is higher than a threshold fixed after a similarity analyses, the web service must be selected in the derived product. to attend our objectif, we use Cosine similarity [22] (eq4) to calculate the mentioned instances, and " sentence transformer" method for sentence embedding [23] (it is the technique to transform (map) words of a language into vectors of real numbers)following its accuracy and its usefulness in measuring similarity between sentence [23]

$$CosineSimilarity = \frac{A.B}{||A||.||B||} \tag{4}$$

where A and B are vectors.

Based on the calculated similarity, we create instances of the similarity concept. The similarity concept denotes the similarity between the core requirement's feature and the DSPL feature in one hand, between core requirement's goal and DSPL goal, and between the core requirement's condition and the service condition in another hand. Then, relationships between similarity instances and the associated instances are created. For instance, a core requirement feature "has-a-similarity" "calculated-with" the DSPL feature. A core requirement condition "has-a-similarity" "calculated-with" the web service condition. A core requirement goal "has-a-similarity" "calculated-with" the web DSPL goal.

In a second step, the created instance and the semantic relation that relate them are used to infer new SO-DSPL knowledge using SWRL rules mentioned in [14]. In addition to the rules created in [14], we have enriched our ontology with new rules presented in Table III. Based on the instanced concepts and the execution of the SWRL rules, products are derived based on the inferred knowledge.

VI. Illustrative Case

All along the present study, many experiments have been fulfilled to evaluate the applicability and the feasibility of our proposed approach to extract core requirement, populate the ontology and derive a service-based product. In this section, we consider an illustrative case which belongs to a product requirement given by a user and in the context of our running example.

In the remainder of this section, we will show the results of applying the different steps of our approach to the selected example: *"My sensor should detect movement. if I get up late night, lights in my house should turn on to enhance convenience and safety"*.

In the first step of the first module, stop words and empty words are removed then the input text is analyzed with Stanford, the mentioned type of chunks are extracted and the analyzer generates their relative POS tags, and typed dependencies of the requirement's token. The second step applies filter rules. Thus, we obtain the following chunks: my sensor, should, detect, movement. If, I, get up, late night, light, in my house, should turn on, to enhance convenience and safety. Table IV presents the chunks, POS tag and types dependencies result given by stanford analyser. In the second phase we apply linguistic rules to match each token with the corresponding concept of the ontology. On the other hand, we derive the product core requirement as a textual form.

Based on the PoS, Chunk and the types dependencies of each token, we choose the category of linguistic rules to be applied.

From this product requirement, these two core requirements are extracted as a textual form:
Core requirement 1: sensor should detect movement
Core requirement 2: lights should turn on if I get up night

The associated product core requirements became: Sensor should detect movement. Lights should turn on if I get up night.

Then, the OntoSO-DSPL ontology is population and the correspond concepts are instanced. Thus, the mentioned SWRL rules are executed, products are derived and web services are selected.

VII. Evaluation

To validate our approach, we have implemented a tool that supports our proposed approach steps including the linguistic rules. OWL (Web Ontology Language) is used to populate the proposed SO-DSPL ontology using data from the input client's product requirements. A series of experiments were performed via the implemented tool in order to validate our work. We first present in Subsect. 6.1, the dataset used. We then highlight in Subsect. 6.2 the selected evaluation measures to perform the evaluation step.

A. Dataset

To evaluate the performance of our implemented approach, we applied our approach the smart home requirements data set [20]. In order to evaluate the performance of our approach on a larger volume of data, we have augmented the existed dataset using data Augmentation algorithms [23], which consists in altering an existing data to create a new one. The objective is to augment the dataset by generating new product requirements with the same meaning as the existing requirements but written in another form. Thus, we have used "nlpaug" libraries using the Substitution by contextual word embeddings RoBERTA technique. The result data collection consists of 9000 textual product requirements. This collection of examples contains different informal texts that express product requirements in different manners.

B. Evaluation measures

In our experiments, we used recall and precision to evaluate our approach. These measures fit well to our objective which consists in identifying core requirements. It should be noted that the set of customers requests were examined to extract different core requirements. This result was compared to the output of our proposed component. For this purpose, we adopted the evaluation measures to our context of work, which we define as follows:

- Precision represents the number of found relevant instances of concepts or relationships between concepts among the found instances.
- Recall represents the number of found relevant instances of concepts or relationships among all the relevant instances to create an intention instance (detected by the expert).

Precision and recall are calculated using the formula 5 and 6 respectively:

$$Precision = \frac{TP}{TP + FP} \tag{5}$$

$$Recall = \frac{TP}{TP + FN} \tag{6}$$

where:

- TP (true positives): are the correct identification of core requirement elements by the core requirement Recognition component.

TABLE III
SOME SWRL RULES (THERE ARE SEVERAL OTHER RULES BUT SPACE LIMITATION)

ID	SWRL Rule	Description
R1	uc:Feature(?f1) $\wedge dspl : Feature(?f2) \wedge Similarity(?s)$ $\wedge$has-a-similarity(?f1, ?s) $\wedge similarity - calculated - with(?s, ?f2)\wedge$ similarityValue(?s, ?v) $\wedge swrlb : greaterThan(?v, 80)$ -> is-similar-to(?f1, ?f2)	if the similarity of a core requirement feature and a DSPL feature is greater than 80 then the two feature are similar.
R2	uc:goal(?g1) $\wedge dspl : goal(?g2) \wedge Similarity(?s)$ $\wedge$has-a-similarity(?g1, ?s) $\wedge similarity - calculated - with(?s, ?g2)\wedge$ similarityValue(?s, ?v) $\wedge swrlb : greaterThan(?v, 80)$ -> is-similar-to(?g1, ?g2)	if the similarity of a core requirement goal and a DSPL goal is greater than 80 then the two goal are similar.
R3	dspl:configuration(?cf) $\wedge uc : coreRequirement(?cr)\wedge$ satisfy(?cf,?uc) $\wedge uc : condition(?c1)\wedge$ is-composed-of(?cr,?c1) $\wedge ws : condition(?c2)\wedge$ triggered-based-on(?s,?c2) $\wedge is - similar - to(?c1, ?c2)$ ->selected(?s,true) $\wedge satisfy(?c1, ?c2) \wedge implement(?s, ?f)$ $\wedge composed - of(?cf, ?f)$	if the similarity of a core requirement condition and a web service condition is greater than 75 then the two condition are similar.
R4	dspl:configuration(?cf) $\wedge composed - of(?cf, f1)\wedge$ recommended-with(?f1,?f2) -> composed-of(?cf,?f2)	if a feature is selected in a configuration and it recommends another feature (with the semantic relation "recommended-with" then the recommended feature is with be selected in the running configuration.
R5	swrlx:makeOWLThing(?S, ?y) $\wedge dspl : Feature(?y)) - >$ implements(?y, ?S)) $\wedge ws : Service(?S)$	For each dspl feature an individual service is created and related by the relationship "implements" to execute its functionalities.
R6	swrlx:makeOWLThing(?f, ?c) $\wedge dspl : Feature(?F) - >$ composed-of(?f, ?c) $\wedge Configuration(?c)$	each configuration must be composed by more than one feature.
R7	uc:CoreRequirement(?CR1) $\wedge uc : CoreRequirement(?CR2)$ $\wedge uc : ProductRequirement(?PR)$ $\wedge uc : composed - of(?PR, ?CR1)\wedge$ uc:composed-of(?PR,?CR2) $\wedge has - priority(?CR1, Desirable)\wedge$ has-priority(?CR2, Essential) $\wedge dspl : Feature(?F1)$ $\wedge dspl : Feature(?F2) \wedge dspl : alternative - with(?F2, ?F1)$ $\wedge dspl : satisfy(?F1, ?CR1)$ $\wedge dspl : satisfy(?F2, ?CR2) \wedge dspl : Configuration(?CF)$ $\wedge satisfy(?CF, ?PR) \wedge dspl : composed - of(?CF, ?F1)$ -> dspl:composed-of(?CF,?F2) $\wedge dspl : selected - for(?CF, ?F2)$ $\wedge dspl : eliminated - for(?CF, ?F1)$	The features associated to a product's core requirements and their are related with the relationship "alternative-with" then an adaptation is triggered to the running configuration by eliminating the optional feature and selecting the essential one.
R8	uc:CoreRequirement(?CR1) $\wedge uc : CoreRequirement(?CR2)$ $\wedge uc : ProductRequirement(?PR)$ $\wedge uc : composed - of(?PR, ?CR1)\wedge$ uc:composed-of(?PR,?CR2) $\wedge has - priority(?CR1, Essential)\wedge$ has-priority(?CR2, Essential) $\wedge dspl : Feature(?F1)$ $\wedge dspl : Feature(?F2) \wedge dspl : alternative - with(?F2, ?F1)$ $\wedge dspl : satisfy(?F1, ?CR1)$ $\wedge dspl : satisfy(?F2, ?CR2) \wedge dspl : Configuration(?CF)$ $\wedge satisfy(?CF, ?PR) \wedge dspl : composed - of(?CF, ?F1)$ -> uc:alternative-conflict(?CR1,?CR2)	The features associated to a product's core requirements and their are related with the relationship "alternative-with" and the two core requirements are essential then a conflict of alternative constraint violation is detected.

- FP (false positives): are the wrong identification of core requirement elements by the core requirement Recognition component.
- FN (false negatives): are the core requirement elements that have not been extracted by the core requirement Recognition component.

C. Experimental Results and Analysis

Table V shows the results across the dataset. We achieve precision scores of up to 89.87 % and recall scores of up to 92.85% by applying the population process while taking into account all the rules. In fact, by analyzing the outputs of our approach corresponding to each client's request in the dataset, errors can be found if the user use a long phrase to express the condition of the requirement. These results can further be improved by intervening, this time, in the first phase of the approach. In fact, as customers freely express their request and requirement, they, sometimes, do not respect the writing rules.

Therefore, the same content can be interpreted differently by the analyzer. For example "4 PM" and "4PM " without spaces, are labeled differently by this chunker. For the first one, it tags the token 4 by the PoS "CD" and by "$" for the "$", but for the second, it considers the whole as "CD" Pos.This type of

TABLE IV
CHUNKS, POS TAG AND TYPES DEPENDENCIES

Chunks	POS tag	Types dependencies
(ROOT (S	nmod:poss(sensor-2, My-1)	nmod:poss(sensor-2, My-1)
(NP (PRP$My)(NNsensor)$)	nsubj(detect-4, sensor-2)	nsubj(detect-4, sensor-2)
(VP (MD should)	aux(detect-4, should-3)	aux(detect-4, should-3)
(VP (VB detect)	root(ROOT-0, detect-4)	root(ROOT-0, detect-4)
(NP (NN movement))))	obj(detect-4, movement-5)	obj(detect-4, movement-5)
(. .)))	mark(get-3, If-1)	mark(get-3, If-1)
(ROOT	nsubj(get-3, i-2)	nsubj(get-3, i-2)
(S	csubj(turn-12, get-3)	csubj(turn-12, get-3)
(SBAR (IN If)	compound:prt(get-3, up-4)	compound:prt(get-3, up-4)
(S	amod(lights-7, late-5)	amod(lights-7, late-5)
(NP (PRP i))	compound(lights-7, night-6)	compound(lights-7, night-6)
(VP (VBP get)	obj(get-3, lights-7)	obj(get-3, lights-7)
(PRT (RP up))	case(house-10, in-8)	case(house-10, in-8)
(NP	nmod:poss(house-10, my-9)	nmod:poss(house-10, my-9)
(NP (JJ late) (NN night) (NNS lights))	nmod(lights-7, house-10)	nmod(lights-7, house-10)
(PP (IN in)	aux(turn-12, should-11)	aux(turn-12, should-11)
(NP (PRP$my)(NNhouse)))))))$	root(ROOT-0, turn-12)	root(ROOT-0, turn-12)
(VP (MD should)	compound:prt(turn-12, on-13)	compound:prt(turn-12, on-13)
(VP (VB turn)	mark(enhance-15, to-14)	mark(enhance-15, to-14)
(PRT (RP on))	xcomp(turn-12, enhance-15)	xcomp(turn-12, enhance-15)
(S	obj(enhance-15, convenience-16)	obj(enhance-15, convenience-16)
(VP (TO to)	cc(safety-18, and-17)	cc(safety-18, and-17)
(VP (VB enhance)	conj(convenience-16, safety-18)	conj(convenience-16, safety-18)
(NP (NN convenience)		
(CC and)		
(NN safety)))))))		

TABLE V
RECALL AND PRECISION OF THE OVERALL APPROACH

	TP	FP	FN	Precision	Recall
DataSet	55400	6241	4261	89.87%	92.85%

tagging error can influence the entire instantiation process. A possible contribution to the improvement of results would be, therefore, to have a text filtering or rectification stage of each input according to the NLP rules.

VIII. CONCLUSION

In order to extract information and knowledge from user requirements and for being able to derive the most appropriate product in the context of a SO-DSPL, we have presented an approach that analyses and understands automatically the user requirement. We reuse the structure of user requirements from SO-DSPL [14]ontology and benefit from the use of NLP algorithms. Indeed, the proposed approach extracts user requirements and builds a requirement in accordance with the core requirement structure. This latter is defined by the basic requirements that must be covered by the derived product to satisfy the user. Our recognition approach is based on a set of linguistic rules and the support of uncertainty. These rules facilitate the building of core requirement structure which is then loaded as an instance of the SO-DSPL ontology. Based on the derived core requirements, relevant knowledge are inferred and relevant services are selected to derive the entire user product. The originality of the proposed approach is, on the one hand, that the entire process of the extraction and population approach is made automatically and in a semantic and intelligent way thanks to ontology reasoning capabilities. This will enhance SPL activities such as: product recommendation, user satisfaction, feature extraction and service (DSPL product) adaptation. On the other hand, it can be applied both on a short and a long text. Our near future work is to continue the experimentation of the approach and to enrich it with linguistic rules that allow the extraction of context changes. In a second step, we aim to combine this work with recommender system that will derive the appropriate services for the generated requirement.

REFERENCES

[1] B. Tanmay, N. Nan, S. Juha and M. Anas, "Leveraging topic modeling and part-of-speech tagging to support combinational creativity in requirements engineering", IN Requirements Engineering, vol. 20, no. 3, pp. 253–280, 2015.

[2] G. Sarita and C. Tanupriya, "An efficient automated design to generate uml diagram from natural language specifications," In Cloud System and Big Data Engineering (Confluence), 2016 6th International Conference, pp. 641–648, IEEE, 2016.

[3] Y. Mu,Y. Wang, and J. Guo, "Extracting software functional requirements from free text documents," in Information and Multimedia Technology, 2009. ICIMT'09. International Conference on, pp. 194–198, IEEE, 2009

[4] C. Arora, M. Sabetzadeh, L. Briand,and F. Zimmer, "Automated extraction and clustering of requirements glossary terms," IEEE Transactions on Software Engineering, 2016.

[5] E. Boutkova, and F. Houdek, "Semi-automatic identification of features in requirement specifications," in 2011 IEEE 19th International Requirements Engineering Conference, pp. 313–318, Aug 2011.

[6] A. Ferrari, G. Spagnolo, and F. Dell'Orletta, "Mining commonalities and variabilities from natural language documents," in Proceedings of the 17th International Software Product Line Conference, pp. 116–120, ACM, 2013.
[7] S. J. Korner and T. Brumm, "Natural language specification improvement with ontologies," International Journal of Semantic Computing, vol. 3, no. 04, pp. 445–470, 2009.
[8] Y. Wang, "Semantic information extraction for software requirements using semantic role labeling," in Progress in Informatics and Computing (PIC), 2015 IEEE International Conference on, pp. 332–337, IEEE, 2015.
[9] G. Capobianco, A. D. Lucia, R. Oliveto, A. Panichella, and S. Panichella, "Improving ir-based traceability recovery via noun-based indexing of software artifacts," Journal of Software: Evolution and Process, vol. 25, no. 7, pp. 743–762, 2013.
[10] G. J. Hahm, M. Y. Yi, J. H. Lee and H. Suh, "A personalized query expansion approach for engineering document retrieval," Advanced Engineering Informatics, vol. 28, no. 4, pp. 344–359, 2014.
[11] S.-P Ma, C.-H. Li Tsai and C.Lan, "Web service discovery using lexical and semantic query expansion," in e-Business Engineering (ICEBE), 2013 IEEE 10th International Conference on, pp. 423–428, IEEE, 2013
[12] N. H. Bakar, Z. M. Kasirun, N. Salleh and H. A Jalab, "Extracting features from online software reviews to aid requirements reuse," Applied Soft Computing, vol. 49, pp. 1297–1315, 2016
[13] M. Arias, A. Buccella and A. Cechich, "A Framework for Managing Requirements of Software Product Lines", Electronic Notes in Theoretical Computer Science, vol. 339, pp. 5-20, 2018
[14] N. Maalaoui, R. beltaifa, L. Labed and R. Mazo, "An Ontology for Service-Oriented Dynamic Software Product Lines Knowledge Management",16th International Conference on Evaluation of Novel Approaches to Software Engineering, vol. 314, pp 314-322, 2021
[15] R. Capilla,J. Bosch,P. Trinidad,A. Ruiz-Cortes and M. Hinchey, "Overview of Dynamic Software Product Line Architectures and Techniques:Observations from Research and Industry",The Journal of Systems and Software,pp 3-23, 2014
[16] C.D. Manning, "Part-of-Speech Tagging from 97% to 100%: Is It Time for Some Linguistics?". In: Gelbukh A.F. (eds) Computational Linguistics and Intelligent Text Processing. CICLing 2011. Lecture Notes in Computer Science, vol 6608. Springer, Berlin, Heidelberg. 2011
[17] A. Mansouri, L.S. Affendey and,A. Mamat, "Named Entity Recognition Approaches",IJCSNS International Journal of Computer Science and Network Security, VOL.8 No.2, February 2008
[18] H. Bo, P. Cook, T. Baldwin, "Lexical normalization for social media text".ACM Transactions on Intelligent Systems and Technology Volume Article No.: 5pp 1–27, 2013
[19] D. Dubois,J. Lang and H. PradeFuzzy, sets in approximate reasoning, Part 2: logical approaches. In "Fuzzy Sets and Systems",pp 203-244,1992
[20] K. Pradeep,A. Nirav, and P. Munindar, "Acquiring Creative Requirements from the Crowd: Understanding the Influences of Personality and Creative Potential in Crowd RE".Proceedings of the IEEE 24th International Requirements Engineering Conference (RE), pp 176–185., September 2016,
[21] A. Arellano, E. Carney, and M.A. Austin, "Natural Language Processing of Textual Requirements," The Tenth International Conference on Systems (ICONS 2015),pp. 93– 97, Barcelona 2015
[22] S. Pinky, P.a. Kritish, T. Pujan and S. Subarna," Comparison of Semantic Similarity Methods for Maximum Human Interpretability",In IEEE, 2019
[23] https://github.com/makcedward/nlpaug,Online; accessed 12-july-2022
[24] M. Hannon, A solution to knowledge's threshold problem. Philosophical Studies: An International Journal for Philosophy in the Analytic Tradition, 174(3), 607–629. http://www.jstor.org/stable/26001716, 2017
[25] A. Arellano, E. Zontek-Carney, A. Austin, Frameworks for Natural Language Processing of Textual Requirements. International Journal on Advances in Systems and Measurements. 8. 230-240,2015

Interactive Visualization Dashboard for Common Attack Pattern Enumeration Classification

Mounika Vanamala
Dept. of Computer Science
University of Wisconsin Eau Claire
Rice Lake, WI, USA
vanamalm@uwec.edu

Walter Smith
Dept. of Computer Science
North Carolina Agricultural and Technical State Univ.
Greensboro, NC, USA
xhyuan@ncat.edu

Xiaohong Yuan
Dept.of Computer Science
North Carolina Agricultural and Technical State Univ.
Greensboro, NC, USA
wsmith12@aggies.ncat.edu

Joi Bennett
Dept. of Computer Science
North Carolina Agricultural and Technical State Univ.
Greensboro, NC, USA
jbbennett1@aggies.ncat.edu

***Abstract*— Attack patterns represent computer attackers' tools, methodologies, and perspective. The Common Attack Pattern Enumeration Classification (CAPEC) provides information about attack patterns which include descriptive textual fields, relationships between different attack patterns, execution flow, mitigations and related Common Weaknesses Enumeration (CWE) weakness and external Mapping. This paper describes an interactive visualization dashboard we developed for displaying the hierarchically structured CAPEC information. The dashboard includes a tree map and a network graph. The tree map visualization displays the hierarchy of CAPEC in a rectangular region in a space-filling manner. The network graph displays the parent child-taxonomy from the CAPEC using nodes and links between nodes. The visualization dashboard displays the external mapping of CAPEC to CWE, Adversarial tactics, techniques, and common knowledge (ATT&CK), The Open Web Application Security Project (OWASP) and Web Application Security Consortium (WASC) taxonomy. This visualization tool improves usability and provides a range of new capabilities for understanding and interacting with the rich content and relationships in CAPEC.**

Keywords-Attack patternss; Common Attack Pattern Enumeration and Classification (CAPEC); visualization, Network graph, tree map.

I. Introduction

To understand the methods for hacking information systems, cyber security experts must consider the attacker's point of view. The Common Attack Pattern Enumeration and Classification (CAPEC) provides a publicly available catalog of common attack patterns that helps users understand how adversaries exploit weaknesses in applications and other cyber-enabled capabilities [1].

CAPEC provides descriptive textual fields, also called elements, for each attack pattern. The current CAPEC release includes a list of 572 specific attack patterns. Each attack pattern may include up to 30 elements to describe the attack details. While CAPEC has addressed the need to create a standard for representing and defining attacks from an attacker's perspective, issues of usability arise because CAPEC does not provide a consistent level of documentation for some elements among the attack patterns. In many cases, attack pattern elements are missing completely. The inconsistent use of elements makes it problematic to discern the relationship, if any, between the descriptive fields. The goal of this research is to improve usability and provide a range of new capabilities for understanding and interacting with the rich content and relationships in CAPEC. Effective visualization helps users analyze and reason about data and evidence. It makes complex data more accessible, understandable, and usable. The goal is to communicate information clearly and efficiently to users. Visualization helps developers to better comprehend large and complex systems [2].

Navigation of CAPEC web content relies on following parent-child hyperlinks in textual content. This makes it difficult to comprehend CAPEC's overall hierarchical structure. To address this, we introduce a new web-based interactive visualization dashboard for CAPEC attack patterns. The visualization includes tree maps consisting of rectangles that represent the hierarchy of a system, and network graph. We describe tree map and network graph visualizations to visualize the parent-child taxonomy of CAPEC. CAPEC attack patterns are mapped onto external databases such as CWE, ATT&CK, OWASP and WASC. We describe how external mappings are displayed in this dashboard. This dashboard can be used by software engineers and security engineers who make use of CAPEC attack patterns for secure software development or other security activities.

The rest of the paper is organized as follows. In Section 2, we discuss the background of CAPEC, visualization techniques and implementation platform. Section 3 describes the visualization dashboard, and Section 4 discusses related work. Section 5 concludes the paper.

II. BACKGROUND

This section provides background on CAPEC, tree map, network graph as well as Dash and Heroku we used to implement the visualization.

A. CAPEC

CAPEC attack patterns help people understand how weaknesses could be exploited and ways to defend against the weakness. CAPEC attack patterns are organized with parent and child hierarchy. For example, CAPEC 122 "Privilege Abuse" is a top level attack pattern with five child attack patterns: CAPEC-1 "Accessing Functionality Not Properly", CAPEC-17 "Using Malicious Files", CAPEC-180 "Exploiting Incorrectly Configured Access", CAPEC-221 "WebView Exposure", and CAPEC 503 "Data Serialization External Entities Blowup". Each of these attack patterns has several child attack patterns, for example, "CAPEC-58 Restful Privilege Elevation" is the child attack pattern of "CAPEC-1 Accessing Functionality Not Properly". Fig. 1 shows an example of the hierarchical parent child relationship in CAPEC attack patterns.

B. Tree Map

Trees maps are one of the most used structures to visualize relational information. Tree maps use a rectangular space-filling layout [3]. Space-filling techniques make maximal use of the display space. The two most common approaches to generating space-filling hierarchies are rectangular and radial layouts. In the basic tree map, a rectangle is recursively divided into slices, alternating horizontal and vertical slicing, based on the populations of the subtrees at a given level. There are many variations of tree maps such as square tree maps [4], and nested tree maps which are used to emphasize the hierarchical structure. These methods are structured using horizontal and vertical divisions to convey the hierarchy. For these and other space-filling techniques, color can be used to convey any attributes, such as a value associated with the node (e.g., classification) or it may display the hierarchical relationships, e.g., siblings and parents may have similarities in color. Symbols and other markings may also be embedded in the rectangular or circular segments to communicate other data features.

In additional rectangular layout, one way to pack a tree display into a smaller space is to employ a radial layout [2]. Also, there is a class of visualization techniques that represents tree relationships implicitly [5], rather than explicitly drawing vertices and edges.

C. Network Graph

The most common representation used to visualize trees or hierarchical relationships is a node-link diagram. This is the most popular form of non-space filling layout. This type of visualization shows how things are interconnected using nodes / vertices and link lines to represent their connections and help illuminate the type of relationships between a group of entities. In network graphs, not all of the nodes and links are created equally: additional variables can be visualized, for example, by making the node size or link stroke weight proportion to an assigned value. By mapping out connected systems, network graphs can be used to interpret the structure of a network through looking for any clustering of the nodes, how densely nodes are connected or by how the diagram layout is arranged [3].

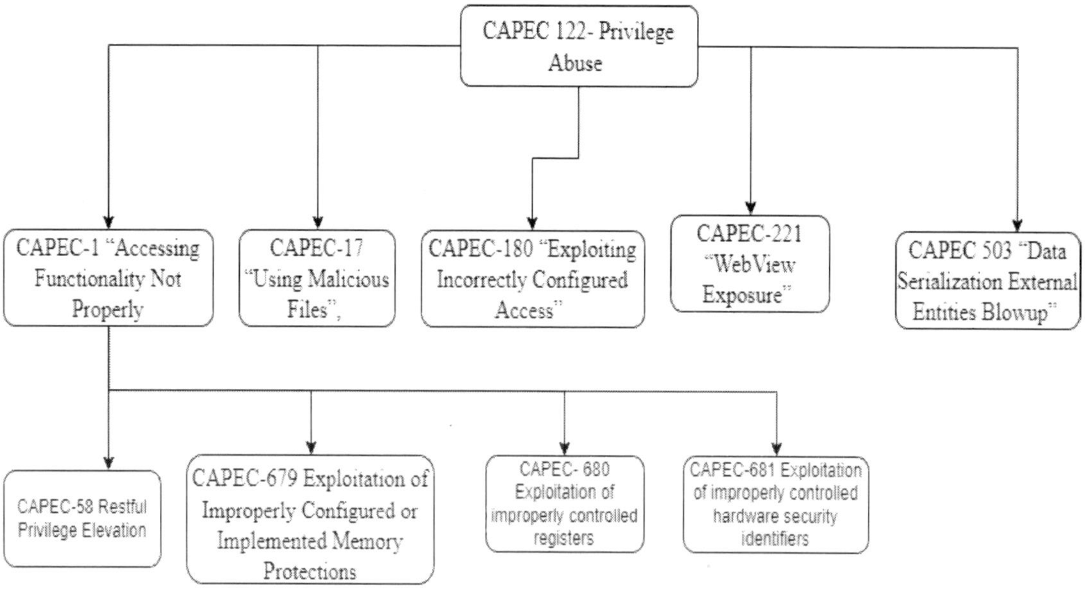

Fig. 1. The hierarchical parent-child relationship in CAPEC attack patterns

D. Dash

Plotly's dash library [6][7] provides a declarative Python interface for developing full-stack web applications ("Dash apps"). In addition to the main dash library, the dash-html-components and dash-core-components packages comprise the building blocks of a Dash app. dash-html-components provides an interface for building the layout of a Dash application that mimics the process of building the layout of a website; dash-core-components is a suite of common tools used for interactions with a Dash app (e.g., dropdowns, text inputs, and sliders) and includes Dash Core Components (DCC). Graph components for interactive graphs are made with plotly.py.

Interactivity is implemented with callbacks. These allow for reading the values of inputs in the Dash app (e.g., text inputs, dropdowns, and sliders), which can subsequently be used to compute the value of one or more "outputs", i.e., properties of other components in the app. The function that computes the outputs is wrapped in a decorator that specifies the aforementioned inputs and outputs; together, they form a callback. The callback is triggered whenever one of the specified inputs changes in value.

E. Heroku

Heroku is a container-based cloud Platform as a Service (PaaS) [8]. It is flexible, easy to use, and offers developers a simple path to getting their apps to market. Heroku is open and extensible, meaning that developers can build any language they desire to use such as: Nodejs, Ruby, PHP, Python, Java and so on. For this research, we use Heroku because of its benefit of security and performance and the large quantity of add-ons available.

III. THE CAPEC VISUALIZATION DASHBOARD

This section describes the visualization dashboard for CAPEC attack patterns. The Visualization Dashboard presents different visualization techniques for navigating the CAPEC taxonomy. Our interactive visualization interfaces including tree maps and network graphs are implemented using Dash, Plotly, Heroku, and MongoDB. The data obtained from MITRE'S CAPEC website in the form of a CSV is hosted on a MongoDB database. The user can choose to visualize the CAPEC attack pattern data or CAPEC attack pattern external mapping.

A. Visualization of the CAPEC Data

Fig. 2 shows the visualization of CAPEC Data. There is a selection menu at the left top from which the user can choose what graph to display: CAPEC Data or External Mapping. The left top part of the visualization is a tree map created using Plotly. Given the data, a CSV is created with the columns parent, child, and severity, which refers to the parent attack pattern ID, the child attack pattern ID, and the severity of the parent attack pattern. The tree map shows the parent attack pattern ID with its child attack patterns within the rectangular space of the parent attack patten. The colors in the tree map are chosen based on the severity with a key on the right of the graph showing the color scale for the severity. If a user hovers over them, they can get the exact numerical value for severity.

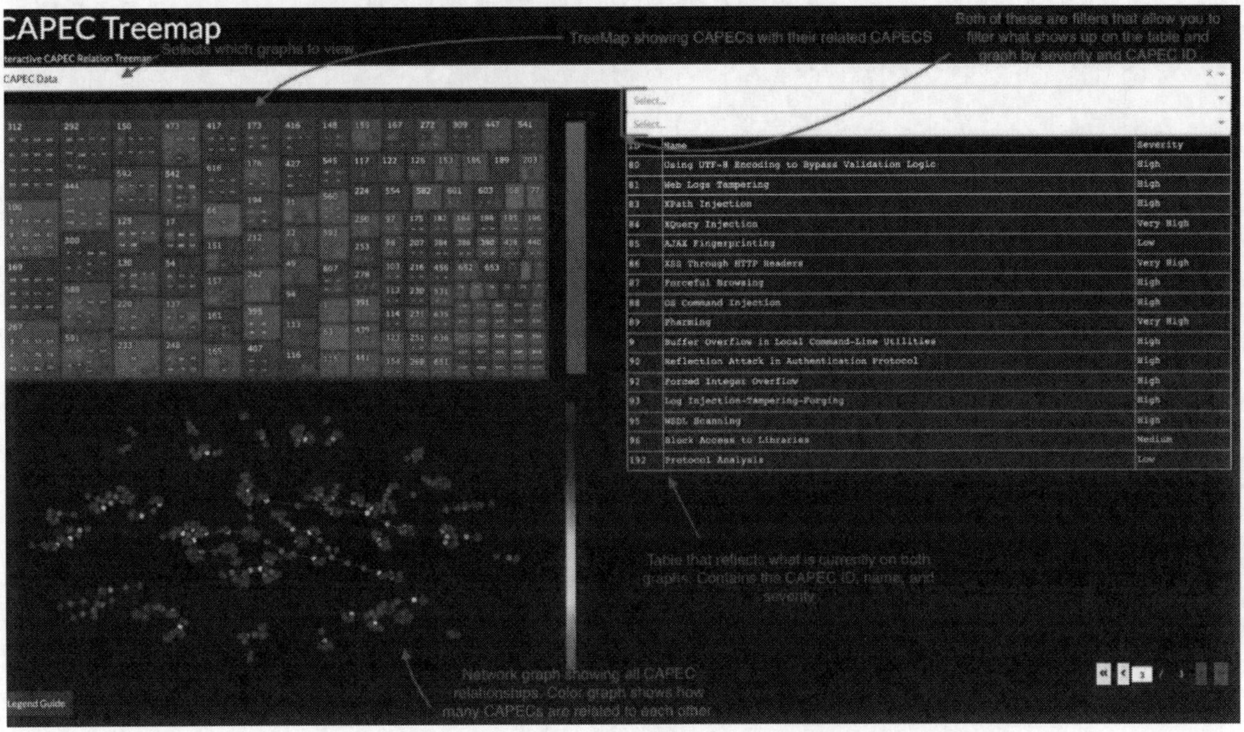

Fig. 2. Tree map and network graph to visualize CAPEC data

Below the tree map in Fig. 2 is a network graph showing how a CAPEC attack pattern is related to other CAPEC attack patterns. Each note represents an attack pattern. The link from one node to another node shows the parent/child relationship between the two nodes linked together. The color of the node indicates the number of nodes connected to this node. The color scale to the right side of the network graph shows a purple color, indicating higher number of connected nodes, and a red color indicating lower number of connected nodes.

The right side of Fig. 2 shows a table that lists all the CAPEC attack patterns shown on the tree map and the network graph. It displays the CAPEC ID, the name of the CAPEC attack pattern, and the severity of the attack pattern. On the top of the table, there are two drop down menus allowing users to select the CAPEC attack pattern IDs, and a severity value to filter out specific CAPEC attack patterns or attack patterns of a selected severity level to display in the tree map, network graph and the table.

From Fig. 2, we can see that tree map effectively utilizes the space it takes to display hierarchical relationship. In the network graph, there is a lot of empty space and a lot of clusters.

The Visualization dashboard allows users to select a CAPEC ID from the tree map to view detailed information of the CAPEC attack pattern. For example, in Fig. 3, if a user clicks on CAPEC-125 in the tree map, a window will pop up showing the description of CAPEC-125. The window also includes buttons "taxonomy", "execution flow", and "mitigation flow". Clicking on each button will provide the corresponding information for CAPEC-125. The network graph changes correspondingly, showing only CAPEC-125 and all the child attack patterns connected to CAPEC-125.

B. *Visualization of the CAPEC External Mapping*

When users select external mapping from the dropdown menu on top of the tree map, the visualization dashboard will show the external mappings of CAPEC attack patterns. The CAPEC attack patterns are mapped to ATT&K [9], OWASP [10], WASC [11] and CWE weaknesses [12]. Fig. 4 shows the attack patterns that are mapped to these taxonomies. In Fig. 4, the left-top rectangle in blue color shows the CAPEC IDs that are mapped to the ATT&K taxonomy. The left-bottom rectangle in orange color shows the CAPEC IDs that are mapped to OWASP, and the right-bottom rectangle in green color shows the CAPEC IDs that are mapped to WASC. The right side of the dashboard is a table that shows the CAPEC ID and the related CWE weaknesses.

The user can select an CAPEC ID, and the dashboard will show the external mapping of the particular attack pattern. For example, in Fig. 5, CAPEC-168 is chosen. A popup window displays the CAPEC attack pattern ID:168, its related CWE weaknesses: 212, 69, and related ATT&CK. A hyperlink to the CAPEC page for this attack pattern is also given.

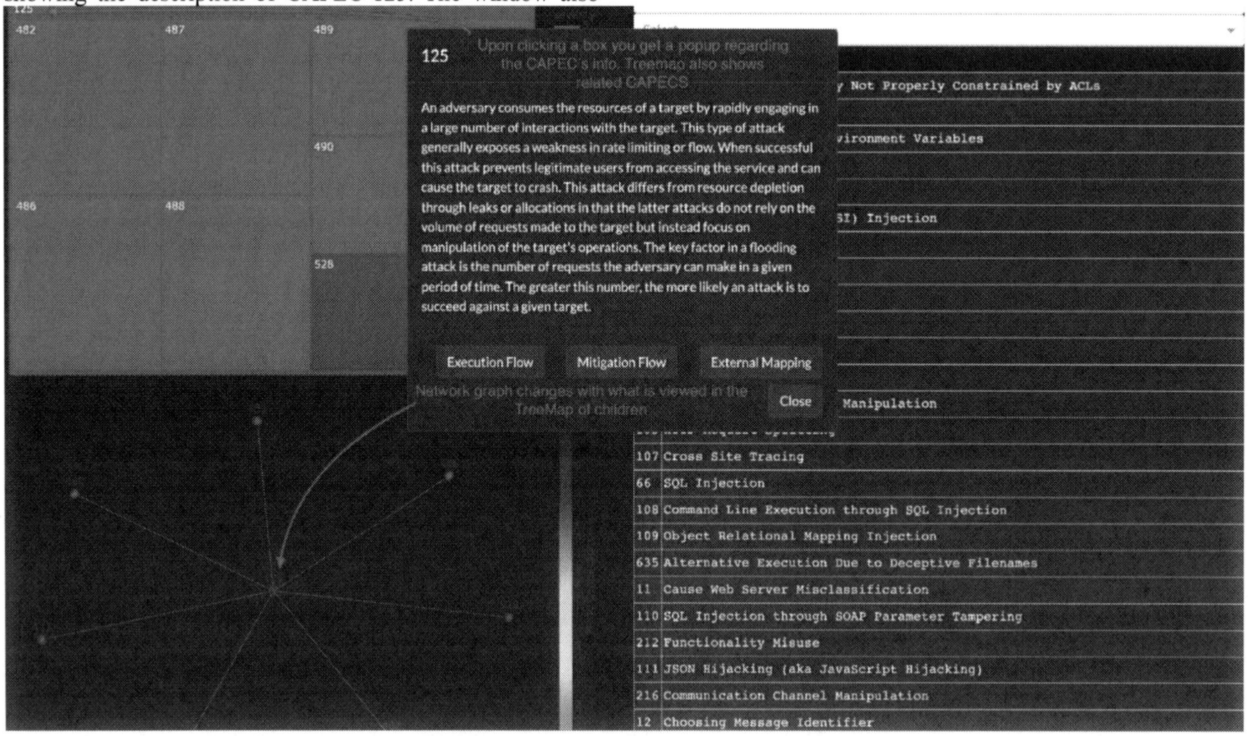

Fig. 3. Interaction between the tree map and network graph.

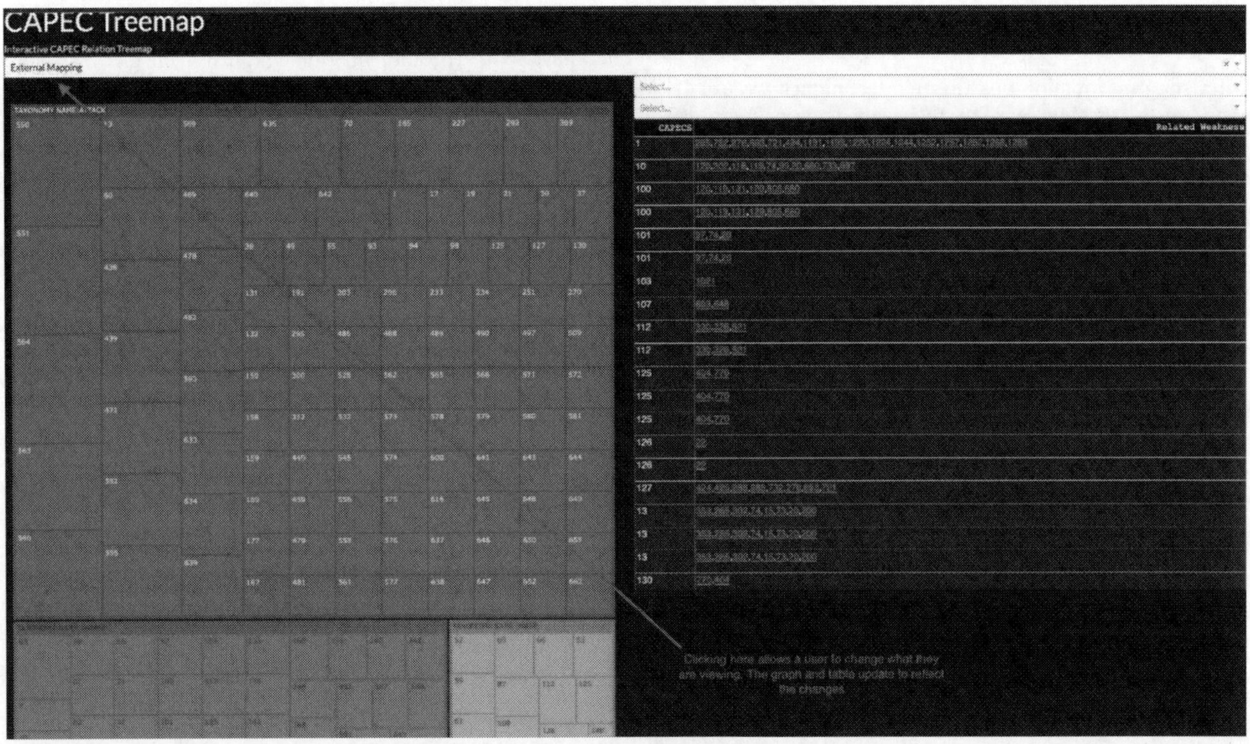

Fig. 4. External mappings of CAPEC attack patterns

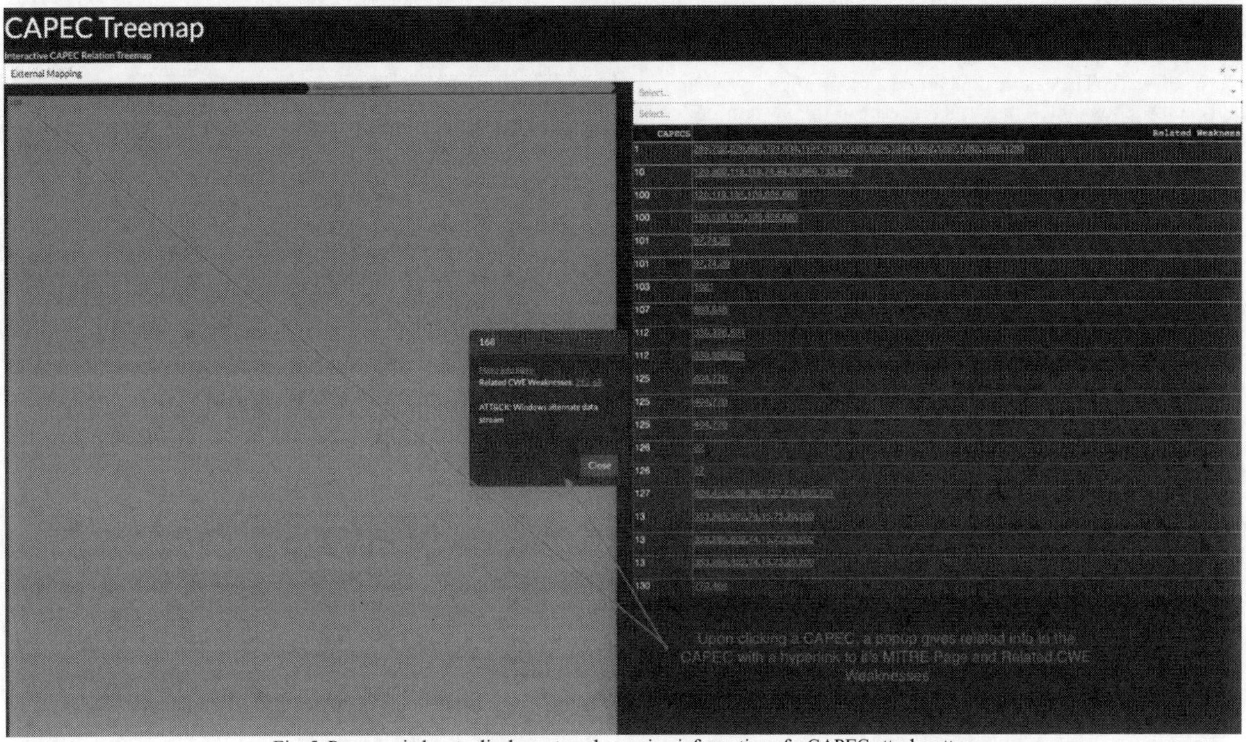

Fig. 5. Pop up window to display external mapping information of a CAPEC attack pattern

IV. RELATED WORK

Existing information visualization techniques are usually limited to the display of a few thousand items or avoid the problem of visualizing large number of items by using aggregation, sampling, and extracting, or by not managing occlusion and overlapping [13]. Among the popular techniques is the use of scatter plots connected to interactive controls such as in Dynamic Queries. We have used the tree visualization in our dashboard to show the parent child taxonomy in CAPEC.

Noel [14] visualized the overall hierarchical structure of CAPEC attack patterns using network graph, Sunburst visualization, Circular tree map, and Voronoi tree map. They also conducted text mining and computed hierarchical clusters and grouped related attack patterns through automated analysis. They used bipartite graph to visualize cross references from CAPEC attack patterns to CWE weaknesses. Our tool used rectangular tree map and network graph to visualize the hierarchical structure of CAPEC attack patterns and display external mapping information including CWE, ATT&CK, OWASP and WASC. The goal of our tool is to allow users to retrieve such information easily.

Regainia and Salva [15] proposed a methodology that takes as inputs CAPEC attack patterns, and infers relationships between attacks, weaknesses, security principles and patterns to generate the classification and Attack Defense Trees. Seehusen [16] proposed to use CAPEC for Risk-Based Security Testing. Vanamala et al. [17] and Vanamala et al. [18] have used software repositories like CVE (Common Vulnerabilities and Exposures) and CAPEC to help develop secure software. They have developed a recommender system that recommends attack patterns relevant to the system under development based on software requirements documents. A software developer can develop security requirements and secure design based on these attack patterns [19].

V. CONCLUSION AND FUTURE WORK

In this paper, we describe a web-based interactive visualization dashboard for the CAPEC attack patterns. This includes visualizing the overall hierarchical structure of CAPEC attack patterns using tree map and network graph. Our visualization techniques provide a range of new capabilities for understanding and interacting with the rich content and relationships in CAPEC. The goal is to be able to effectively communicate this information to a user in a user-friendly way. This tool will help users to make use of CAPEC attack patterns in developing secure software or conducting other security activities such as threat modeling, security testing, training, and education. Our future work is to conduct a user study for the dashboard to assess the effectiveness of the tool in helping users understand the structure of CAPEC and to make use of CAPEC attack patterns in their security tasks.

ACKNOWLEDGMENT

This work is partially supported by the National Center of Academic Excellence in Cybersecurity (NCAE-C) under the grant H98230-20-1-0404. Any opinions, findings, and conclusions or recommendations expressed in this material are those of the author(s) and do not necessarily reflect the views of the sponsor.

REFERENCES

[1] The Common Attack Pattern Enumeration and Classification. [Online]. Available from: https://capec.mitre.org/ [last accessed on 2022.10.12]

[2] M. Balzer, A. Noack, O. Deussen, and C. Lewerentz, "Software landscapes: visualizing the structure of large software systems," IEEE TCVG, 2004. doi: 10.2312/VisSym/VisSym04/261-266

[3] B. Johnson, "TreeViz: treemap visualization of hierarchically structured information," Proceedings of the SIGCHI Conference on Human Factors in Computing Systems, June 1992, pp. 369-370.

[4] W. Scheibel, M. Trapp, D. Limberger, and J. Döllner, "A taxonomy of tree map visualization techniques" VISIGRAPP (3: IVAPP), 2020, pp. 273-280.

[5] R. Vliegen, J. J. Van Wijk, and E. J. van der Linden, "Visualizing business data with generalized treemaps," IEEE Transactions on visualization and computer graphics, vol. 12, no. 5, pp. 789-796, 2006.

[6] I. Stančin and A. Jović, "An overview and comparison of free Python libraries for data mining and big data analysis," The 42nd International Convention on Information and Communication Technology, Electronics and Microelectronics (MIPRO), May 2019, pp. 977-982.

[7] Plotly. "Introduction to Dash". [Online]. Available from: https://dash.plotly.com/introduction [last accessed on 2022.10.12]

[8] Heroku. [Online]. Available from: https://www.heroku.com/home [last accessed on 2022.10.12]

[9] MITRE ATT&CK. [Online]. Available from: https://attack.mitre.org/ [last accessed on 2022.10.12]

[10] OWASP. [Online]. Available from: https://owasp.org/ [last accessed on 2022.10.22]

[11] The Web Application Security Consortium (WASC). Threat Classification. [Online]. Available from: http://projects.webappsec.org/w/page/13246978/Threat%20Classification [last accessed on 2022.10.12]

[12] Common Weakness Enumeration. [Online]. Available from. https://cwe.mitre.org/ [last accessed on 2022.10.12]

[13] J. D. Fekete and C. Plaisant, "Interactive information visualization of a million items," The IEEE Symposium on Information Visualization, (INFOVIS 2002), 2002, pp. 117-124.

[14] S. Noel, "Interactive visualization and text mining for the CAPEC cyber-attack catalog," Proceedings of the ACM Intelligent User Interfaces Workshop on Visual Text Analytics, 2015. pp. 1-8.

[15] L. Regainia and S. Salva, "A Methodology of security pattern classification and of attack-defense tree generation," The 3rd International Conference on Information Systems Security and Privacy, 2017, pp. 136-146, doi:10.5220/0006198301360146.

[16] F. Seehusen, "Using CAPEC for risk-based security testing," International Workshop on Risk Assessment and Risk-driven Testing, 2015, Springer, Cham, pp. 77-92.

[17] M. Vanamala, X. Yuan and K. Roy, "Topic modeling and classification of common vulnerabilities and exposures database," 2020 International Conference on Artificial Intelligence, Big Data, Computing and Data Communication Systems (icABCD 2020), IEEE, 2020, pp. 1-5. doi: 10.1109/icABCD49160.2020.9183814

[18] M. Vanamala, X. Yuan and K. Bandaru, "Analyzing CVE database using unsupervised Topic Modelling," 2019 International Conference on Computational Science and Computational Intelligence (CSCI), 2019, pp. 72-77, doi: 10.1109/CSCI49370.2019.00019.

[19] M. Vanamala, J. Gilmore, X. Yuan and K. Roy, "Recommending attack patterns for software requirements document," The 2020 International Conference on Computational Science and Computational Intelligence (CSCI), 2020, pp. 1813-1818, doi: 10.1109/CSCI51800.2020.00334.

Prepare Students for Software Industry

A Case Study on an Agile Full Stack Project

José Carlos Metrôlho[1,2], Fernando Reinaldo Ribeiro[1,2], Rodrigo Batista[2]
[1]R&D Unit in Digital Services, Applications and Content
[2]Polytechnic Institute of Castelo Branco
Castelo Branco, Portugal
e-mail: metrolho@ipcb.pt, fribeiro@ipcb.pt, rodrigo.batista@ipcbcampus.pt

Paula Graça
DEETC of Instituto Superior de Engenharia de Lisboa
Instituto Politécnico de Lisboa
Lisbon, Portugal
e-mail: paula.graca@isel.pt

***Abstract*— Reducing the gap between Software Engineering education and the needs in the software industry is a goal for Academia. Advancement in terms of cutting-edge technical skills and good soft skills preparation is the desired goal to shorten the onboarding in the labour market. Generally, in computer science or computer engineering courses, separate subjects exist to teach requirements engineering, analysis and design, coding, or validation. However, integrating all these phases normally requires experience in developing a complete project. The approach presented in this paper has involved the staff of a software company in collaboration with the staff of an academic Institution and resulted in a student's involvement in a full-stack software development project. The student was involved in an agile team composed of teachers and Information Technology (IT) professionals. Scrum framework was followed, and the product was developed using a low-code development platform. Results show that this agile and full stack approach allows students to develop cutting-edge technical and non-technical skills. The paper presents the approach, the achieved results, some lessons learned and some guidelines for the future.**

Keywords- agile software development; cognitive services; form recogniser; Scrum; software engineering; invoice.

I. INTRODUCTION

Nowadays, technology, namely software, is part of ordinary people's lives, and so there is a considerable demand for well-prepared professionals in this area of knowledge. Preparing professionals in these areas is not easy. If, on the one hand, they must have deep knowledge in specific technical subjects (databases, programming languages, requirements analysis, Web development, mobile development, etc.), it is also increasingly important that they have the skills to integrate or explore features in more complex systems. This broader view of specific software ecosystems requires a well-prepared new generation of engineers using new approaches and a more holistic experience of modern software development activity. These approaches can be enablers for accelerating development performance and obtaining better designed and high-quality software products.

In the software industry, many advances are also happening to speed up development. Examples of this are the low-code development platforms, which provide an abstraction layer that allows the developers to handle more of the inherent complexity of application development and simultaneously explore reuse and integrate different frameworks. They allow fast learning development processes, enable a more systemic view of software projects, and provide easy integration with other application endpoints. However, software engineering gains importance here because its inherent abstraction requires good development practices to be followed.

Another essential aspect nowadays is the great possibility of integration and interconnection between various systems. This makes it increasingly important that the new generation of IT professionals knows the services available and what mechanisms to use to integrate them into their applications. This holistic knowledge can be acquired in theory, but nothing better than consolidating it through developing projects that use this integration and other technologies. Cloud service providers (Amazon Web Services, Microsoft® Azure Cloud Platform or Google Cloud Platform) are cases in point.

Full stack development has changed, with new areas and skill sets becoming important. In the works published in [1], [2], in addition to the traditional definition of full stack, new scope and challenges are presented in this development field. In [1], the authors argue that students are "in a better position concerning their employment opportunities if they possess hands-on skills on the entire spectrum of full stack technologies". Also, the authors make clear that full stack does not mean "all" technologies and that "students should learn how to recognise fundamental problems to solve them with the appropriate conceptual tools using the corresponding technology of the day". In this paper, we share a case study that aims to prepare students for this reality, still in the academic environment and in close collaboration with partners from the software development industry.

In turn, the job market needs more technically well-prepared graduates with good soft skills. Thus, preparing the new generation of engineers requires training not only in the technical subjects that are the knowledge base, but also the vision, and more holistic experience about the paths followed today by software companies and the soft skills. Tackling all these aspects can be achieved with strategies and case studies like the one presented in this article. The product developed in this case was an application for household accounting, automatically recognising data from existing invoices in digital format (pdf, photo) using cognitive services.

In this case study, an important fact was that a company that develops software for the international market was involved. The company defined the product/goal. A student from a higher education institution (academy), integrated into a distributed team, developed it, using Scrum [3] as a software development process. This combination of several contributions and developing a full stack project using an agile software development process allows the student to acquire the knowledge and preparation necessary for today's challenges in the modern competitive software development market. The main goal is to contribute to reduce the gap that sometimes exists between what is learned in academia and what is needed in the industry. In this paper, based on the experience observed in a successful case, we share some practices in the teaching of software engineering to best prepare students for software industry.

The remainder of this article is organised as follows. Section II presents a background and related work. In Section III, the case study is presented. In Section IV, results and discussion about lessons learned are presented. Finally, some conclusions are presented in Section V.

II. BACKGROUND

Developers often do not just play a single role in software development; they must be multifaceted, often taking on the role of designers, coders, and database specialists. Therefore, having this knowledge and multi-tasking skills is essential and allows the developer to use them to complete a project or software development independently. This is also an advantage because it will enable the developer to be more familiar with all stages of the development process, making cooperation inside and outside the team more optimised, and contributing to reducing software development costs. These professionals should be able to work both in Web and mobile platforms with also knowledge of design through the Web like Hyper Text Markup Language (HTML) and Cascading Style Sheets (CSS). In addition, they should be able to use software development tools and techniques that allow the development team to be at its highest level of productivity.

However, higher education institutions face a challenging task in preparing students to work proactively in these high-performance teams. Many approaches have been proposed to teach and learn Software Engineering subjects. Some attempt to motivate students to take a more active role in their training and provide them more realistic experiences by replicating the settings used in the software development profession. Project-based Learning (e.g., [4]), flipped classroom (e.g., [5]), and gamification (e.g., [6], [7]) are some of these strategies that are frequently used to teach Software Engineering. Some other strategies promote a closer involvement of software companies to reduce the gap between Software Engineering education and the needs and practice in the software industry. For instance, in the approach described in [8], the industry actively supervises software product development. Another approach is to create supplementary training programs that aid in the screening of qualified candidates, as presented in [9]. These approaches are essential for students because they provide real challenges, more realistic experiences, and recreating industry software development environments. Nevertheless, they are also crucial for companies. For them, networking with students and other corporate sponsors, building ties with faculty, and promoting their business and products among college students are some potential advantages.

From a different perspective, software engineering teaching has been adapting to new developments and trends, namely the agile methodologies. Frequently, teaching agile methodologies have focused on teaching a specific framework like Scrum (e.g., [10]–[12]) or Extreme Programming (e.g., [13][14]). A study on using Agile Methods in Software Engineering Education [15] concluded that using Agile practices would positively influence the teaching process, stimulating communication, good relationships among students, active team participation, and motivation for present and future learning.

Besides the good results obtained by several of these strategies, software engineering teaching and learning can still benefit from a more participative and closer involvement of software development companies in the training process. This can enable students to join distributed teams, enhance their non-technical skills, and engage themselves in the practices used in these companies.

III. THE CASE STUDY

A. People/Team

In this case, the agile team was composed of 6 members. This is following the recommendations of Scrum [3]. Regarding the role of each one: 1 member of the company acted as product owner; 2 members of the company (with vast experience in terms of development using the adopted platforms) acted as coaches/development technical support; 1 member was the student that acted as a developer; 2 teachers acted as Scrum masters and, for some tasks, as coaches (involved in documentation, timeline, etc.). In this process, the student, the central element of the approach, interacted with the other people. Besides getting support for the development of the project/product, he also gained experience in terms of teamwork (soft skills), realising the difficulties and aspects that are common in business projects of this type. The members' posture was demanding and methodical, continually adopting practices equal to what is done in the day-to-day business activity.

B. Process

Tools were adopted for this purpose to carry out the development process. Thus, Jira [16] was used to manage all stages so that details of the evolution of the project and its rhythm could be adequately monitored in an articulated manner. This choice requires everyone to follow good communication practices and compliance with activity logs and user stories in this case.

Figure 1 presents the timeline of one of the semesters, and in Figure 2, we can see the Jira interface with part of the product backlog (the content is in Portuguese because it was the language agreed by the team for it).

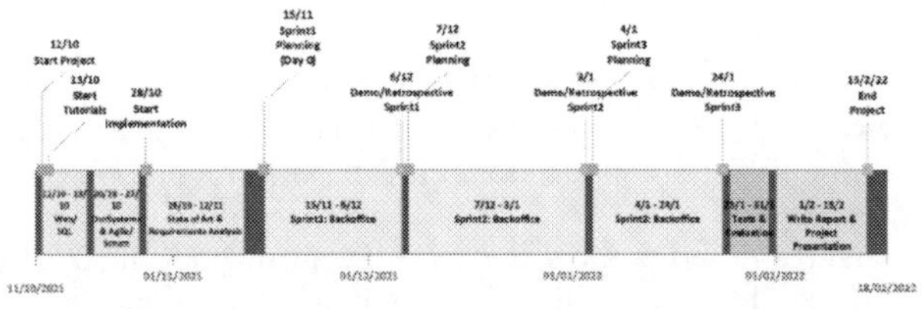

Figure 1. Timeline.

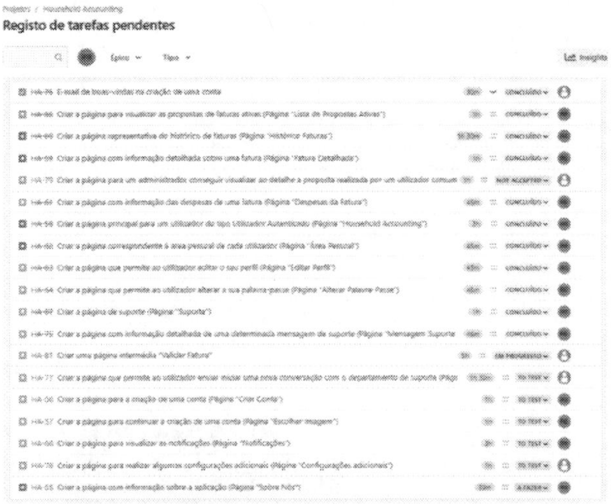

Figure 2. View of backlog in Jira UI.

On the left side of the Jira interface of Figure 2, we can see the list of user stories and, on the right side, the corresponding status (finished, in progress, not accepted or to test).

Scrum's artefacts [3] were all met, such as having a product backlog, sprint backlog, etc. In addition, there were daily meetings between the student and his mentors and checkpoints to clear any impediments to progress. The sprints were 2-4 weeks long, but every week there was a meeting (weekly meeting) between all the team members to review the progress of the work. There were sprints for development, but there were also periods when the goal was to learn how to develop or optimise the project. For example, how to integrate Azure [17] cognitive services into the product under development. In addition, the definition of the sprint periods were not unrelated to the academic activity, which took place in parallel, so that the student could also be able to fulfil the academic requirements in his other subjects. Thus, there were different sprint periods as there were also different workloads.

C. Project

Since an agile approach was adopted, it followed the value [18]:

"Working software over comprehensive documentation."

In terms of requirements documentation and modelling, the requirements were documented using user stories, and in addition, we used wireframes and the Entity-Relationship (ER) model. The team did not follow an extensive and deeper documentation approach because the student knew it from previous work in other curricular units. However, taking advantage of this knowledge, the student also represented the use cases and the ER model for the final report.

The research work was demanding for the student and the other members involved. New challenges were posed that required research, pre-experimentation, and analysis. For example, to implement the synchronism between the mobile application and the backend, it was necessary to analyse several patterns and adjust them to the concrete objective of this new product. The same happened in relation to security aspects of the application or the use of Azure cognitive services. In other words, the fact that it is an application with ambitious goals also posed interesting challenges to all team members. The product owner defined the initial requirements and documented them in the product backlog. For the user stories, the acceptance criteria were defined, which helped to design the test cases and thus contribute to a robust application.

Although the student had general knowledge about Artificial Intelligence (AI), it required him to be prepared on how to take advantage of the resources provided by Azure not only in terms of parameterisation and integration, but also in training to get the best performance. This is important because what was at stake in this challenge was to implement the functional requirements and user stories and obtain a final product with the highest possible accuracy in terms of automatic detection of fields of interest present in invoices.

Thus, the project involved research, development, software integration, application synchronisation (Web and mobile), security, agile Scrum framework, teamwork, and new tools (low-code platform, integration with cloud Azure, cognitive services, Jira, etc.). A detailed report of all phases and details of each aspect covered during the implementation process was also made. In the final stage of the project, acceptance tests were done to determine if the implemented features were useful and satisfied the users' needs.

This work covered many aspects of a software project, which could hardly be contemplated in a purely academic project. In addition to the technical-scientific coverage evidence, the agile methodology was chosen, and the fact that there was permanent communication between all its members was central. This leads us to verify in practice that one more value of the agile manifesto followed results in a successful path [18]:

"Individuals and interactions over processes and tools"

All these aspects mentioned above were considered, and the project includes documentation on user stories, database modelling, wireframes, and systems software architecture, among other valuable and necessary documentation.

Figure 3 shows the general architecture of the implemented system.

This work involved full-stack Web and mobile development using the OutSystems low-code platform [19]. This choice, teamwork, and adopting the agile framework (Scrum) allowed us to design from scratch, implement and test a complex and challenging software product during the normal period of a school year.

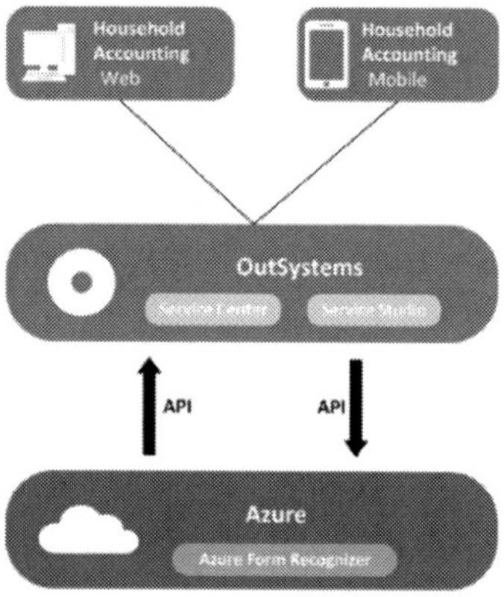

Figure 3. Systems Architecture.

D. Product

The recognition and automatic extraction of data from documents (invoices, receipts, etc.) are complex to implement and require various aspects to make it work successfully. With this project, we intended to apply mechanisms to recognise and extract data from invoices and store, organise and manage these data.

Using the OutSystems platform to develop the current project was a requirement from the company. The company proposed this product idea to develop a Web and mobile application using the OutSystems low-code platform, allowing users to manage their expenses in a digital format, independently of the users receiving the documents digitally or on paper. One of the characteristics of this platform is the speed of development and the integration with other necessary tools for the implementation of the objectives of this work (e.g., integration with Azure services). It allows to build and deploy full-stack Web and mobile applications [19].

The product owner proposed the product backlog. However, in each sprint review meeting, there were adjustments to the user stories. A sprint retrospective was always carried out so that the improvement process was constant from sprint to the next sprint, fostering a continuous pace. This demonstrates to the student the importance of the 3rd and 4th values of [18]:

"Customer collaboration over contract negotiation"

and

"Responding to change over following a plan".

The final product was developed on time, and all goals were achieved. In other words, at the end of the project, the resulting product was an application (Web and mobile) that was developed in OutSystems with the integration of Azure cognitive services (Azure form recogniser [20]) that allows (among other functionalities) the user to:

- Register invoices automatically.
- Process invoices (recognise and extract) data from pdf or an image captured by a smartphone.
- See spending statistics of a specific type and period.

The mobile application was implemented to be used even when it is offline. Because of that, mechanisms to synchronise both applications (Web and mobile) were implemented.

Figures 4 and 5 show the final layout of both the Web portal User Interface (UI) and one of the mobile applications UI.

Figure 4. Examples of portal Web UIs (On top: Invoice's historic view; Bellow: Output of automatic processed invoice view).

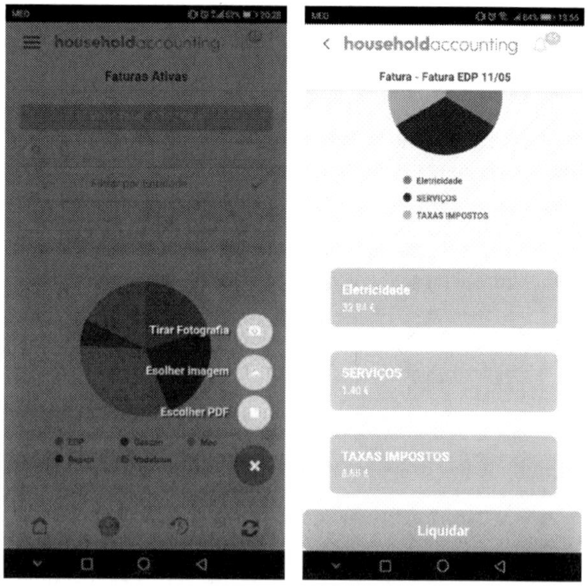

Figure 5. Examples of mobile app UIs (Left: select new invoice; Right: expenses).

In Figure 4 (top), we can see a dashboard to consult invoice's historic, with filters, charts presenting the collected data of different service providers (Telecommunications companies, electricity suppliers, etc.) and the list of stored invoices by designation, date, service provider, and monetary value. In Figure 4 (bellow), we can see the result of an automatically processed invoice view, presenting the invoice's file and the automatically captured fields.

Invoice templates can be configured in the administration portal for different service providers. The training and configuration of the recognition algorithms, using Azure cognitive services, can be configured through a dedicated Web portal.

The company's representatives validated the visual aspects (UI/User Experience (UX)), the synchronisation between the Web and the mobile applications, and security issues. The performance results obtained with the recognition of invoices were also analysed and improved.

IV. RESULTS AND LESSONS LEARNED

According to the opinion of all those involved, the result of the project was very positive. In addition to completing the entire system within the planned period of 2 semesters, a high-quality software product was developed (all requirements implemented and good acceptance from potential external end-users). In other words, in addition to providing all the intended features identified throughout the project, the developed software also performs with good performance results. After several tests with invoices from various service providers, the performance was excellent in all cases. As in any of these cases, the better organised the information on the invoice is (input), the easier it will be to train the system and, obviously, the better the accuracy of the data obtained (output). In the tests carried out, in most cases, all data was recognised automatically from the original pdf invoices received by email from the service providers (e.g., gas company, energy company or telecommunications providers). A lower accuracy rate was achieved if the invoices were digitised using the smartphone camera (even so, in the performed experiments, at least 46.5% of the fields were well recognised, and the user manually entered the remaining fields). After having a first version of the system available (Web and mobile), several potential users were asked to install and use the application and to respond to a survey. The survey included 14 questions. Twelve questions were answered using the Likert Scale (1–5), and one question asked for a numerical answer. The other question was an optional free response question where respondents could include any information. The results obtained at this stage serve three crucial goals: 1) to provide a better insight into the platform, which may identify novel issues/problems to consider; 2) to obtain initial feedback on potential users' acceptance and perception of the platform's key features and 3) to evaluate the usefulness of the proposed system. Twelve users completed the survey. To exclude the outliers, the survey with the best evaluation and the survey with the worst evaluation were excluded. This resulted in 10 valid answered questionnaires.

The analysis of the responses shows that:

- 90% of respondents rated the application as useful or very useful.
- 80% of respondents rated the application as easy or very easy to use.
- All the respondents were satisfied or very satisfied with the automatic reading of invoice information.
- Importing invoices in pdf format was considered very important by 80% of respondents. The import of invoices from a photo was considered important or very important by 60% of the respondents.
- In the open answer question, it was possible to obtain some feedback on usability improvements and the reporting of some bugs.

In terms of lessons learned, this approach requires a dedication of at least one h/week (average) from the teachers and the company's members. In the case of the mentor, this period was longer due to all the daily meetings. The dedication paid off because the result (resulting product, preparation of the student (technical and non-technical skills)) was very positive. The fact that everyone was engaged in developing a comprehensive project that involved all stages and components of the proposed architecture was challenging, motivating and clearly beneficial for all parties, that is, for teachers, students, and staff involved from the partner company.

V. CONCLUSIONS

The presented case study shares an agile approach to preparing students for the job market regarding Software Engineering (SE) practices in the context of final year projects (in the 5th and 6th semesters of the course curricular plan to complete the degree). This approach reduces the gap between SE education and practice in the software industry. The student was involved in a distributed team with teachers and IT professionals from a software house to develop a product that demanded full stack development and agile best practices. The case study presented illustrates the work methodology and the resulting product. In other words, the paper described people, the process, the project, and the product.

These industry-academia partnerships helps students become better and quickly prepared to work in high-performing teams. They raise students´ employment opportunities by preparing them in cutting-edge fields and improving their soft skills to have better performance in software development teams. These partnerships are also advantageous for the other involved partners. Hiring qualified human resources is good for the companies, as well as for the participating higher education institutions (contributes to improve their employability rate).

ACKNOWLEDGMENT

We thank the members of the company Do iT Lean who were also involved in this case study providing technical support.

References

[1] A. Taivalsaari, T. Mikkonen, C. Pautasso, and K. Systä, "Full Stack Is Not What It Used to Be," in *International Conference on Web Engineering*, 2021, pp. 363–371.

[2] A. R. C. Akshat Dalmia, "The New Era of Full Stack Development," *Int. J. Eng. Res. Technol.*, vol. 9, no. 4, pp. 7–11, 2020, doi: 10.17577/IJERTV9IS040016.

[3] K. Schwaber and J. Sutherland, "The Scrum Guide. The Definitive Guide to Scrum: The Rules of the Game.," 2016. https://www.scrum.org (accessed Jul. 20, 2022).

[4] R. Brungel, J. Ruckert, and C. M. Friedrich, "Project-Based Learning in a Machine Learning Course with Differentiated Industrial Projects for Various Computer Science Master Programs," in *2020 IEEE 32nd Conference on Software Engineering Education and Training, CSEE and T 2020*, 2020, pp. 50–54, doi: 10.1109/CSEET49119.2020.9206229.

[5] L. Gren, "A Flipped Classroom Approach to Teaching Empirical Software Engineering," *IEEE Trans. Educ.*, vol. 63, no. 3, pp. 155–163, 2020, doi: 10.1109/TE.2019.2960264.

[6] P. Rodrigues, M. Souza, and E. Figueiredo, "Games and gamification in software engineering education: A survey with educators," in *2018 IEEE Frontiers in Education Conference*, 2018, vol. 2018-Octob, pp. 1–9, doi: 10.1109/FIE.2018.8658524.

[7] R. Malhotra, M. Massoudi, and R. Jindal, "An innovative approach: Coupling project-based learning and game-based learning approach in teaching software engineering course," in *Proceedings of 2020 IEEE International Conference on Technology, Engineering, Management for Societal Impact Using Marketing, Entrepreneurship and Talent, TEMSMET 2020*, 2020, pp. 1–5, doi: 10.1109/TEMSMET51618.2020.9557522.

[8] W. E. Wong, "Industry Involvement in an Undergraduate Software Engineering Project Course: Everybody Wins," in *120th ASEE Annual Conference and Exposition*, 2013, pp. 23.742.1-23.742.12, doi: 10.18260/1-2--19756.

[9] E. Tuzun, H. Erdogmus, and I. G. Ozbilgin, "Are Computer Science and Engineering Graduates Ready for the Software Industry? Experiences from an Industrial Student Training Program," in *2018 IEEE/ACM 40th International Conference on Software Engineering: Software Engineering Education and Training (ICSE-SEET)*, 2018, pp. 68–77.

[10] A. Heberle, R. Neumann, I. Stengel, and S. Regier, "Teaching agile principles and software engineering concepts through real-life projects," in *2018 IEEE Global Engineering Education Conference (EDUCON)*, 2018, pp. 1723–1728, doi: 10.1109/EDUCON.2018.8363442.

[11] G. Wedemann, "Scrum as a Method of Teaching Software Architecture," in *Proceedings of the 3rd European Conference of Software Engineering Education*, 2018, pp. 108–112, doi: 10.1145/3209087.3209096.

[12] I. Bosnić, F. Ciccozzi, I. Čavrak, E. Di Nitto, J. Feljan, and R. Mirandola, "Introducing SCRUM into a Distributed Software Development Course," in *Proceedings of the 2015 European Conference on Software Architecture Workshops*, 2015, pp. 1–8, doi: 10.1145/2797433.2797469.

[13] J. J. Chen and M. M. Wu, "Integrating extreme programming with software engineering education," in *38th International Convention on Information and Communication Technology, Electronics and Microelectronics*, 2015, pp. 577–582, doi: 10.1109/MIPRO.2015.7160338.

[14] B. S. Akpolat and W. Slany, "Enhancing software engineering student team engagement in a high-intensity extreme programming course using gamification," in *27th Conference on Software Engineering Education and Training*, 2014, pp. 149–153, doi: 10.1109/CSEET.2014.6816792.

[15] S. Al-Ratrout, "Impact of using Agile Methods in Software Engineering Education: A Case Study," in *2019 6th International Conference on Control, Decision and Information Technologies (CoDIT)*, 2019, pp. 1986–1991, doi: 10.1109/CoDIT.2019.8820377.

[16] ATLASSIAN, "Jira Software." https://www.atlassian.com/br/software/jira (accessed Oct. 13, 2022).

[17] Microsoft Corporation, "AZURE. INVENT WITH PURPOSE. Learn, connect, and explore." https://azure.microsoft.com/en-us/ (accessed Oct. 13, 2022).

[18] "Manifesto for Agile Software Development," 2001. https://agilemanifesto.org (accessed Jul. 20, 2022).

[19] OutSystems, "OutSystems Developers: Develop more. Ship more. Get more done." https://www.outsystems.com/developers/ (accessed Jul. 26, 2022).

[20] Microsoft Corporation, "Azure Form Recognizer." https://azure.microsoft.com/en-us/services/form-recognizer (accessed Jul. 20, 2022).

Using a Combined Approach of Software Engineering and XR Engineering to Create Virtual Job Onboarding Environment: A Case Study

Marko Jäntti
Centre for Measurement and Information Systems
Kajaani University of Applied Sciences
Ketunpolku 1, 87100 Kajaani, Finland
Email: marko.jantti@cemis.fi

Abstract—**Digital transformation projects, such as creating virtual collaboration spaces with Extended Reality (XR), require new types of skills and knowledge from software engineers. While fundamental elements of software engineering and managing software projects are still useful, there are many new aspects that software engineers need to manage in Extended Reality (XR) projects. In this paper, we present results of a case study focusing on creating a virtual job onboarding environment for a Finnish forest machine operator. The content that was selected for the virtual onboarding space included company-related material for increasing awareness of green transition, such as recycling waste resulted by forest logging operations and training mandatory issues on occupational safety. The research problem presented in this study focuses on how software engineering and XR engineering can be used together to create virtual job onboarding spaces. Differences between traditional software engineering and XR engineering are also addressed. This study contributes towards practical implementation of commercial and open source resources for building a virtual job onboarding environment, through the combination of software engineering and XR engineering processes. We argue that this combined approach offers a good choice for managing the development of virtual spaces.**

Keywords—Digital transformation; Software Engineering; job onboarding; virtual collaboration space; Extended Reality (XR).

I. Introduction

Digital transformation is changing the way how organizations are training their employees, partners and end-users. An increasing number of training events is organized in virtual learning platforms instead of traditional classrooms. The job onboarding is a business process where quality of training and introduction plays a critical role. Through the process, organization aims at transforming job candidates into top-performing employees It is a process that also directly affects employee satisfaction and employee productivity.

Unfortunately, many organizations fail in making the job onboarding process employee-friendly. According to Sibisi and Kappers [1], poor onboarding may result in lower confidence among employees in their new roles, worsened levels of engagement, and an increased risk to quit job and start working for a competitor. Caruzzi [2] reveals that organizations with a standardized onboarding process experience 62 % greater new hire productivity and 50 % greater new hire retention.

Virtual reality has been widely used by various domains. Military domain has been the forerunner in applying virtual reality (VR) technologies. The military has used VR for various military tasks such as simulating combat first-aid and surgical procedures to correct battlefield injuries [3]; team training, battlefield review and tactics development [4]; and providing Virtual Reality Exposure Therapy (VRET) for veterans with Post-Traumatic Stress Disorder [5].

Additionally, virtual reality provides new opportunities for increasing safety awareness in industrial sites such as factories and mines. Bell and Fogler [6] have applied VR to chemical engineering education, for example, demonstrating the consequences of not following proper lab safety procedures. Liang et al. [7] have developed a VR-based interactive game for safety trainings in underground mines. Moreover, many companies started their virtual reality journey because of COVID 19 health measures. Boyd et al. [8] report findings on using virtual reality for minimizing the spread of Covid-19 on construction sites.

In this study, we focus on virtual onboarding spaces and instead of VR and use a broader term Extended Reality (XR) instead of VR. Extended reality consists of three main elements: Virtual Reality (VR), Augmented Reality (AR), and Mixed Reality (MR). Development of XR spaces and applications (we call this process XR engineering) requires new types of skills and knowledge from software engineers. While fundamental elements of software engineering and managing software projects are still useful, there are many new aspects software engineers need to manage in Extended Reality (XR) projects.

In the IEEE Standard Glossary of Software Engineering [9], software engineering is defined as the application of a systematic, disciplined, quantifiable approach to the development, operation, and maintenance of software. In XR engineering, development, operation and maintenance activities aim typically at producing and maintaining either games or virtual spaces. From this paper, game development is excluded. Software engineering lifecycle activities can also be a target where XR can be used. Elliott et al. [10] have studied the benefits of using virtual reality for live coding and code reviews. Virtual reality environments have also been used for collaborative software modeling [11].

According to Sommerville [12], a system is a purposeful

collection of interrelated components of different kinds that work together to deliver a set of services to the system owner and its users. An XR-based system is typically produced by using game engine software (Unity, Blender, or similar) or cloud-based services (e.g. Amazon Sumerian, Google ARCore) and used by end-users through virtual reality glasses or XR-enabled web browsers. WebXR is an open standard which allows VR apps to run directly from web browsers. WebXR Device API removes interoperability problems because it brings AR and VR capabilities to the web [13] and a user can thus avoid downloading heavy installatioin packages.

In this paper, the goal is to answer the research problem: How software engineering and XR engineering can be used together to create virtual job onboarding spaces? The main contribution of this paper is to show findings of a case study where we trialled and implemented both commercial and open source instances of a virtual job onboarding environment by using a combination of software engineering and XR engineering methods. The case study was performed by a Finnish digital innovation hub. The case organization is a forest machine operator company located in Eastern Finland Nurmes. The study was implemented in October 2021 - May 2022.

In Section 2, research methodology of the study is presented. In Section 3, case study results are presented. Section 4 is the analysis and finally, the conclusions are given in Section 5.

II. Research Problem & Methodology

According to Yin [14], a case study is an empirical inquiry that investigates a contemporary phenomenon in depth and within its real-life context especially when the bondaries between phenomenon and context are not clearly evident.

The case study research method was selected to study and increase understanding of a real-life phenomenon: improvement of job onboarding. The context for the research is also interesting. We got access to a Finnish forest machine operator company through EU-funded digital experiment. This was a new type of case organization for us. For the case organization, job onboarding was a high priority improvement target.

The research problem of this study is: How software engineering and XR engineering can be used together to create virtual job onboarding spaces? The research problem was divided into the following research questions: 1) How software engineering and XR engineering fit together in creating virtual job onboarding environment and how they differ from each other? 2) How employees express benefits of virtual job onboarding? 3) What types of challenges may exist in creating virtual job onboarding environments?

A. Case Organization

Motoajo is a family company, whose experience in forestry contracting begun in the 50's. As a result of organized development and patient growth, the company (an SME) offers job for 70 workers. The company's office is located in Nurmes, Eastern Finland, where the company also mainly operates. While loggin and transporting roundwood and coppice, Motoajo always pays attention to the nature and operates by all means to protect it. The company's vehicles are modern and made according to current emission standards. With harvesters the company follows the Measuring Instruments Act with random sampling of tree trunks. All the vehicles are equipped with loader scales. Motoajo's aim is to work cost-effective and on schedule with professional staff and modern vehicles also in challenging environments, not forgetting safety at work.

Motoajo's personnel consists of trained and experienced professionals. Drivers' workmanship is constantly improved by taking part to courses of quality, environmental and work safety. Motoajo Oy has a comprehensive spare part stock and a service with professionals and vehicles. Through the experiment, Motoajo seeks solutions organizing delivery of forestry liquids to remote locations as well as innovative methods to carry out job introduction to new forestry employees. The company consumes annually around million litres of fuel and huge amount of forest machine supplies. Job onboarding is important for Motoajo from following reasons: First, it is an effective way to increase productivity of employees. Second, it is directly linked to occupational safety. Job onboarding ensures that employees are aware of issues affecting their job safety and are able to perform their work activities both safely and effectively. The existing way to conduct job onboarding is baically based on personal job introduction performed by a senior employee. New employees shall receive access to job introduction (general overview of the organization, organizational policies, occupational safety, maintenance of machines etc.) material in Google Forms.

B. Data Collection Methods

The data collection for the study was performed by Arctic Data Intelligence Digital Innovation Hub. The goal of AIKA Digital Innovation Hub is to act as a one-stop shop that helps companies of Kainuu region in tackling digital challenges (especially AI, HPC, data analytics and digital transformation). Case study evidence was collected during Green and Digital Forest Service Management experiment from multiple sources:

- Documentation: Quality manual, experiment hand book, 3D model import guidelines document
- Archival records: Job onboarding material in Google forms, video scenarios from a foreman
- Interviews/discussions: Focused interview with CEO (February 9th, 2022, 30 min), discussions with virtual space providers
- Participative observation: field visits in Motoajo's storage, participation in digital experiment work meetings, Towards digital and sustainable forestry webinar (Youtube)
- Direct observations: Observations during the field visit in logging destination, how a forest machine driver operates in the forest, how fuel container has been placed on the logging site.
- Physical artefacts: Matterport 3D models, plastic IBC containers, recycling containers

C. Data Analysis

The case material was analyzed by a within case analysis technique [15] by using researcher and method triangulation

[16]. The research team consisted of Digital Innovation Hub employees and external consult of Motoajo. The digital experiment progress was reported to the case organization systematically and frequently and communicated also to non-academic audience such as stakeholders of the digital innovation hub. A qualitative content analysis technique was applied for case study material.

III. Results of the Study: Design and Implementation of a Virtual Job Onboarding Environment

Next, we describe the activities of design, implementation and testing/evaluation regarding the virtual job onboarding environment.

A. Service Design

The service design phase started with a field visit to the Motoajo's storage in Nurmes, Eastern Finland. The case organization's representatives indicated the need to address green transition and recycling of forestry waste in job onboarding material. There was a need to increase awareness of staff how to sort different types of forestry waste (chainsaw bars, lubricant tubes, oil filters), to show location of various pieces of equipment, what type of protection is required while dealing with the fungicide, and what an employee should do to prevent fuel leaks while operating in the forest with a forest machine (how to position fuel container safely in the ground). The following list of design and implementation issues was created in the design phase:

- Implementation of IoT based monitoring system for forestry liquids including Tekelek tank level sensors that were installed into plastic IBC containers containing marking dye and Adblue (Diesel Exhaust Fluid)
- Development of mobile app (managing refilling process, monitoring liquid levels, alerts on critical levels), two phase authentication possible / Google authenticator
- Creating first draft of the virtual job introduction environment by using 360 viewer Lapentor
- Creating 3D models of the storage
- Recording videos for hotspots both in logging destination and in storage (video material how to recycle waste such as oil canisters and metal waster coming from logging operations and how to position fuel containers safely in the forest).
- Organizing dissemination activities: two webinars (Digital Afternoon, Towards Green and Digital Forest Service Management) and creation of online articles
- Exploring opportunities for further exploitation of experiment results

For project dissemination purposes, we organized an interview with CEO of the case organization. The CEO highlighted the importance of job onboarding for organizational productivity. Additionally, we conducted 2 webinars where a foreman of the case organization communicated the benefits of job onboarding. Next, a summary of the interview and discussions is provided (narratives related to job onboarding).

Fig. 1. A virtual job onboarding environment in Lapentor

- "We have been thinking forest machine -related job onboarding. The forest side is even more important for productivity than recycling-related job onboarding."
- "This job onboarding system could be sold to any other domain, not only for forest domain."
- "It would ge great if a new employee would watch the job onboarding video material during the first working days. Then, he/she would be much more prepared for work tasks."
- "An employee can watch videos and repeat them as many times as needed."
- "Job onboarding needs to be well documented. It gives as a lot of credibility."
- "We have several remote storage areas. We have improved monitoring of liquid containers and job onboarding of new employees. Previously, we have provided personal job onboarding. However, if the new employee is going to work in Vehmersalmi, it's a long way to travel there to take care of job onboarding."

B. Service Implementation

The prototype of virtual job introduction was created by using open source 360 virtual tour service Lapentor (see Figure 1). Video content was captured by using mobile phone and was later uploaded to Vimeo video sharing platfrom and embedded to Lapentor hotspots. These videos dealt with several work scenarios, such as sorting metal waste, sorting oil canisters, placing a warning sign for a logging site, operating safely with liquids and maintenance of a fuel pump.

In the next phase, we decided to study whether it would be possible to create a virtual collaboration space where a trainee and trainer could meet. For this purpose, we contacted a VR specialist in Kajaani University of Applied Sciences that had a long experience in creating virtual spaces and capturing 3D

Fig. 2. A virtual job onboarding environment in Matterport: how to recycle chainsaw bars

models with Matterport cameras. Figure 2 shows our virtual storage in Matterport environment.

We needed to purchase server space for Matterport 3D models because we did not want to make the 3D models of the storage publicly available. The following step was to start the bidding process for purchasing the virtual collaboration space. We decided to use Glue Collaboration as a platform to our virtual collaboration space because they seemed to have a clear process and guidelines how to import custom 3D models (a document showing requirements for importing 3D models). However, they stated that importing custom 3D models requires some manual work effort (around 1 working day) from them. The bidding also involved Glue licences for 2 persons. After we had started bidding process, we observed that we should had been more careful in describing 3D rendering requirements to Invitation for Tenders (lightning, objects we wanted to have in the storage). The third party consultant of the virtual collaboration space provider stated that point cloud needs 3D rendering. Luckily, one of the 3D experts of our own organization's VR laboratory was available and took care of 3D rendering.

C. Testing and Evaluating the Service

One of the interesting aspects we planned to have in our virtual job onboarding environment was a digital twin of an IBC container that would have provided a realistic real time data on the liquid levels. This required a significant amount of work effort such as purchasing, installing, configuring sensors, setting up IoT dashboards, creating a mobile app for retrieving data on container refilling events and events when forest machine drivers pick up liquids from the container. Development of real time liquids monitoring system and integrating data to the job onboarding system required more software engineering expertise than XR engineering. Here we applied traditional software engineering activities, such as sofware test cases.

The virtual job onboarding system was presented to the case organization multiple times. In trialling the system, a foreman of the case organization used both laptop and also Oculus Quest 2 VR glasses. As a feedback, they stated that most likely the organization's employees would use the open source version of the job onboarding system (Lapentor) from their laptops or mobile phones. Lapentor is a cost-effective solution for job onboarding and it is easy to add new job onboarding content (hotspots) to the system. New employees can see the realistic view on the storage including waste containers and can click the hotspots in the virtual storage to access the video material. The job onboarding material is available 24/7 for employees and there is no need to purchase expensive XR equipment. As part of the evaluatioin, the CEO of the case organization mentioned that the usage of the system could be extended to the optimizing settings of forest machines. The system was considered very easy-to-use. The drawback of the Lapentor system is that it is not a virtual collaboration environment. If a trainee and a trainer like would like to meet in the storage, they need to access a virtual collaboration space, such as Glue or Mozilla Hubs.

IV. ANALYSIS

The data analysis was performed by using qualitative analysis technique for the case study data. The goal of the analysis was to compare software engineering and XR engineering with 7 patterns. Thus, our analysis technique can be considered as pattern matching. Regarding the first research question, we identifed both differences and similarities (Table I) between software engineering (software development with Java as an example) and Extended Reality (XR) engineering.

TABLE I. SOFTWARE ENGINEERING VS XR ENGINEERING

Topic	Soft Engineering	XR Engineering
Focus	Code and data	Media and content
Files	.java, .class, .jar, .dll	.fbx, .stl, .gltf, .obj
SDKs	Java SDK	XR SDK for each VR headset
Skills	Coding, UI, bus. logic, data	Coding, UX, 3D model., rendering
Dev types	Web dev, mobile dev	Web dev, mobile dev, game dev
Reqs	Non-func., func, data	File reqs for 3D models
Navigation	Menus	Teleporting, hotspots, floorplan
Comput.	CPU	GPU
Project mgmt	Agile, increment,, waterfall	Agile

According to our case study findings, XR engineering focuses on dealing with media files and game engines requiring knowhow on 3D modeling, compatibility of media files, 3D rendering such as configuring lightining to virtual spaces and visualizing the storage. One of the issues we learnt during the study was that XR SDKs (for example, Oculus SDK for Windows) vary between VR headsets. While Java developers could enjoy a pretty good interoperability of Java SDK, XR developers need to struggle with headset-specific requirements if they want to test and release their own XR apps. However, in our case study, we did not have to deal with device SDKs because we decided to use existing well-tested virtual tour and virtual space platforms. Rendering scenes in Lapentor is done with krpano software that enables showing panoramic images on the web.

While three architectural layers (user interface UI, business logic BL, data layer) act as a basis of design and development in software engineering, XR engineering focuses on designing interactions and may involve head tracking, motion tracking, hand tracking and eye tracking. These are quite standard interaction design elements for game developers but a new world for a typical software engineer.

Navigation within the virtual space is very different compared to the navigation within a web-based system. Virtual spaces enable teleporting users between virtual rooms. Both in

Matterport and Lapentor, content for end-users can be added through hotspots (in Matterport these are called Mattertags). Matterport also produces a floorplan view that helps end-users navigating to the desired room easier. While performance of traditional software systems depends on computing nodes, XR developers typically utilize Graphics Processing Units (GPUs). By using GPUs models can be rendered much quicker than by using Computing Processing Units (CPUs).

Regarding project management approach, both software engineers and XR engineers are using agile approaches or some kind of modification of them. Software engineers used to utilize waterfall lifecycle model, incremental models such as Rational Unified Process RUP [17] decades ago. However, agile project management is nowadays a mainstream choice. We did one observation on strict file requirements for 3D models that do not exist in typical software engineering projects. Our XR engineer understood file requirements immediately but researchers with some SE background were not in their comfort zone while reading the 3D model import guidelines.

In order to increase the system quality, we decided to create test cases (typical artifacts in software development) for IoT based container monitoring system that we aimed to link to the virtual job onboarding system as a digital twin of the container. These test cases revealed some interesting defects that were later communicated to system developers. With no doubt, software engineering has more rigorous approach for ensuring software quality than XR engineering. Software testing knowhow would be very useful also for XR engineers to ensure that interactions and hotspots become thoroughly tested. Therefore, we propose a combined approach of software engineering and XR engineering for producing high-quality XR spaces.

Table II shows the analysis of the second research question: How employees express the benefits of virtual job onboarding. The source of the evidence is indicated in the first column.

TABLE II. BENEFITS

Source	Issue
INT	Enables repeated playing of onboarding content
INT	Prepares staff better for their job tasks
DIS	Saves travelling costs and time
DIS	Compliance with regulations
DIS	Eliminates unnecessary waste sorting
PO	Increases productivity
PO	Enables importing custom 3D models
PO	Collaboration in virtual space

It was interesting to follow the discussion and analyze the narratives of interviews and webinars to capture expressions for benefits of virtual onboarding. The case organization's management emphasized the productivity and preparedness of the staff for job activities. The middle management of the case organization highlighted cost savings and time savings and transition to a different model of job onboarding (from personal job onboarding to more scalable job onboarding).

During the study, our research team observed that forest machine drivers need to update their skills and knowledge continously to be able to operate the forest machine. Forest machine drivers need to be aware of the procedures, rules and regulations set by the forest certificates (FSC, PEFC) and contractors.

The last research question focused on the challenges in creating virtual job onboarding spaces. The following list contains a summary of identified challenges.

- Deciding which 360 platform or virtual collaboration platform could be best for our purposes (possibility to import custom 3D models, import custom 3D assets, quality of avatars, number of existing interactions, price of licences, cross-device usage).
- Planning the bidding process for virtual spaces is difficult. How to set a quality criteria and describe it in Invitation for Tenders? XR-engineers are needed to answer the questions from potential service providers.
- Making a plan on 3D rendering. Which textures / objects should be included? What is the quality of lightning? In our case, we had very limited time and a large storage space and we prioritized that waste containers are of high priority.
- Conducting video shootings and 3D model creation in winter conditions. Arctic conditions (-25 celsius outside, -5 to -10 celsius inside the storage) caused challenges for battery duration of cameras.
- Creating digital twin and integrating it to the virtual job onboarding system. Unfortunately, we were not able to bring real time sensor data to our virtual job onboarding environment. Very likely this challenge was related to API/integration limitations of Lapentor and we had very limited resources to investigate the issue.
- Creating job onboarding video content without predefined scripts. While we were in the cold storage and in a logging site in the forest, we did not use any scripts. Usage of scripts might have increased the quality of video material and decreased the time we spent for video recording. On the other hand. we feel that we received more authentic job onboarding material by ignoring the scripts.
- Multi-provider network of actors. Although we had an excellent team, multi-provider network caused communication gaps in implementation of the virtual job onboarding system. As an example, our XR specialist had generated a high-quality, rendered 3D model of the storage. Somehow, the insufficient 3D model was still used in creating the virtual collaboration space (a large part of the storage was of point cloud quality)

It would be very interesting to compare our XR challenges to the challenges encountered by other academians especially on the forest sector. Conducting this case study has remarkably increased our knowledge on opportunities and limitations of XR spaces and their benefits for job onboarding.

V. CONCLUSION

In this paper, we aimed at answering the research problem: How software engineering and XR engineering can be used together to create virtual job onboarding spaces? We used a case study research method to collect data from a Finnish forest machine operator company. Our results and experiences may be useful both for software engineers and for XR engineers. The job onboarding system that we developed supports also the Green Transition approach. Thus, our findings can also be beneficial to sustainability engineers.

Next, our findings related to three research questions are summarized. Concerning the first research question (How software engineering and XR engineering fit together in creating virtual job onboarding environment and how they differ from each other?), we observed that software development and XR development have a lot of common. It is fair to state that many academians and practitioners shall really likely consider XR as just one additional type of software development.

However, XR engineering has its own terminology and concepts (polycounts, realt-time rendering, heatmap) that most software engineers might have never heard of. While software engineers' skillsets include software development, cloud, database, and mobile app development, XR engineers typically need the same skills but also game development knowhow. Of course, programming skills are key skills for both XR engineers and software engineers. During our study, we observed that software development lifecycle activities help especially in improving the quality of XR development and planning test coverage. Software test cases are useful in identifying defects in any type of software including XR and virtual spaces. During a relatively short testing period, our test cases manage to reveal some interesting defects during the case study. One defect was found by using administrator priviledges.

For the second research question (How employees express benefits of virtual job onboarding), we captured narratives that referred to benefits of job onboarding. According to our findings, case organization considered as expected benefits of virtual job onboarding: preparing staff better for their job tasks, saving travelling costs and time, ensuring compliance with regulations, eliiminating unnecessary waste sorting and increasing productivity. The organization's top management emphasized overall productivity increase due to better job onboarding.

Our final research question dealt with virtual job onboarding implementation challenges. During our case study, the following challenges were identified: deciding which 360 platform or virtual collaboration platform could be best; challenges in planning the bidding process for virtual spaces; conducting video shootings and 3D model creation in winter conditions; planning and performing 3D rendering; failure in creating digital twin and integrating it to the job onboarding system; creating job onboarding video content without predefined scripts; communication gaps due to multi-provider network of actors in the XR engineering project.

There are certain limitations related to the case study method that we utilized. First, data was collected during a relatively short time period (during a 6-month digital experiment). Interviewing and engaging more end-users to trial the new job onboarding system could have provided new insights and ideas for further development. Second, only qualitative data was used and collected during the study. In the future, quantitative data, for example, from a controlled experiment with new employees could be collected to analyze the impact of more immersive job onboarding. Further research could also focus on extending the scope of job onboarding to adjustment of forest machine settings.

Acknowledgment

We would like to thank the case organization for valuable collaboration. This paper is based on research in Development of AIKA Arctic Data Intelligence and Supercomputing Ecosystem in Kainuu project (A78688) funded by European Regional Development Fund and Regional Council of Kainuu. The prototype of the virtual job onboarding platform was created in DIH World experiment co-funded by the Horizon 2020 Framework Programme of the European Union under grant agreement no 952176.

References

[1] S. Sibisi and G. Kappers, "Onboarding can make or break a new hire's experience," *Harvard Business Review*, April 2022.

[2] J. Caruzzi, "To retain new hires, spend more time onboarding them," *Harvard Business Review*, April 2018.

[3] R. Satava and S. Jones, "An integrated medical virtual reality program. the military application," *IEEE Engineering in Medicine and Biology Magazine*, vol. 15, no. 2, pp. 94–97, 1996.

[4] M. Moshell, "Three views of virtual reality: virtual environments in the us military," *Computer*, vol. 26, no. 2, pp. 81–82, 1993.

[5] A. Vianez, A. Marques, and R. Almeida, "Virtual reality exposure therapy for armed forces veterans with post-traumatic stress disorder: A systematic review and focus group," *International Journal of Environmental Research and Public Health*, vol. 19, p. 464, 01 2022.

[6] J. Bell and S. Fogler, "The application of virtual reality to (chemical engineering) education." 01 2004, pp. 217–218.

[7] Z. Liang, K. Zhou, and K. Gao, "Development of virtual reality serious game for underground rock-related hazards safety training," *IEEE Access*, vol. 7, pp. 118 639–118 649, 2019.

[8] A. Boyd, C. Bradley, and L. Waugh, "Use of virtual reality to minimize the spread of covid-19 on construction sites," in *Proceedings of the Canadian Society of Civil Engineering Annual Conference 2021*. Singapore: Springer Nature Singapore, 2023, pp. 273–281.

[9] IEEE Standard 729-1983 1, *IEEE Standard Glossary of Software Engineering Terminology*. IEEE, 1990.

[10] A. Elliott, B. Peiris, and C. Parnin, "Virtual reality in software engineering: Affordances, applications, and challenges," in *2015 IEEE/ACM 37th IEEE International Conference on Software Engineering*, vol. 2, 2015, pp. 547–550.

[11] E. Yigitbas, S. Gorissen, N. Weidmann, and G. Engels, "Collaborative software modeling in virtual reality," in *2021 ACM/IEEE 24th International Conference on Model Driven Engineering Languages and Systems (MODELS)*, 2021, pp. 261–272.

[12] I. Sommerville, *Software Engineering*. Pearson Education Limited, USA, 2016.

[13] B. Blair MacIntyre and T. Smith, "Thoughts on the future of webxr and the immersive web," in *2018 IEEE International Symposium on Mixed and Augmented Reality Adjunct (ISMAR-Adjunct)*, 2018, pp. 338–342.

[14] R. Yin, *Case Study Research: Design and Methods, Fourth edition*. Beverly Hills, CA: Sage Publishing, 2009.

[15] K. Eisenhardt, "Building theories from case study research," *Academy of Management Review*, vol. 14, pp. 532–550, 1989.

[16] R. Yin, *Case Study Research: Design and Methods*. Beverly Hills, CA: Sage Publishing, 1994.

[17] P. Kruchten, *The Rational Unified Process: An Introduction*. Addison-Wesley, 2001.

Bootstrapping Meta-Circular and Autogenous Code Generation

Herwig Mannaert
Normalized Systems Institute
University of Antwerp, Belgium
Email: herwig.mannaert@uantwerp.be

Koen De Cock
Research and Development
NSX bv, Belgium
Email: koen.de.cock@nsx.normalizedsystems.org

***Abstract*—Metaprogramming or automated code generation has been pursued for a long time, and is often considered crucial to increase programming productivity. It has been argued in previous work that evolvability of software is equally important, and that a meta-circular metaprogramming architecture may be crucial to addressing some fundamental evolvability issues in metaprogramming. At the same time, the field of software engineering struggles to provide firm technical guidance to computer programmers, and often reverts to heuristics and documented patterns. As metaprogramming is in general more complex than traditional programming, it seems even more crucial to provide technical guidance to metaprogrammers. In this contribution, the bootstrapping of an elementary meta-circular metaprogramming environment is investigated. Its main purpose is to serve as a pathfinder for the development of design patterns and techniques that can support and guide metaprogramming.**

***Index Terms*—Evolvability; Metaprogramming; Design Patterns; Meta-Circularity.**

I. INTRODUCTION

Metaprogramming or automated code generation has been pursued for a long time. Among other things, it is often seen as one of the most promising approaches to increase the productivity in computer programming. We have argued in our previous work that it is equally important to increase the evolvability of software systems [1], although this receives less attention within the Information Systems (IS) research area [2]. We have also argued that some fundamental issues hamper the evolvability of metaprogramming software [3], and that a meta-circular architecture seems suitable to address this. At the same time, it seems hard to provide strict guidance to computer programmers [4], and the field of software engineering often reverts to heuristic design patterns and craftsmanship practices. As metaprogramming is in general more complex than programming, and meta-circular metaprogramming even more complex, it seems imperative to provide some solid design patterns for such metaprogramming environments. In this contribution, we investigate the bootstrapping of a basic meta-circular metaprogramming environment, that could serve as a pathfinder to extract such envisioned design patterns, or even more fundamental techniques.

The remainder of this paper is structured as follows. In Section II, we briefly discuss automatic or metaprogramming, and its relationship with the broader field of software engineering. In Section III, we describe the overall architecture and the implementation setup of our elementary metaprogramming environment. Section IV presents the detailed procedure to bootstrap the meta-circular and autogenous metaprogramming environment. The details and characteristics of this environment are discussed in Section V. Finally, we present some conclusions in Section VI.

II. METAPROGRAMMING AND SOFTWARE ENGINEERING

In this section, we give a brief overview of the field of metaprogramming, and discuss its importance and position in the discipline of software engineering.

A. Automatic or Metaprogramming

The automatic generation of code, i.e., *writing code that writes code*, is probably as old as coding or software programming itself. Not unlike many other areas in information technology, several different terms are used to describe this activity, and their associated meanings may vary both over time and between authors. We briefly go through some terms and concepts, which we have explained in more detail in [3].

Though it has been argued for a long time that the mechanisms are quite similar [5], a distinction is often made between *code generation*, where a compiler generates executable code from a high-level programming language, and *automatic programming*, where source code is generated from a model or template. Related terms include *generative programming*, highlighting the similarity to automated manufacturing in the industrial sector [6], and *metaprogramming*, emphasizing the fact that this is a meta-level activity, and often defined as a programming technique in which computer programs have the ability to treat other programs as their data [7].

One of the main goals of automatic programming has always been to improve programmer productivity. Therefore, several terms in software development methodologies and tools are closely related to automatic programming. Methodologies like *Model-Driven Engineering (MDE)* and *Model-Driven Architecture (MDA)* focus on the creation and exploitation of conceptual domain models and ontologies, and assume the presence of software tools for the automatic generation of code. Such model-driven code generation tools that provide an environment for programmers to create application software through graphical user interfaces and configuration, are now often referred to as *Low-Code Development Platforms (LCDP)* or *No-Code Development Platforms (NCDP)*. Despite all the terms and tools, the realization of automatic programming on an industrial scale remains not straightforward [8].

B. Engineering Metaprogramming

Software engineering is sometimes considered to be an eclectic field. To guide software developers, various paradigms, techniques, process models and tools exist. Even a vast amount of *software development methodologies*, i.e., a comprehensive guide to developing a system [9], have been available for decades. Though this resulted in a widespread belief that adherence to systems development methodologies is beneficial [10], the adoption of systems development methods remained limited [9] [10]. This led to more pragmatic strategies for concrete guidance, like the use of *design patterns* [11], solutions to common development problems that have proven their quality empirically, *agile methodologies* like SCRUM [12] that value self-organizing teams and adaptive collaboration with customers over strict planning and comprehensive processes, and *software craftsmanship* practices like clean code [13]. It seems that we have not found the fundamental laws of software that would play the role that the fundamental laws of physics play for other engineering disciplines [4], which could explain the renewed emphasis on best practices and heuristics in postmodern software engineering.

Though metaprogramming would seem in general to be more complicated than standard programming, structured techniques and guidance seem even scarcer for metaprogramming. Nevertheless, we have argued in our previous work that some fundamental issues need to be addressed to achieve productive and scalable adoption of automatic programming techniques [3]. First, to cope with the increasing complexity due to changes, we have proposed to combine automatic programming with the evolvability approach of *Normalized Systems Theory (NST)* providing (re)generation of the recurring structure and re-injection of the custom code [1], [3]. Second, we have proposed a meta-circular architecture to regenerate the metaprogramming code itself as well [14], [15]. The term meta-circularity dates back to Reynolds [16], and is related to the concept of homoiconic languages [17], enabling a program to be manipulated as data using the same language, and allowing the program's internal representation to be inferred just by reading the program itself.

Such a meta-circular architecture offers several potential benefits. It could avoid the growing burden of maintaining the often complex meta-code and continuously adapting it to new technologies [3], and could facilitate a more scalable collaboration between metaprogrammers through the exchange of meta-models. At least, a unified view on both the metaprogramming code and the source code being generated would reduce the cognitive load for the metaprogrammers, and would enable us to apply advancements in programming techniques simultaneously to both the generative and generated code.

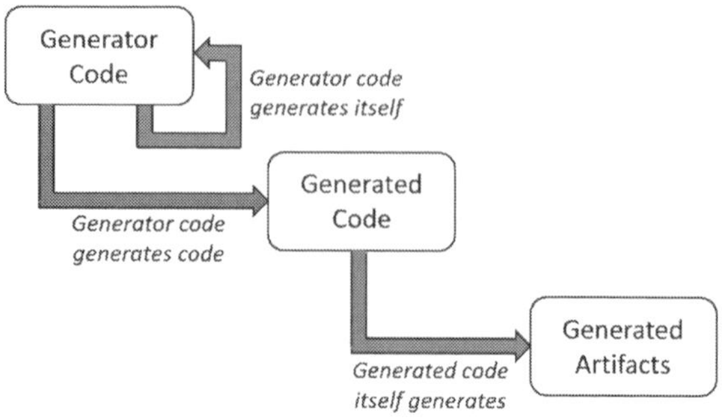

Figure 1. Representation of meta-circular and autogenous generation.

As one could expect meta-circular metaprogramming to be even more complicated than standard metaprogramming, it seems imperative to provide guidance to the metaprogrammers through structured concepts, techniques, and patterns. In this contribution, we investigate the bootstrapping of an elementary meta-circular metaprogramming environment in a very basic Java programming environment. The main purpose of such an elementary environment is to clarify the basic concepts, and to serve as a pathfinder to extract some future design patterns — and maybe even more fundamental techniques or basic primitives — to guide metaprogrammers.

III. An Elementary Metaprogramming Environment

In this section, we explain the scope, purpose, architecture, and implementation environment of the elementary metaprogramming environment presented in this paper.

A. Purpose and Overall Architecture

The scope of the code generation needs to be very basic but nevertheless realistic. As data models such as *Entity Relationship Diagrams (ERD)* are common and widespread, we decided to use basic representations of data entities as the models of the metaprogramming environment. The generated code needs to be able to represent such basic data entities, featuring both data attributes and relationships or references, and to import or read instances of these data entities. An example of such a data entity would be an invoice, having an invoice number and client as attributes, and references to the various invoice lines as relationships.

The goal is to create an elementary metaprogramming environment with a clear and simple structure, completely devoid of unnecessary complexities. At the same time, we want the metaprogramming environment to exhibit two additional fundamental characteristics. These fundamental properties are schematically represented in Figure 1.

- Meta-Circular generation:
  The generator code needs to be able to generate itself. This requires, of course, a bootstrapping process, i.e., the generator code needs to be handcrafted first before it can be enabled to (re)generate itself.

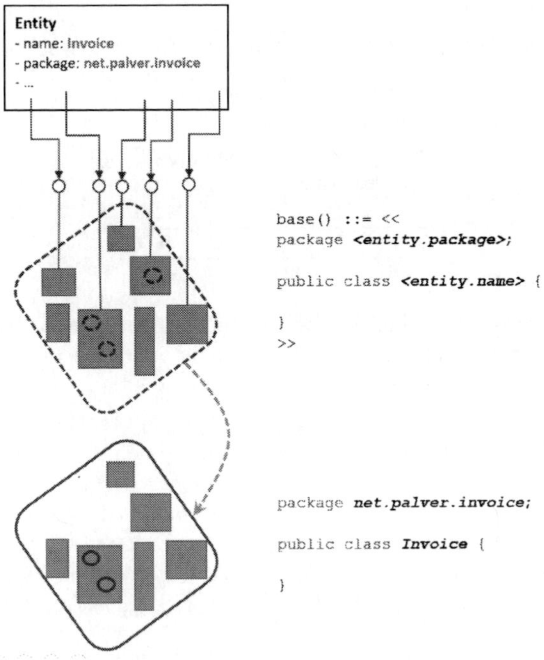

Figure 2. Instantiating a coding template with model parameters.

- Autogenous generation:
  The generated code itself needs to be able to generate. The artifacts that the generated code could generate should in general be related to the domain entity, e.g., invoice classes could generate an invoice document.

B. A Basic Implementation Environment

To represent data, both the model parameters such as entities and attributes, and the actual instances of the data entities such as invoice numbers, we decided to use the extremely simple and widespread format of *Comma-Separated Values (CSV)*. As templating engine, we have opted for *StringTemplate* [18], as it allows hardly any logic in the templates [19]. In this way, we ensure that the templating engine serves as a plain off-the-shelf tool to replace parameter strings with actual values.

To feed the data of the model into the templating engine, we use an elementary kernel function of the metaprogramming environment described in [3]. Based on this functionality, the model consisting of linked data instances is made available to the coding templates through *Object Graph Navigation Language (OGNL)* expressions [20] using the *Apache Commons OGNL* library [21]. More specifically, every model data *entity* is passed as a linked data tree to the template, where we can select individual properties like name by `entity.name`, or access a linked list of attributes by `entity.attributes` and loop through them. The templating engine simply replaces the parameters in the template with the actual values from the linked data tree. This procedure, a kind of *convolution* between a template and a linked data tree, seems to us one of the most basic mechanisms for code generation.

Figure 2 provides a schematic representation of such an elementary code generation. An instance of a model *entity*, with name *Invoice* and belonging to a package *net.palver.invoice*, is fed into a coding template for a base class. In this template, the values of the model entities are represented as parameters. The generator code will resolve these parameters and replace them with the actual values of the model entity, resulting in real source code for that domain entity.

IV. Toward Meta-Circular and Autogenous Expansion in Ten Steps

In this section, we present a detailed procedure to bootstrap in ten steps an elementary meta-circular and autogenous metaprogramming environment. The ten steps are grouped in four cohesive subprocedures.

A. Create Basic Generator Code

1) Read basic entity model: We create a base *DTO (Data Transfer Object)* class *EntityComposite* to represent the individual entities with basic attributes like name and package name, and an *EntityReader* that reads a CSV file *Entitys.csv*, and makes a list of DTO instances based on the entries. As a test, we print the list of instances after reading.

2) Expand basic entity class: We introduce a base class expander template *CompositeExpander* for a DTO class representing a domain entity, and a generator class *EntityGenerator* that reads the entities using the *EntityReader*, and feeds them to the template to create the DTOs. We check whether the base classes, similar to Figure 2, are correctly generated.

B. Generate Viable Data Entities

1) Support entity attributes: We provide support for attributes having a type and name through an *AttributeComposite* and *AttributeReader* class, include a variable list of attribute composites in the *EntityComposite* DTO, and introduce get-set-methods in the *CompositeExpander* template. The *EntityReader* is extended to read for every entity the list of attributes from a *<Entity.name>Attributes.csv* file. As a test, we define number and client as invoice attributes, and read some sample data.

2) Generate an entity reader: We introduce a *ReaderExpander* template based on the reader class that we have programmed, and extend the *EntityGenerator* to instantiate for every entity a reader class together with a composite class. The generated classes are compiled for an invoice entity, and tested by reading some sample data.

3) Introduce linked entities: We introduce *list type attributes* and extend the *CompositeExpander* template to support the variable definition and get-set-methods for such list fields. We also extend the *ReaderExpander* template to read these linked entities, in the same way that the *EntityReader* supports invoking the *AttributeReader*. We test this by defining an *InvoiceLine* entity, an *invoiceLines* attribute in the invoice entity, and reading some sample invoices and invoice lines.

C. Regenerate the Generator Code

1) Generate the meta-entities: The model to represent data models is implicitly based on data entities itself, being *Entity* and *Attribute*. So, we define them in the CSV files *Entitys*, *EntityAttributes*, and *AttributeAttributes*, and run the *EntityGenerator* to regenerate the composite and reader classes for entity and attribute. After comparing the generated classes with the origonal ones, we make them available.

2) Replace original base code: We now retire the original composite and reader classes, and replace them in our test setup. Using the newly generated composite and reader classes, and the still original *EntityGenerator* class, we perform regression testing by reading the models for invoice and invoice line, and generating their composite and reader classes.

3) Replace the generator code: We are now ready to generate the generator class itself through a *GeneratorExpander* template. To avoid hardcoding the specific expander templates to be used, we introduce an additional model entity *ExpanderPath* and define the actual expander templates to be used for the entity *Entity* in a CSV file *EntityExpanderPaths*. The generated *EntityGenerator* class will use this CSV file to guide the instantiation fo templates. We also introduce an *expandable* attribute on the entity, as this generator class does not need to be generated for the traditional domain entities. Figure 3 represents the code template for the generator class and its instantiation for the *Invoice* entity, similar to the base class instantiation represented in Figure 2.

D. Enable Autogenous Generation

1) Create autogenous generator: All Java source code has now been retired. A traditional domain entity like invoice can now be enabled to perform generation itself, i.e., autogenous generation, by simply setting the *expandable* attribute, resulting in the generation of an *InvoiceGenerator* class. This generator class will use the list of templates through a CSV file *InvoiceExpanderPaths*, and instantiate these templates. The artifacts to be created by these domain entities are not necessarily programming files. As a test example, we used an *InvoiceTexExpander* template, generating a Latex file for every invoice instance.

2) Generate derived artifacts: We are now able to generate additional artifacts for instances of domain entities like *Invoice* by simply defining additional templates and defining them in the *InvoiceExpanderPaths* CSV file. For instance, we have introduced *HyperText Markup Language (HTML)* and *Universal Business Language (UBL)* expansion templates to instantiate and exchange invoices.

V. Results and Discussion

Figure 4 presents a schematic overview of the various artifacts and their interrelationships. These artifacts include model parameter data files, domain entity data files, (generated) source code classes, runtime object instances, source code templates, and artifacts generated by the domain classes. The green area filling symbolizes the fact that the artifacts are generated, and the light blue contours indicate run-time objects instantiated by classes.

TABLE I.
SIZE OF THE REMAINING TEMPLATE SOURCE CODE.

Expander	LOC	#Bytes
Composite	29	735
Reader	35	1180
ExpansionContext	26	726
Generator	34	1230
Total	**124**	**3871**

At the upper or meta-level, an *EntityReader* reads the entities and their attributes, and instantiates object instances of the *EntityComposite* class. These object instances of the domain entities are used by the *EntityGenerator* to instantiate the code templates and to generate domain classes like *InvoiceComposite* and *InvoiceReader*. At the central or domain level, a generated reader class like *InvoiceReader* reads the invoices and their invoice lines.

This basic code generation or metaprogramming framework has been extended to include the two additional characteristics.

- The metaprogramming becomes *meta-circular* by representing and reading the meta-entities in the same way as the domain entities, enabling the generation of the various classes at the meta-level itself.
- The metaprogramming becomes *autogenous* by generating a generator class for the domain entities as well, allowing to generate various artifacts for the instances of the domain entities themselves.

In the resulting meta-circular and autogenous code generation environment, there is not a single line of actual Java source code left. The only remaining source code consists of the four Java coding templates. Table I presents an overview of the size of the Java code in the four coding templates, detailing both the number of *Lines Of Code (LOC)* and the number of bytes. The *ExpansionContextExpander* template has not been mentioned yet, as it is a small technical helper class used mainly to setup some basic technical details, including the file paths for the CSV input files and the generated artifacts.

The small number of artifacts, and the very limited size of the final codebase, indicates that we have indeed created a quite elementary metaprogramming environment, that nevertheless exhibits meta-circular and autogenous code generation. The complete absence of any remaining source code is another confirmation of the elementary nature and limited complexity of the environment. In our opinion, this shows that the instantiation of coding templates through the evaluation of OGNL expressions in object data trees is a valuable metaprogramming pattern, and may even be close to being a fundamental technique for metaprogramming.

As mentioned before, the meta-circular nature of the metaprogramming environment avoids the complexity of two programming environments, i.e., one for the generator code

```
base() ::= <<
package $entity.packageName$;
public class $entity.name$Generator {
  public static void main(String [] args) throws Exception {
    String domainUri = "file:/"+args[0];
    ArrayList<$entity.name$Composite> instances = $entity.name$Reader.read$entity.name$s(domainUri);
    ArrayList<ExpanderPathComposite> expanders = ExpanderPathReader.readExpanderPaths(domainUri+"$entity.name$ExpanderPaths");
    ExpansionEngine expansionEngine = new ExpansionEngine(domainUri);
    Context expansionContext = expansionEngine.getExpansionContext();
    ArrayList<ExpanderComposite> expanderComposites = expansionEngine.getExpanders(expanders);
    for ($entity.name$Composite instance : instances) {
      $entity.name$ExpansionContext instanceContext = new $entity.name$ExpansionContext(instance, expansionContext);
      for (ExpanderComposite expanderComposite : expanderComposites) {
        expansionEngine.expand(instanceContext, expanderComposite);
      }
    }
  }
}
>>

package net.palver.invoice;
public class InvoiceGenerator {
  public static void main(String [] args) throws Exception {
    String domainUri = "file:/"+args[0];
    ArrayList<InvoiceComposite> instances = InvoiceReader.readInvoices(domainUri);
    ArrayList<ExpanderPathComposite> expanders = ExpanderPathReader.readExpanderPaths(domainUri+"InvoiceExpanderPaths");
    ExpansionEngine expansionEngine = new ExpansionEngine(domainUri);
    Context expansionContext = expansionEngine.getExpansionContext();
    ArrayList<ExpanderComposite> expanderComposites = expansionEngine.getExpanders(expanders);
    for (InvoiceComposite instance : instances) {
      InvoiceExpansionContext instanceContext = new InvoiceExpansionContext(instance, expansionContext);
      for (ExpanderComposite expanderComposite : expanderComposites) {
        expansionEngine.expand(instanceContext, expanderComposite);
      }
    }
  }
}
```

Figure 3. Representation of the instantiation of the generator code template for the *Invoice* entity.

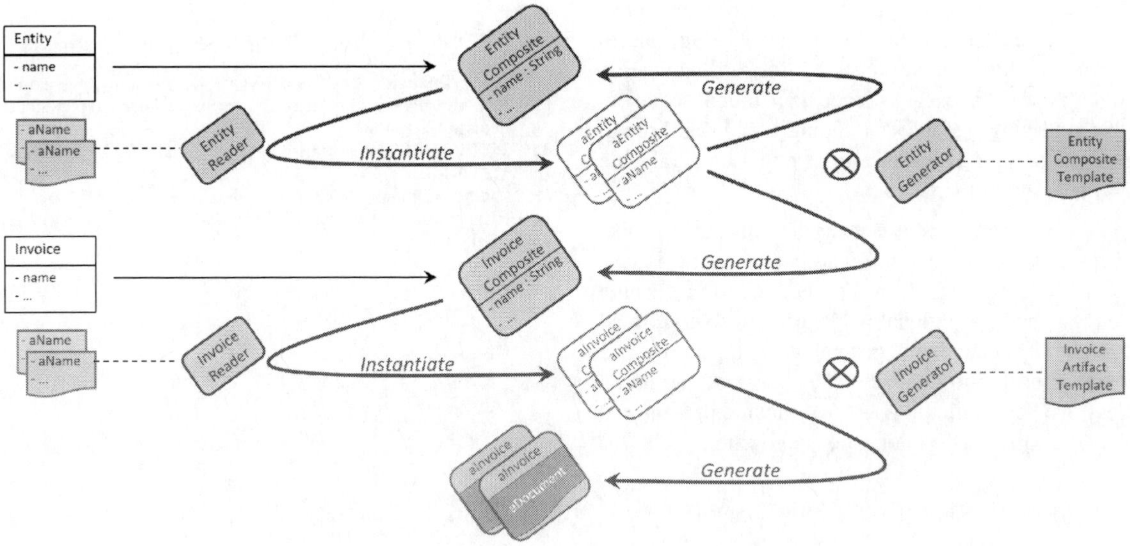

Figure 4. A graphical representation of the overall expansion.

and one for the generated code, and enables the simultaneous introduction of improved and/or extended programming techniques in *both generator code and the code that is generated.* Moreover, it fundamentally decreases the barrier to port such a (meta)programming environment to another programming platform and/or language. Indeed, porting the coding templates and target systems to another language would automatically port the metaprogramming software as well.

VI. Conclusion

Automated code generation or metaprogramming is often seen as an important, and maybe even crucial, approach to increase programming productivity. We have argued in previous work that, for reasons of software evolvability and scalable collaboration, such a metaprogramming environment should preferably exhibit a meta-circular architecture. As meta-circular metaprogramming might entail additional complexity, it seems desirable to provide guidance to metaprogrammers through structured concepts and techniques.

In this contribution, we have presented a detailed procedure to bootstrap an elementary but realistic meta-circular metaprogramming environment. Its purpose was to serve as an architectural pathfinder to clarify some basic concepts, and to support the future extraction of metaprogramming design patterns, or even more fundamental techniques.

The bootstrapping of this meta-circular metaprogramming environment is believed to make some contributions. First, the elementary nature of the environment offers a clear and structured view on both the concept of meta-circularity in code generation environments, and on the bootstrapping process that is needed to realize such an architecture. Second, we have also presented the emergence and basic mechanism of autogenous code generation, i.e., the generated code itself being able to generate artifacts. Third, the rather straightforward realization of meta-circular and autogenous code generation seems to indicate that replacing variables in coding templates through OGNL expressions in data instance trees might be a valuable pattern for metaprogramming.

Next to these contributions, it is clear that this paper is also subject to a number of limitations. The bootstrapping is performed for a single elementary metaprogramming in a single language environment. Additional work needs to be performed to extract and formulate more general design patterns and structured techniques for (meta-circular) metaprogramming. Nevertheless, we believe that this is a worthwhile pursuit, and we are planning to further explore this approach.

References

[1] H. Mannaert, J. Verelst, and P. De Bruyn, Normalized Systems Theory: From Foundations for Evolvable Software Toward a General Theory for Evolvable Design. Koppa, 2016.

[2] R. Agarwal and A. Tiwana, "Editorial—evolvable systems: Through the looking glass of IS," Information Systems Research, vol. 26, no. 3, 2015, pp. 473–479.

[3] H. Mannaert, K. De Cock, P. Uhnak, and J. Verelst, "On the realization of meta-circular code generation and two-sided collaborative metaprogramming," International Journal on Advances in Software, no. 13, 2020, pp. 149–159.

[4] P. Kruchten, "Introduction: Software design in a postmodern era," IEEE Software, vol. 22, no. 2, 2005, pp. 16–18.

[5] D. Parnas, "Software aspects of strategic defense systems," Communications of the ACM, vol. 28, no. 12, 1985, pp. 1326–1335.

[6] P. Cointe, "Towards generative programming," Unconventional Programming Paradigms. Lecture Notes in Computer Science, vol. 3566, 2005, pp. 86–100.

[7] K. Czarnecki and U. W. Eisenecker, Generative programming: methods, tools, and applications. Reading, MA, USA: Addison-Wesley, 2000.

[8] J. R. Rymer and C. Richardson, "Low-code platforms deliver customer-facing apps fast, but will they scale up?" Forrester Research, Tech. Rep., 08 2015.

[9] C. Riemenschneider, B. Hardgrave, and F. Davis, "Explaining software developer acceptance of methodologies: A comparison of five theoretical models," IEEE Transactions on Software Engineering, vol. 28, no. 12, 2002, pp. 1135–1145.

[10] M. Huisman and J. Iivari, "The individual deployment of systems development methodologies," in Lecture Notes in Computer Science, A. Banks Pidduck, Ed., vol. 2348. Springer-Verlag, 2002, pp. 134–150.

[11] E. Gamma, Design Patterns: Elements of Reusable Object-Oriented Software. Addison-Wesley, 1994.

[12] K. Schwaber, Agile Software Development with Scrum. New Jersey, US: Prentice Hall, 2002.

[13] R. C. Martin, Design of modular structures for evolvable and versatile document management based on normalized systems theory. London, UK: Pearson, 2008.

[14] H. Mannaert, K. De Cock, and P. Uhnák, "On the realization of meta-circular code generation: The case of the normalized systems expanders," in Proceedings of the Fourteenth International Conference on Software Engineering Advances (ICSEA), November 2019, pp. 171–176.

[15] H. Mannaert, K. De Cock, P. Uhnák, and J. Verelst, "On the realization of meta-circular code generation and two-sided collaborative metaprogramming," International journal on advances in software, vol. 13, no. 3-4, 2020, pp. 149–159.

[16] J. Reynolds, "Definitional interpreters for higher-order programming languages," Higher-Order and Symbolic Computation, vol. 11, no. 4, 1998, pp. 363–397.

[17] C. Mooers and L. Deutsch, "Trac, a text-handling language," in ACM '65 Proceedings of the 1965 20th National Conference, 1965, pp. 229–246.

[18] "StringTemplate," URL: https://www.stringtemplate.org/, 2022, [accessed: 2022-06-15].

[19] T. Parr, "Enforcing Strict Model-View Separation in Template Engines," URL: https://www.cs.usfca.edu/ parrt/papers/mvc.templates.pdf, 2022, [accessed: 2022-06-15].

[20] "OGNL," URL: https://en.wikipedia.org/wiki/OGNL, 2022, [accessed: 2022-06-15].

[21] "Apache Commons OGNL - Object Graph Navigation Library," URL: https://commons.apache.org/proper/commons-ognl/, 2022, [accessed: 2022-06-15].

Strategy for Early Recognition and Proactive Handling of Disruptions Regarding the Service of Computer Centres and IT Infrastructures Based on Statistical Methods

Martin Zinner, Kim Feldhoff, Wolfgang E. Nagel
Center for Information Services and High Performance Computing (ZIH)
Technische Universität Dresden
Dresden, Germany
E-mail: {martin.zinner1, kim.feldhoff, wolfgang.nagel}@tu-dresden.de

***Abstract*—Ensuring smooth operations of data centres is key to a company's success. This endeavour is becoming more and more difficult. Given the continuously increasing amount of data, real-time demands and continuous system availability requirements, the Information Technology (IT) infrastructure is increasingly becoming more and more complex and unmanageable. Humans are not able to manually identify in time the breakdowns of the IT systems, let alone predict or avoid them. Hence, there is a need for an overall strategy regarding the early recognition or rather, the avoidance of outages. In the focus of our attention are technologies in the area of artificial intelligence, data analytics, anomaly detection, logging, and parsing, etc. We define an overall strategy in this regard, such that by automating and/or reducing routine activities the support team can concentrate its activity on setting up leading edge technologies rather than relying on the individual skills of some team members in fixing or preventing the failures. To conclude, our strategy supports a paradigm shift from more or less subjectively designed individualistic conceptions in handling of disruptions regarding the service of computer centres and IT infrastructures towards objectively established optimal solutions.**

***Index Terms*—Computer centre; Data Analytics; Statistical methods; Anomaly detection; Artificial Intelligence; Trend analysis; Failure diagnosis; Failure prevention; Monitoring system; Event logs.**

I. INTRODUCTION

Given the continuously increasing amount of data, cloud enabling of applications, virtualisation and software as a service, the IT infrastructure is increasingly becoming more and more complex, such that the Information Technology (IT) departments lose the overview of their systems [1] [2]. Moreover, the aging legacy systems, which are critical to day-to-day operations, but are based on outdated technologies, additionally contribute to the confusions within the IT departments. Hence, humans are not able to manually identify in time the failures (breakdowns) of the IT systems, not to mention their ability to identify the cause of the failure and remedy the outage within the required time frame as specified by the support agreements. An IT system includes all hardware, software, and peripheral equipment, operated by a limited group of IT specialists. Hence, the IT system can be an application, a *Virtual Machine* (VM), a server, the whole computer centre or IT infrastructure.

Moreover, cascading of failures should be avoided, since they can cause a partial or a complete breakdown of the IT systems, leading to production outages. Hence, by reacting in time to failures, often far below the legal required response time imposed by contracts, possible negative side effects and subsequent failures can be avoided or their number can be considerably reduced. The optimal functioning of the computer centres can be measured by the *Quality of Service* (QoS) they deliver [3]. The QoS describes the overall performance of a service as seen by the users of the service or measured by appropriate metrics. A metric is a quantitative measure used to characterise, evaluate, and compare performance, whereas measurement is the process by which numbers or symbols are assigned to attributes of entities [4].

An experienced car driver knows that while the engine is running and the oil pressure fails, after a short period of time, the pressure control system stops the compressor and consequently, – in order to avoid damage – shuts down the engine. A much better strategy is to avoid low oil pressure by monitoring the values of the sensors and by taking appropriate proactive actions if these values reach some predefined thresholds.

Regarding our study, two major perspectives on the health of a specified IT system have been identified:

a) Objective perspective - the view which the surrounding system has on the specified IT system,
b) Subjective perspective - the view which the IT system has regarding his own health.

For example, the event log files, which an application generates, are part of the subjective perspective of the application regarding its own health. On the other hand, metrics like the daily standard deviation of the *Central Processing Unit* (CPU) load and *Random Access Memory* (RAM) usage regarding the application, is part of the objective perspective, the operating system has on the application. The subjective perspective, an application has regarding his own health, may be inaccurate, since for example, the log files may be incomplete or even erroneous. On these grounds, it is essential to set up a proper objective perspective. Within this article, we suppose that the objective perspective is reliable and accurate. This is not true per se, since the operating system, which gathers the metrics, may also be buggy, but a discussion in this regard is outside the scope of this article. Although, the objective perspective is accurate, the default metrics delivered by the usual applications like the operating systems do not deliver enough information regarding the health of the IT systems. The ultimate challenge is to set up an appropriate strategy regarding the estimation of the health of the IT systems based on the available basic information delivered by the operating systems, log files, including the system log files, sensors, etc.

A. Motivation

1) Rapidly increasing data amount: The total amount of data created, captured, and consumed globally is forecast to increase rapidly, reaching more than 180 Zettabytes in 2025, as opposed to 64.2 Zettabytes in 2020 and 15.5 Zettabytes in 2015 [5]. Worldwide by 2022, over 50 billion *Internet of Things* (IoT) devices including sensors and actuators are predicted to be installed in machines, vehicles, buildings, and environments and/or used by humans.

2) Real-time demands: Real-time information processing has become a significant requirement for the optimal functioning of the manufacturing plants [6]. Demand is also huge for the real-time utilisation of data streams [7]. The operations of a real-time system are subject to *time constraints* (deadlines), i.e., if specified timing requirements are not met, the corresponding operation is degraded and/or the QoS suffer and it can lead even to system failure [8]. There is a general tendency that real-time requirements are becoming crucial requisites.

Travellers require current flight schedules on their portable devices to be able to select and book flights; in order to avoid overbooking, the flight plans and the filled seats must be kept reasonably current. Similarly, people expect instant access to their business-critical data in order to make informed decisions. Moreover, they may require up-to-date aggregated data or even ad-hoc requests. This instant access to critical information may be crucial for the competitiveness of the company [9].

3) 24/7/365 (round-the-clock) system availability: Continuous availability requirements for production-support IT systems, for example in the semiconductor industry, are the general rule. Many companies consider their tolerance for factory non-scheduled downtimes, due to their revenue losses, plain and simple to be zero. Manufacturing systems tend towards fully automated production systems. Moreover, in the semiconductor industry, in order to avoid chaotic situations, even the outage of some central IT systems, like the *Manufacturing Execution System* (MES) leads to a graceful shutdown of the production.

B. Aim

Our intention is to define an implementable strategy to achieve *Early Recognition and Proactive Handling of Disruptions* (ERPHD) regarding the service of computer centres and IT infrastructures. Furthermore, the objective of our strategy is to keep operational expenses low, such that by reducing routine activities, the IT staff can focus mainly on innovation. We need a strategy of maximising outcome through leading edge technologies while minimising maintenance and support effort.

In conclusion, our strategy is enabling a new overall perspective on handling the disruptions regarding the service of computer centres and IT infrastructures, such that it contributes to a paradigm shift from more or less subjectively designed individualistic conceptions in handling of disruptions towards objectively established optimal solutions.

C. Paper organisation

The remainder of the paper is structured as follows: Section II gives an overview regarding existing work related to the described problem. An informal description of our strategy is presented in Section III. The presentation of the main results and discussions based upon these results constitute the content of Section IV, whereas Section V summarises our contributions and draws perspectives for future work.

II. Related work

The focus of this section is primarily on the existing industry-specific solutions. We are not aware of similar open source implementations.

A. HPE InfoSight

Hewlett Packard Enterprise (HPE) helps customers address potential infrastructure issues with HPE *InfoSight*, a cloud-based *Automated Infrastructure Operations* (AIOps) platform, that applies InfoSight *Artificial Intelligence* (AI) and advanced machine learning to go beyond simple troubleshooting. HPE InfoSight puts the focus on prevention. It uses predictive analytics to predict, prevent, and auto-resolve problems from storage to VMs. HPE InfoSight prevents customers from ever seeing a known issue through advanced pattern-matching algorithms. HPE InfoSight eliminates most of the pain of managing HPE infrastructure alone by automatically predicting and being able to resolve most of the issues automatically. For example, InfoSight might identify performance issues between the VMs and the storage system. This allows for increased application availability and reduced costs, while avoiding the typical headaches of manually digging into log files. In order to achieve the above benefits, HPE must collect telemetry data from the systems [10] [11].

B. Ironstream

Ironstream® integrates machine data from traditional legacy IBM systems into leading IT analytics platforms to work seamlessly with Splunk®, ServiceNow®, Micro Focus®, Microsoft®SCOM, Elastic, Apache Kafka® [12] [13]. Hence, organisations can monitor and manage their IT systems from a single management console by integrating event and system performance data from these traditional IBM systems into their platforms.

C. Splunk

Splunk offers a central platform for analysing machine generated data by developing advanced analytics [14] [15]. It can gather data from various log files including also applications event logs. Splunk can collect data from various location and combines it into centralised indexes and aggregates the log files from many sources to make them centrally searchable. It can drill down to the period when the problem occurred in order to be able to determine its cause. Appropriate alerts can be generated to avoid similar problems in the future. Moreover, important patterns and data analytics can be derived. A Search Processing Language (SPL) [16]–[18] has been developed in order to filter, summarise, and visualise large amount of data.

D. SAP HANA Troubleshooting and Performance Analysis Tool

In order to support its in-memory database HANA, the software company SAP introduce onto the market a troubleshooting and performance analysis tool [19]. This tool fulfils the expected requirements, like performance and high resource utilisation, has a section of common symptoms and troubleshooting, root causes and solutions, etc. for the general part. For example the section root causes and solutions has a part regarding thread monitoring: "What and how many threads are running, what are they working on, and are any of these threads blocked?" or "Are any operations running for a significantly long time and consuming a lot of resources? If so, when will they be finished?".

Moreover, the tool has a part corresponding to database issues, like SQL statement analysis, query plan analysis, advanced analysis, etc. For example, the advance analysis comprises analysing column searches, analysing table joins, etc. The troubleshooting and performance analysis strategy of SAP regarding HANA is very complex and fulfils the requirement and expectations of the users. Unfortunately, it is built by considering the implementation and particularities of a proprietary in-memory database. Of course, some concepts as the importance of the thread monitoring can be considered.

E. Toward Resilience in HPC

High-Performance Computing (HPC) is a technology that harnesses the power of supercomputers or computer clusters to solve complex problems requiring massive computation. In addition to parallel processing, HPC jobs also require fast disks and high-speed memory. Therefore, HPC systems include computing and data-intensive servers with powerful CPUs that can be vertically scaled. HPC systems can also scale horizontally by way of clusters. These clusters consist of networked computers, including scheduler, compute, and storage capabilities [20]. At the University of Technology Dresden/Germany, "jam–e jam", a prototype to analyse and predict system behaviour based on statistical analysis has been developed. It detects node-level failures on HPC systems, as early as possible, in order to employ appropriate protective measures in useful time. The main source of monitoring data are the system log entries – data using the syslog protocol – due to their availability and information richness [21].

In conclusion: the main focus of the existing industry-specific solutions is primarily system performance data on proprietary hardware like HPE InfoSight and Ironstream, and software like SAP HANA. Additionally, Splunk focuses on gathering and interpreting event log data based on a proprietary language (SPL), which increases the learning curve. In contrast, our strategy comprises an overall solution, which is vendor-independent, it does not need inside knowledge regarding the implementation and functioning of the applications and it is based on leading edge but harmonised technologies. It can be conceived as a central monitoring and troubleshooting environment. Additionally, it proposes a uniform event log parsing and analysis strategy, which does not assume inside knowledge of the structure. We are not aware of any commercially available tool which uses this approach.

III. Strategy Description

In a nutshell, the strategy regarding the disruptions of the services of computer centres and IT infrastructures might be:

a) Monitoring the health of the IT systems,
b) Predicting possible malfunctions, interruptions, and downtimes,
c) Proactive actions in order to avoid possible degradation of the QoS delivered by the IT systems,
d) Immediate alerts on failures,
e) Appropriate actions in order to avoid subsequent degradation of the QoS delivered by the IT systems,
f) Corrective actions in order to facilitate the resumption of the failed activity, automatic if possible, else manual actions, including bypass solutions (workarounds),
g) Appropriate actions to avoid similar cases in the future.

A. Event logs

Generally speaking, an event log is an automatically produced, usually, but not necessary time-stamped documentation of events relevant to a particular IT system. We analyse the advantages and disadvantages of the event logs within the ERPHD strategy and make proposals in order to be able to use them advantageously.

1) Importance of the event logs: Event logs are semi-structured text which are generated by logging statements in software code [22]. Unfortunately, event logs may be inaccurate, they may not unequivocally identify the cause of the anomaly and the subsequent steps that have to be taken in order to remedy the failure. According to at least two studies, around 60% of failures due to software faults do not leave any trace in event logs, and 70% of the logging patterns aim to detect errors via a checking code placed at the end of a block of instructions [22].

The event logs are written in general by application developers in order to facilitate the debugging and error finding in their programs. The purpose of the event logs, especially of those written by developers, is to support the development process and not to ease troubleshooting once the product goes productive. Ideally, the information delivered by the event logs should be enough to unequivocally identify the cause of the anomaly, and hence to enable the support team to take appropriate corrective actions. Unfortunately, in real-world systems this is not always the case. Hence, the findings in the entries delivered by the event logs should be augmented by additional sources of information.

The event log files are generally human readable, they are either plain format text files, in XML or JSON format, etc., and enable an efficient and simple one way of communication of the applications with the outside world and they probably will still widely be used in the future. The biggest advantage of the event log files represents also the major difficulty when trying to parse them, namely their flexibility and designing freedom. The effort to harmonise the information parsed from the event log files should not be underestimated.

2) Parsing strategies: To parse signifies to break something into its parts, parsing comprises a syntactic analysis of a string, such that it is separated into more easily processable components by identifying tokens and looking for recognisable patterns. It converts formatted text into a data structure. When parsing the message, the footprint of the actual text message – i.e., the identification mark of the message without considering irrelevant numbers – should be stored additionally. This is advantageous, since this way, the text of the message can be uniquely identified independent of the included numbers. Hence, to each message, an additional *Unique Text Identifier* (UTID) is associated as its text part. Additionally, some keywords like "error", "warning", etc., and time stamps can/should be tracked. Thus, an *Unique Identifier* (UID) can be defined by using the UTID and some additional attributes. This way, the complexity of the event logs has been reduced to a tuple of identifiers, including UTID, UID, and additional keywords. These tuples can be historised/aggregated and used for evaluations. Obviously, a mapping of the UID to the original message should be set up, such that the stored information can be human readable and interpretable.

Generally, multilingual event log files should not pose difficulties, if the event log entry of a particular statement of the monitored application does not switch the language aleatorily. We are only interested in the footprint of the respective message and are not analysing its content. Moreover, keywords or key phrases such as "error", "warning", etc., which are evaluated, can be mapped to the corresponding English idiom [23] [24].

In conclusion: event logs could/should be extensively used within our strategy, but since they are highly unreliable, they should be used with precaution in the classical sense. Moreover, the history of their behaviour should be carefully analysed and appropriate decision should be taken based on deviation from the expected appearance. There is no set of rules regarding the form and content of the event logs, which makes the analysis of the logs even more difficult.

B. Failures

Generally, a *failure* is an issue with the IT system that prevents it from functioning properly and it is an observed property of the run-time behaviour of the system [25]. It occurs when the "delivered service no longer complies with the specifications, the latter being an agreed description of the system's expected function and/or service" [26]–[28]. The IT system may end abnormally if a failure occurs [29]. We analyse the types of failures which can occur within an IT system and examine the high level strategies to address them.

1) General considerations: The handling of incorrect results, which do not produce abnormal termination is outside the scope of this work. For example, if the mathematical formula is incorrectly implemented and delivers wrong results, but the programs terminates in the usual way then this is a debugging issue for the development or for the testing team, and it is considered a defect or a bug.

A *crash* is a serious software failure, such that the software process terminates unexpectedly. Crashes can be reproducible (e.g., triggering an unhandled exception) or non-reproducible (e.g., accessing invalid memory addresses). We do not make any difference between a failure and a crash which is reproducible. It seems that the most difficult problem besides preventing outages is troubleshooting, i.e., finding the cause of the crash. Troubleshooting is the process of identifying and resolving a problem, error or fault within a software or computer system, whereas debugging requires finding the cause of a problem related to software code and fixing it. A fault is an incorrect part of an IT system, which leads to unintended behaviour and in the end to its failure, whereas an error describes any issue that arises unexpectedly that cause a computer to not function properly [30].

Finding the cause for a non-reproducible crash may be a very cumbersome problem, which is hard to debug or predict. For example, dump analysis can help. In some other cases, the cause is a consequence of traceable malfunctions, for example memory leaks can cause the crash of a program.

An *outage* is a discontinuity in the provision of the service of an IT system or group of IT systems including the computer centre or the IT infrastructure. Analogously, a *disruption* is an unplanned event that causes the general system or major application to be inoperable for an unacceptable length of time (e.g., minor or extended power outage, extended unavailable network/equipment or facility damage/destruction) [31].

2) Detecting the cause of the crash: Using our strategy, finding the cause of a crash becomes a routine activity, and one does not have to rely on the "inside knowledge" of some highly qualified IT personnel. Moreover, the time to restrict the cause of the crash can be reduced to minutes instead of hours.

Our aim is to avoid failures, but this intent is not realistic, bearing in mind the complexity of the present-day computer centres. Hence, methodologies should be set up, such that a very fast reaction to overcome the drawback of failures is generally possible:

a) Sound methods should unequivocally determine that a failure has happened, i.e., the crash is instantly recognised as such,
b) Within short time, reliable techniques should localise and subsequently identify the cause of the failure,
c) Apply the predefined workaround (e.g., by deleting some wrong data, etc.),
d) Restart the application, if necessary,
e) Setup a solution, such that similar failures can be avoided in the future.

In conclusion: The collaboration of a couple of specialists in order to narrow the cause of outages is not any more necessary. We are seeking a *paradigm change*: from art (troubleshooting) to very well founded rules.

C. Leading edge technologies

We provide a very general overview of the leading edge technologies which can be applied within our strategy. A detailed consideration would go beyond the size of this article.

1) Artificial Intelligence: There are many definitions of *Artificial Intelligence* (AI) depending of the goals one is trying to achieve with an AI system. Amazon defines AI as "the field of computer science dedicated to solving cognitive problems commonly associated with human intelligence, such as learning, problem solving, and pattern recognition" [32].

2) Data Analytics: Data Analytics is the science of analysing data in order to draw conclusions based upon the analysed data. There are couple of basic types, as descriptive, diagnostic, predictive and prescriptive. Their names also suggest their functionality, e.g. predictive analytics forecast possible events, the prescriptive analytics propose an action plan [33].

3) Trend Analysis: Trend analysis attempts to predict future events, it uses historical data in order to forecast future directions [34]. It is based on the idea that what happened in the past gives hints regarding the future. There is no guarantee that the forecast will be correct.

4) Machine learning: Machine learning (ML) is a branch of AI which focuses on the use of data and algorithms to imitate the way that human learn [35]. For example, Amazon builds a lot of its business on machine learning systems. Machine learning is so important to Amazon, they stated, "Without ML, Amazon.com couldn't grow its business, improve its customer experience and selection, and optimise its logistic speed and quality" [32]. The roots of machine learning dates back to Arthur L. Samuel 1959, see a revised version of his research paper [36]. Nowadays, due to the technological advances in storage and processing power, we are witnesses of the revival and further development of innovative machine learning technologies [35].

5) Anomaly Detection: Anomaly detection refers to finding data instances that do not fit the established patterns. *Outlier detection* is similarly defined. Detecting outliers or anomalies in data has been studied in the statistics community since the end of the 19th century [37] [38]. Outliers are not necessary "bad" data, they are extreme data points within data. On the other hand anomalies are outside what is defined as "good" data. Hence, if the model is accurate, both anomaly detection and outlier detection yield the same results, if this is not the case, the model has to be adapted accordingly.

In conclusion: The fundamentals of the leading edge technologies in order to set up our failure prevention strategy have been known in the statistics community for decades. The importance and renaissance of these technologies is due to the progress in the storage and computer processing power area, such that a much higher amount of data can nowadays be evaluated at lower costs.

D. Historisation

Historisation is the process of keeping data available over time. It offers additional aggregation possibilities and hence extended analysis possibilities. It is indispensable to consider historical information in order to compare past and present and therefore to be able to make predictions. Moreover, we need appropriate strategies to detect the alterations due to version upgrades and if possible avoid false alarms. Nowadays, the monitoring possibilities of the technical parameters of networks and VMs are very good. The primary goal of these monitoring systems is to offer current information regarding those metrics in order to support the production requirements. But we need historisation of the data of the VMs to be able to perform trend analysis.

In conclusion: Historisation is absolutely essential in order to be aware of previous correct states, usually up to one year, definitely as long as aggregated data is evaluated for trend analysis, etc.

E. Strategies for failure recognition and troubleshooting

There is a need to recognise instantly that an application has stopped functioning in the expected way. There should be a method in place, such that crashed application can be unequivocally distinguished from the non-responding ones. The latter can resume their normal activity after the cause of non-responsiveness has been eliminated, for example high CPU load or short network outage. Moreover, large SQL-queries (e.g. full table scans) can block some database application as long as the query is running. For example, an unusual number of threads can be an indication that the application has crashed.

Troubleshooting an application crash may be sometimes very difficult and time consuming. Using statistical methods, the number of possible suspicions can be meaningfully reduced. Moreover, these methods can give hints for possible malfunctions, such that the identification of the cause of the failure should be more or less straightforward. All available historised information including event log files, input/output information, consumed resources, etc., can/should be evaluated. This is advisable since the event log files are unreliable and for example outliers are not necessarily a sign of malfunctions; the challenge is to deliver reliable results using unreliable methods. Thankfully, there are reliable techniques, such that a raised suspicion can be confirmed or not. For example, for a database application, an unexpected or a corrupt dataset value can cause a failure if there is no appropriate catch mechanism in place, which detects the unexpected value at the time of its first use. The error propagates, and finally, when the exception is catched, there is no hint in the event logs regarding the real cause of the failure. Hence, multiple diagnosis methods can make the difference. For example, machine learning strategies can be used to identify unusual data sets in data entry.

In conclusion: Failure diagnosis can be a cumbersome issue, since the event log files do not always contain accurate hints regarding the cause of the failure. Multiple methods, like the evaluation of the event log files, statistics based on the metrics of the resource utilisation, etc., should be simultaneously used in order to improve the accuracy of the failure suspicions and exclude proper functioning IT systems.

F. Strategies for failure avoidance

Generally speaking, the strategies presented in Subsection III-E regarding failure diagnosis can be used for failure prevention. In fact, the technology of identifying non-suspicious IT-systems and the strategy for failure prevention are very similar. Strategies such as the rigour in the development process, verification and validation activities, automated testing using comprehensive test cases, etc., would go beyond the scope of this study [39]. These strategies should be deployed before the roll-out process of the application.

Setting up appropriate metrics and historisation of their values facilitates trend analysis, predictive analytics, and outlier detection. As already mentioned, outliers are not necessarily faulty data, but they can give hints regarding further out of order functioning. Furthermore, a reliable notification infrastructure should be set up in order to be able to react in a timely manner if suspicions occur. For example, by setting up the metric "memory consumption" on application level and by applying trend analysis, potentially large memory consumption, i.e., memory leaks can be detected. This way, by taking appropriate actions, the deterioration of the QoS delivered by the application can be prevented.

In conclusion: by applying statistical methods, the future behaviour of an IT system can be anticipated. The major challenge is to set up the appropriate metrics – i.e. quantitative measures used to characterise, evaluate, and predict anomalies – to best model trend analysis, anomaly detection, failure diagnosis and prevention, etc.

G. Monitoring

Monitoring is the process of gathering metrics regarding the activity of the IT systems. We give a general overview of the overall monitoring strategy with subsequent detailed explanations.

1) General considerations: Commercially available monitoring systems are expected to gather data necessary to be able to decide whether an application is working correctly or not. Unfortunately, while this may be usually the case, the default vendor-delivered metrics are not fully suitable for solving the problem as above. Additional effort is necessary for:

a) Resource monitoring on the application side,
b) Resource monitoring on the server side,
c) Event log monitoring,
d) Input/output monitoring,
e) Direct health validation including threads surveillance,
f) Historisation of the collected information,
g) Using leading edge technologies in order to establish trends and pattern recognition,
h) Establishing strategies for error recognition and efficient troubleshooting,
i) Appropriate strategy in order to avoid the occurrence of crashes.

2) Strategy: The monitoring and evaluation strategy should be set up such that it can be carried out with a medium educated stuff. We are looking now in detail to each of the above items.

a) In order to be able to identify the resources used by the application, commercial or self-made solutions can be used. These information should be historised, such that comparison with successful completion can be done. Every deviation which is behind some thresholds could indicate an anomaly that can lead to failures.
b) Resource monitoring on the server side is similar to resource monitoring on the application side, the additional benefit is that if some resources on the server side surpass for an extended time some threshold, the server may become inoperable. For example, if the CPU is at 100% utilisation, the application may become unresponsive, although it is functioning correctly. If the application has its own VM then the distinction as above is obsolete.
c) There is a need to parse and structure the event logs as indicated above. Furthermore, the event log files along with the newly created structure should be historised, such that statistical evaluations can be performed on the newly created structures.
d) Furthermore, of crucial interest is input/output monitoring, although it is almost always neglected. Unfortunately, unforeseen changes in the input stream can cause unwanted behaviour of the application. For example, for database application an unexpected input value can cause unexpected application reactions, which is almost impossible to predict, since no one counted with this situation. This is also a good counterexample, where possible crash prediction is improbable. To remedy issues as above, an appropriate filter on the input data stream can be set up, but the problem in principle remains.
e) Under the heading *direct health validation* we understand the strategy of gathering direct information from the application itself regarding his health status. For example, a database application can automatically be queried by standard SQL statements within self-made tools. For example, metrics like the response time of the application can be tracked and historised. If the response time degrades under some predefined thresholds then certainly the QoS of the application will degrade accordingly. Furthermore, the behaviour of the threads, possibly including their resource use, can be further supervised. For example, if an application alternates between 4 and 8 threads and the *Operating System* (OS) detects only 2 threads, then the application has crashed, although the OS does not classify it as terminated.
f) Generally speaking, all of the collected information regarding the health of an IT system should be historised in order to allow comparison with earlier behaviour. Commonly, historisation for example using a *Data Warehouse* (DWH) is not a primordial concern of the vendors of monitoring systems, their primary focus is on the

operative part.

g) The leading edge technologies to establish trends, outliers, and pattern recognition have been summarised in Subsection III-C. The presented technologies are complementary, such that multiple technologies can be used in order to achieve our goals.
h) Establishing strategies for error recognition and efficient troubleshooting is one of the most ambitious phases of our strategy. Since not all crashes are recorded in the event logs, establishing whether an application has crashed or not, is not always a straightforward task. Moreover, application may be irresponsive having some residual threads detectable by the operating system, compare Subsection II-D. Well suited technologies are available in the area of anomaly detection in order to identify patterns, which are out of order and give hints regarding application crash, see Subsection III-E for more details.
i) In order to anticipate malfunctions, trend analysis and pattern recognition can be promising approaches, see Subsection III-F for more details.

In conclusion: Monitoring is a complex activity, which involves taking into account all available information regarding the IT systems to be considered. But monitoring alone is not sufficient, the collected data has to be historised in order to be able to compare successful historical operational sequences with the current ones. Additionally, methodologies have to be set up on the historical data based on statistical methods in order to automatically detect failures, their causes, and forecasts malfunctions of the IT systems.

IV. Outline of the Results

The main achievement of this work is the cognition that an overall strategy termed ERPHD regarding instant recognition and preventions of failures of the IT systems of a computer centre and/or the IT infrastructure using statistical methods is realisable. This strategy also includes the evaluation of the event log files using similar approaches as for machine or system performance data. Thus, a central point of surveillance can be set up. We give an overview of the pros and cons of the ERPHD strategy and close the section with some general remarks.

1) Advantages of ERPHD strategy: the strategy for early recognition and proactive handling of disruptions provides the technology, such that:

a) Involving almost the same effort, all event logs can be taken into account due to harmonised parsing strategy,
b) All existing applications can be monitored regarding early recognition and proactive handling of disruptions due to the general properties of our strategy,
c) The routine support activity decreases, hence the actual support team can be kept smaller due to the failure prevention strategy,
d) A central monitoring system can be set up, versus many monitoring tools due to our uniform strategy,
e) The learning curve of the support team is manageable due to a central monitoring system,
f) There is an automated evaluation of the event log files, long manual search is obsolete due to the harmonised parsing strategy for all event logs,
g) It is based on reliable leading edge technology,
h) Enables real-time computer centres and IT infrastructure due to our failure prevention strategy,
i) Supports straightforward design strategies due to clear, easy understandable architectural and implementation principles,
j) Avoids or reduces "hot working phases" at night for the IT personnel due the failure prevention capabilities,
k) Ensures very good scalability due to uniform design strategies,
l) Supports easy maintenance due to transparent and straightforward software development process, and last but not least,
m) Supports early detection of erroneous data sets due the advanced statistical methods.

2) Difficulties of ERPHD strategy:

a) There is no open-source or commercially available out-of-the-box product,
b) Difficult architectural set-up, i.e., new algorithms have to be designed and implemented,
c) Longer development times due to a new architectural design strategy,
d) IT staff has to be additionally trained due to unconventional architectural and maintenance strategies,
e) Heterogeneous development teams including mathematicians and data scientist should be built upon, i.e., the algorithmic part of the development may be sophisticated,
f) Increased development costs due to the unconventional development strategies, and last but not least,
g) Strong management commitment to overcome the difficulties due to the anticipated challenges.

3) Final considerations: Assuring and/or improving the QoS of a data centre is a very complex endeavour, in which the human component also plays a very important role. There should be rules set up, such that the actions or decisions taken by the service team should not be based upon the individual skills of its members, but on generally accepted guidelines. In this respect, the experience and know-how of an individual employee should not be lost if he leaves the company.

In conclusion: If the computer centre or the IT infrastructure exceeds a certain size and importance, the advantages of the ERPHD strategy may prevail over its disadvantages. Definitely, if the computer centre supports a round-the-clock production, if there are real-time requirements in place, or high requirements regarding the QoS then the advantages of the ERPHD strategy outweigh the implementation costs.

V. Conclusion and Future Research Perspective

A. Conclusion

There is an increased request for real-time application capability in the industry and research amid rapidly increasing data amount. Furthermore, there is a need for round-the-clock IT systems availability due to 24/7/365 production requirements. If these requirements cannot be met then the outage of the IT systems leads to production outages with catastrophic consequences for the business. In addition, the complexity of the present day computer centres and IT infrastructures makes it very difficult to manually assure their reliable operability. Hence, to overcome the difficulties as above, there is a need for an overall failure and outage prevention strategy as well as very fast failure detection and diagnosis methodology. Our article is a contribution in this direction.

The existing industrial implementations focus primarily on vendor dependent machine and system performance data, using inside knowledge of the respective IT systems. In contrast, our strategy relies on well-established leading edge statistical methods and takes into account all data generated by the IT systems, including the event logs. The main advantage of our strategy, termed ERPHD is the possibility to centrally monitor the computer centre and IT infrastructure using vendor independent technologies. Moreover, all IT systems including all applications can be monitored using the same technology, hence once the technology has been set up, the effort to extend the monitoring by additional IT systems should pose no problems. This way, once the technology is in place, the QoS of all applications can be substantially improved, raising the QoS of non-production relevant applications with minimal additional effort. Our contribution is a step away from an artisanal approach in handling disruptions towards objectively established optimal solutions. The real challenge is to set up the metrics to best model the IT system.

B. Future research perspectives

A substantial question one can ask himself is the meaningfulness of the objective (e.g. system performance data) versus subjective (e.g. event log files) approach. Additionally, the relevancy of the statistical approach applied on event logs versus the classical approach, where the event logs are content-wise analysed, is of utmost interest. Identifying the weak points of statistical approaches including the limits of applicability, may be of advantage. Last, but not least, the question arises whether there are alternative approaches, which do not rely on proprietary information regarding the IT systems.

REFERENCES

[1] C. Schinko, "Künstliche Intelligenz im Rechenzentrum: So vermeiden Sie IT-Störungen proaktiv [in English: Artificial intelligence in the data center: How to proactively prevent IT disruptions]," *CANCOM.info*, 2018, retrieved: September 2022. [Online]. Available: https://www.cancom.info/2018/11/kuenstliche-intelligenz-rechenzentrum-it-stoerungen-vermeiden/

[2] E. E. Ogheneovo, "On the Relationship between Software Complexity and Maintenance Costs," *Journal of Computer and Communications*, vol. 2, pp. 1–16, 2014, retrieved: September 2022. [Online]. Available: https://doi.org/10.1016/j.procir.2020.05.012

[3] M. Zinner *et al.*, "Techniques and Methodologies for Measuring and Increasing the Quality of Services: a Case Study Based on Data Centers," *International Journal On Advances in Intelligent Systems, volume 13, numbers 1 and 2, 2020*, vol. 13, no. 1 & 2, pp. 19–35, 2020, retrieved: September 2022. [Online]. Available: http://www.thinkmind.org/articles/intsys_v13_n12_2020_2.pdf

[4] N. Fenton and J. Bieman, *Software metrics: a rigorous and practical approach*. CRC press, 2014.

[5] Statista, "Volume of data/information created, captured, copied, and consumed worldwide from 2010 to 2025," 2021, retrieved: September 2022. [Online]. Available: https://www.statista.com/statistics/871513/worldwide-data-created/

[6] R. Sousa, R. Miranda, A. Moreira, C. Alves, N. Lori, and J. Machado, "Software tools for conducting real-time information processing and visualization in industry: An up-to-date review," *Applied Sciences*, vol. 11, no. 11, p. 4800, 2021, retrieved: September 2022. [Online]. Available: https://www.mdpi.com/2076-3417/11/11/4800

[7] K. Yasumoto, H. Yamaguchi, and H. Shigeno, "Survey of real-time processing technologies of iot data streams," *Journal of Information Processing*, vol. 24, no. 2, pp. 195–202, 2016, retrieved: September 2022. [Online]. Available: https://doi.org/10.2197/ipsjjip.24.195

[8] I. Sommerville, "Software engineering 9th edition," *ISBN-10*, vol. 137035152, p. 18, 2011.

[9] Zinner *et al.*, "Real-time information systems and methodology based on continuous homomorphic processing in linear information spaces," 2015, retrieved: September 2022. [Online]. Available: https://patentimages.storage.googleapis.com/ed/fa/37/6069417bdcc3eb/US20170032016A1.pdf

[10] R. Sheldon, "How HPE InfoSight AI proactively spots, solves infrastructure issues," *SearchStorage*, 2019, retrieved: September 2022. [Online]. Available: https://www.techtarget.com/searchstorage/tip/How-HPE-InfoSight-AI-proactively-spots-solves-infrastructure-issues

[11] "HPE InfoSight for Servers User Guide," *Hewlett Packard Enterprise*, 2021, retrieved: September 2022. [Online]. Available: https://www.hpe.com/psnow/doc/a00061446en_us

[12] "Unlocking Real-time Mainframe Operational Intelligence," *Syncsort Ironstream*, 2015, retrieved: September 2022. [Online]. Available: https://www-50.ibm.com/partnerworld/gsd/showimage.do?id=41083

[13] *Precisely Ironstream*, 2022, retrieved: September 2022. [Online]. Available: https://www.precisely.com/product/precisely-ironstream/ironstream

[14] D. Carasso, "Exploring Splunk Search Processing Language (SPL) Primer and Cookbook," *CITO Research New York, NY*, 2012, retrieved: September 2022. [Online]. Available: https://www.splunk.com/pdfs/exploring-splunk.pdf

[15] J. Miller, "Mastering Splunk Optimize your machine-generated data effectively by developing advanced analytics with Splunk," *PACKT Publishing*, 2012, retrieved: September 2022. [Online]. Available: https://www.splunk.com/pdfs/exploring-splunk.pdf

[16] S. Luedtke, "Power Of Splunk SPL," *splunk*, 2016, retrieved: September 2022. [Online]. Available: https://conf.splunk.com/files/2016/slides/power-of-spl.pdf

[17] "Quick Reference Guide," *splunk*, retrieved: September 2022. [Online]. Available: https://www.splunk.com/pdfs/solution-guides/splunk-quick-reference-guide.pdf

[18] K. Subramanian, "Practical splunk search processing language: A guide for mastering spl commands for maximum efficiency and outcome." Springer, 2020, p. 349.

[19] SAP HANA, "Troubleshooting and Performance Analysis Guide," *SAP Help Portal*, 2018, retrieved: September 2022. [Online]. Available: https://help.sap.com/docs/SAP_HANA_PLATFORM/bed8c14f9f024763b0777aa72b5436f6/7d28bc8c4e54413caf2716731494da88.html?version=2.0.03

[20] IBM, "What is high-performance computing (HPC)?" *IBM Homepage*, 2022, retrieved: September 2022. [Online]. Available: https://www.ibm.com/topics/hpc

[21] S. Ghiasvand, "Toward resilience in high performance computing: A prototype to analyze and predict system behavior," Ph.D. dissertation, Dresden University of Technology, Germany, 2020, retrieved: September 2022. [Online]. Available: https://tud.qucosa.de/api/qucosa%3A72457/attachment/ATT-0/

[22] S. He *et al.*, "A survey on automated log analysis for reliability engineering," *ACM Computing Surveys (CSUR)*, vol. 54, no. 6, pp. 1–37, 2021, retrieved: September 2022. [Online]. Available: https://arxiv.org/pdf/2009.07237.pdf

[23] M. R. Ghorab, J. Leveling, D. Zhou, G. J. Jones, and V. Wade, "Identifying common user behaviour in multilingual search logs," in *Workshop of the cross-language evaluation forum for European languages*. Springer, 2009, pp. 518–525, retrieved: September 2022.

[Online]. Available: https://doras.dcu.ie/16037/1/Identifying_Common_User_Behaviour_in.pdf

[24] G. M. D. Nunzio, J. Leveling, and T. Mandl, "Multilingual log analysis: Logclef," in *European Conference on Information Retrieval*. Springer, 2011, pp. 675–678, retrieved: September 2022. [Online]. Available: https://doras.dcu.ie/16438/1/Multilingual_Log_Analysis_LogCLEF.pdf

[25] L. Hatton, "Characterising the diagnosis of software failure," *IEEE Software*, vol. 18, no. 4, pp. 34–39, 2001, retrieved: September 2022. [Online]. Available: https://www.leshatton.org/Documents/Diag_IS799.pdf

[26] J.-C. Laprie, "Dependability: Basic concepts and terminology," in *Dependability: Basic Concepts and Terminology*. Springer, 1992, pp. 3–245.

[27] D. V. L. Bartlett, "The failure phenomenon: a critique," *International Journal of Performability Engineering*, vol. 6, no. 2, p. 181, 2010, retrieved: September 2022. [Online]. Available: http://www.ijpe-online.com/EN/article/downloadArticleFile.do?attachType=PDF&id=3362

[28] B. Randell and M. Koutny, "Failures: Their definition, modelling and analysis," in *International Colloquium on Theoretical Aspects of Computing*. Springer, 2007, pp. 260–274.

[29] S. Dalal and R. S. Chhillar, "Case studies of most common and severe types of software system failure," *International Journal of Advanced Research in Computer Science and Software Engineering*, vol. 2, no. 8, 2012, retrieved: September 2022. [Online]. Available: https://citeseerx.ist.psu.edu/viewdoc/download?doi=10.1.1.1073.5008&rep=rep1&type=pdf

[30] "E-Definitions," *ComputerHope*, 2021, retrieved: September 2022. [Online]. Available: https://www.computerhope.com/jargon/e/error.htm

[31] "CNSSI 4009-2015 [Superseded] from NIST SP 800-34 Rev. 1 - Adapted," 2015, retrieved: September 2022. [Online]. Available: https://csrc.nist.gov/glossary/term/disruption

[32] B. Marr, "The Key Definitions Of Artificial Intelligence (AI) That Explain Its Importance," *Enterprise Tech*, 2018, retrieved: September 2022. [Online]. Available: https://www.forbes.com/sites/bernardmarr/2018/02/14/the-key-definitions-of-artificial-intelligence-ai-that-explain-its-importance/?sh=7a87d4734f5d

[33] J. Frankenfield, "Data Analytics," *Investopedia*, 2022, retrieved: September 2022. [Online]. Available: https://www.investopedia.com/terms/d/data-analytics.asp

[34] A. Hayes, "Trend Analysis," *Investopedia*, 2021, retrieved: September 2022. [Online]. Available: https://www.investopedia.com/terms/t/trendanalysis.asp

[35] "Machine Learning," *IBM Cloud Education*, 2020, retrieved: September 2022. [Online]. Available: https://www.ibm.com/cloud/learn/machine-learning

[36] F. Gabel, "Artificial Intelligence for Games: Seminar," , 2019, retrieved: September 2022. [Online]. Available: https://hci.iwr.uni-heidelberg.de/system/files/private/downloads/636026949/report_frank_gabel.pdf

[37] V. Chandola, A. Banerjee, and V. Kumar, "Anomaly detection: A survey," *ACM computing surveys (CSUR)*, vol. 41, no. 3, pp. 1–58, 2009.

[38] ——, "Outlier detection: A survey," *ACM Computing Surveys*, vol. 14, p. 15, 2007.

[39] ScienceDirect, "Fault Prevention," *Elsevier*, 2022, retrieved: September 2022. [Online]. Available: https://www.sciencedirect.com/topics/computer-science/fault-prevention

On the Applicability of ALF Language in Real Software Projects

Radek Kočí and Lukáš Osadský

Brno University of Technology, Faculty of Information Technology
Bozetechova 2, 612 66 Brno, Czech Republic
emails: koci@fit.vut.cz, xosads00@stud.fit.vutbr.cz

***Abstract*—Modeling is one of the critical activities in specifying requirements and designing a software system. In the design and development of software systems, there has been a long-term trend of shifting from static software models to feasible models. These models include, for example, state diagrams or techniques using automated model transformations, which are based on a subset of Unified Modeling Language (UML) models and supplement them with special languages, such as Action Language for Foundational UML (ALF). A common feature is to move part of the verification and testing from the implementation stage to the design stage and eliminate the implementation process. In this paper, we will focus on the possibilities of using one direction of application of models in software development, namely the Foundational Subset of Executable UML (fUML), in conjunction with the specification language ALF. The paper provides a literature search on the fundamental essence of the Model-Driven Engineering approaches, namely fUML and ALF language. Then, we tried to apply it to the case study of a conference system and captured all the problems. Due to the nature of the issues, we will not present this case study, as the substance is not essential for the paper.**

***Keywords*—modeling; software systems; model-driven engineering; ALF language.**

I. INTRODUCTION

Modeling is one of the critical activities in specifying requirements and designing a software system. The model can be understood as an abstraction of the system, over which the simulation can be performed, as well as part of the design process in the development of new systems. In the design and development of software systems, there has been a long-term trend of shifting from static software models to feasible models, which allow analyzing and verifying design properties in a simulation way, i.e., without the need to implement models. This category of use includes, for example, state diagrams or techniques using automated model transformations, which are based on a subset of UML models and supplement them with special languages, such as ALF. A common feature is to move part of the verification and testing from the implementation stage to the design stage and eliminate the implementation process.

Model-driven approaches assume that it would be more advantageous for application development if the requirements modeling and prototyping steps were combined. The resulting model could, with minor modifications, directly serve as a functional prototype of the application. The basis is the transformation of models according to their purpose. The process begins with the creation of specification models, which are further transformed into executable models that can be verified in a simulation manner. Models can be transformed into different forms, according to their purpose.

In this paper, we will focus on the possibilities of using one direction of application of models in software development, namely the Foundational Subset of Executable UML (fUML), in conjunction with the specification language ALF. The paper describes the fundamental essence of these approaches and summarizes the problems associated with fUML and ALF's case study of a conference system. Due to the nature of the issues, we will not present this case study, as the substance is not essential for the paper.

The paper is structured as follows. First, we briefly summarize concepts od modeling (Section II) and Model-Driven Development (MDD, Section III) of software systems. The current development environments for MDD with ALF language are presented in Section IV. A literature search of essential papers is presented in Section V. Section VI evaluates an applicability of MDD and ALF language in software projects. Finally, the possible development of these techniques is discussed in Section VII.

II. MODELING

The next section is devoted to modeling, various approaches, and resources related to this activity. Models are the basis of modeling and are used throughout all parts of the software development cycle. They are used for the needs of specification, documentation, design, and the like. The German philosopher Herbert Stachowiak described them on the basis of three characteristics.

- *Mapping*. The model is always a model of the original. The original can be something real or imaginary.
- *Reduction*. Models generally do not capture all the original attributes, but only those that are relevant for modeling purposes.
- *Pragmatism*. Models are not assigned to their originals in a one-to-one relationship; they always perform the function of replacement. To fulfill their purpose, they must be used instead of the original.

It is a form of abstraction that describes the state, properties, dynamics, or structure of the modeled object, system, or part of them. Several models can describe the entity we are modeling. One model can describe its structure, other properties, or behavior in different degrees of abstraction. In software engineering, models are used, for example, in the specifications of the customers' requirements. Their purpose is to capture the required system properties, which are used as a model for the creation of the system. In other cases, models may serve as major artifacts in the implementation of systems.

When modeling, we can encounter several terms related to it. Model-Based Engineering (MBE) or Model-Driven Engineering (MDE) is a software paradigm that applies the principles of visual modeling during the software development lifecycle. It is an umbrella term for disciplines such as Model-Driven Development (MDD), Model-Based System Engineering (MBSE), Business Process Modeling (BPM), and OntologyEngineering. MDD is a sub-discipline dealing with the application of model-driven technologies to software development activities. Another discipline dealing with software development is the Model-Driven Architecture (MDA). It is a specific implementation of MDD. MBE is a discipline of systems engineering, whose primary goal is to use the model of information exchange between engineers. BPM is used to describe business processes using diagrams. Ontology Engineering is a discipline specialized in creating ontologies. This work will deal in more detail with the discipline of MDD and MDA.

III. Model-Driven Development

MDD is a sub-discipline of Model-Driven Engineering dealing with applying model-driven techniques to software development activities. It is an approach that uses models as first-class entities to create products. The motivation for using model-driven approaches is that standard software is continually evolving, and the platforms on which this software works are also changing. Thus, it is necessary to continuously modify the products for the platforms they are to operate, which brings with it the need to invest more time and resources in their modifications. One of the goals of model-driven approaches is to prevent this and save resources. MDE takes software development to a higher level of abstraction, so there is no need to adapt models to every platform change. One abstract model can be re-used for multiple platforms without intervention. Besides, they are easier to maintain.

Models as development artifacts are easier to understand even for non-interested parties. One of the problems with using models for development is capturing all implementation details [1].

A. Model-Driven Architecture

MDA is a specific implementation of MDD from Object Management Group (OMG). This implementation is based on several OMG standards, such as the Meta-Object Facility (MOF), XML Metadata Interchange (XMI), Object Constraint Language (OCL), UML, and others. MDA works with basic UML models, which are described using Domain Specific Language (DSL). DSL is a language that specializes in a particular application domain. An example might be SQL or ALF languages. MDA is based on three principles [1].

- *Direct representation.* It allows you to combine problems with solutions using DSL.
- *Automation.* Elements introduced by DSL are to be processed by tools that connect the gap of domain concepts with implementation technologies.
- *Standard.* It allows us to connect technical solutions.

The main idea of MDA is that each software can be used on different platforms. For this reason, MDA uses models that are transformed into other models using transformation rules. The individual transformations are based on the Query/View/Transformation (QVT) standard [2].

B. Executable MDA

Executable UML (xUML) is a software development concept and a highly abstract language that aims to compile and run UML models. xUML is a modification of UML, in which it is possible to describe the details of the model to such a level that it is possible to run it or generate functional code from it. xUML combines a subset of UML models with executable semantics. Models in this environment can be run, debugged, tested, and compiled by the domain of abstract languages. xUML supports MDA, for example allowing the translation of Platform Independent Models (PIMs) into Platform Specific Models (PSMs) [3].

C. Foundational Subset for Executable UML

fUML is an OMG standard. It is a platform-independent executable subset of standard UML that provides modeling concepts for defining UML classes and the behavior of these classes. This subset includes typical UML modeling constructs such as classes, data types, associations, and enumerations. It also provides the means to define model behavior using UML activities. fUML uses different types of diagrams from UML, i.e., it uses class diagrams to define a static structure and activity diagrams to define the behavior [4].

D. Foundational Subset for Executable UML

Modeling systems using graphical representation may not always be sufficient. It is not possible to capture all the details of the system, so text representation is also used to describe the models. There are several options for a textual description of the model. One of them is ALF language from OMG. In addition to the specific textual syntax for describing fUML models, ALF also provides execution semantics by mapping ALF syntax to the abstract syntax of fUML models. The specific syntax of the ALF language is based on a context-free grammar written in Enhanced-Backus-Naur-Form (EBNF) form, and its abstract syntax is represented by the UML model [11]. The primary goal of ALF is to use text syntax to specify executable behavior within a model, i.e., specify the bodies of the class methods needed for the operations contained in the class diagrams. The syntax of the ALF language is similar to the Java language's syntax, uses the default type system, and has static type checking. According to the specification, the ALF code can be executed in three ways [5].

- *Interpretive Execution.* The ALF model can be directly interpreted and triggered.

- *Compilated execution.* The ALF model is translated into a UML model to match fUML and is run according to the semantics specified by fUML.
- *Translation execution.* The ALF model is translated into code that is executable on the selected platform.

IV. Environments

While working on this paper two environments, which can be used for ALF development, were tested.

A. Eclipse IDE

Eclipse IDE is primarily used for developing Java applications, but with the integration of several plugins, it is possible to use ALF language. To use ALF with Eclipse IDE, it is needed to add plugins like Papyrus Modeling Environment for modeling, Moka for model execution/debugging, and Nebula to add custom widgets. We followed the manual [6] to set up this environment and run and debug ALF models and Papyrus Software designer. After installing all necessary plugins, it is needed to display widgets to work with ALF like debugging widgets, model properties widgets, and others. After all this, the environment is ready to use. This environment is suited to use ALF for describing the behavior and fUML models for describing the structure, but it is also possible to use ALF for both. For complete-textual usage, it is better to use the ALF reference implementation [7]. An example model mentioned in the manual [6] was used to test the environment. The given model can be modified, run, and debugged. The first complications occurred with the generation of code from this model. Papyrus Software designer allows us to generate code from UML models when trying to generate code. Nevertheless, only the class skeleton was created; the behavior implemented using the ALF language was not generated. It was not generated because Papyrus Software Designer does not support ALF code generation. For additional code generation options, it is needed to add the Acceleo extension to the Eclipse environment, which serves as a code generator or allows us to define our own code generation rules. Like Papyrus Software Designer, Acceleo does not support ALF, so it is needed to implement its own code generation template.

B. MagicDraw

Furthermore, the commercial tool MagicDraw from NoMagic is used as the primary tool for ALF. Because MagicDraw does not have a free license, its demo version was used. Installation and deployment of the environment are much more comfortable than in the case of Eclipse. It only needs to install MagicDraw and add the ALF integrated editor extension and Cameo Simulation Toolkit extension used to run fUML models. Like Papyrus, MagicDraw allows us to describe the structure using diagrams and model behavior with ALF. But, it is not possible to specify the system structure in ALF, the only thing which can be described is the behavior of parts of the model. As part of product testing, simple class diagrams were created with methods whose behavior was described in the ALF language. Subsequently, it is possible to run the whole model or part of it directly in MagicDraw. Once launched, a simulation window opens with a console. It is possible to start the simulation of behavior described with ALF, set breakpoints, and change the animation's speed. It is also possible to write simple tests with the help of activities. To create a simple model in this environment, these instructions were followed [8]. To generate code, it is necessary to create a "Code Engineering Set", in which the target language and the set of models from which the code is to be generated are selected. There is a manual related to code generation [9]. The problem with code generation is that only the UML model's skeleton is generated during code generation, and the behavior written in ALF is not. MagicDraw does not support code generation from ALF to target language.

Originally, ALF's focus was to ease the writing of complete executable UML models. Due to low market demand, this idea was abandoned, and today ALF serves primarily as an action language in the context of SysML model simulations. So, this is also the primary intention of its use in the MagicDraw environment.

V. Studies

Several studies show the possibilities of the ALF language and the technologies associated with it. Several sources have been studied for this work, and several of them are worth mentioning.

A. Combining ALF and UML in Modeling Tools

One of these works is [10], which deals with the use of the ALF language in the Papyrus environment. It briefly describes the ALF language, the Papyrus environment, its limits, and demonstrates its use on the example of a product order model. At the end of the work, it is mentioned that the Papyrus environment provides only essential functions for describing models using the ALF language. It will still take some time if new generation tools are available that would match the common use of programming languages.

B. Executable Modeling with fUML and ALF in Papyrus: Tooling and Experiments

[11] describes the use of ALF and fUML in Papyrus. This work has a similar topic to [10], but it focuses on experimentation and describes ALF's limits.

C. On Open Source Tools for Behavioral Modeling and Analysis with fUML and ALF

Another interesting work is [12], which describes available tools, that can be used for the ALF language. As mentioned in the work of [10], the conclusion is that although the instruments exist, their possibilities are limited, and they are still in the incubation phase.

Of other studies and articles studied for this work, the most relevant sources of information were [5], [13], and [14]. In these three works, it was possible to generate code from ALF, using different approaches.

D. On the Generation of Full-fledged Code from UML Profiles and ALF for Complex Systems

[14] deals with the generation of C++ code for more complex systems. It uses a combination of ALF language, CHESS tool, and the CHESS-ML modeling language. The CHESS-ML model is a model defined by a UML profile that describes the structure. Behavior is defined using ALF. The work describes the overall transformation, which includes the generation of structural and behavioral aspects of the modeled system. A simplified Asynchronous Transfer Mode (ATM) Adaptation Layer 2 (AAL2) subsystem used in telecommunications for voice transmission was adopted to demonstrate code generation. The code generation consists of a set of transformations such as the conversion of a CHESS-ML model into an unspecified Intermediate Model (InterM) using a model-to-model transformation (M2M) using QVT. Further transformation of the behavior model is defined in the ALF language into InterM using QVT to extend the existing model. The code generation is handled by a model-to-text (M2T) transformation using Xpand [15]. For the needs of transformation between individual models, transformation rules were created within the work, which consisted of approximately 6000 lines of code.

E. Unifying Modeling and Programming with ALF

Standard tools for working with the ALF language are not used in [13]. Instead, they implemented their tools. As described in work, for development in ALF language, it is possible to create own text editor using Eclipse framework Xtext [16], which is primarily used to develop programming and domain-specific languages. It allows to build a language infrastructure directly above the Eclipse environment, including linking, parsing and code validation, syntax highlighting, and more. It also allows to modify standard environment components using Xtend [17]. For the ALF language needs, it is necessary to implement own validation rules for displaying meaningful error messages and modify grammar rules in Xtext, given that ALF uses left-recursive rules, and the Xtext parsing generator does not support them by default. It is also necessary to modify the rules for determining the scope for the needs of importing ALF elements and implement their own type system [13]. Regarding code generation, ALF code is not generated directly, but using model transformations. The idea of transformations is that the ALF model is transformed with the help of transformation rules into another model, specifically the MoDisco Java model. The code is generated with the help of existing generators. The transformation between the ALF model and the MoDisco Java model is performed using the Atlas Transformation Language (ATL) [18], in which it is necessary to define own rules. The paper states that the creation of transformation rules was problematic, mainly because the abstraction of the ALF language is significantly higher than in Java. There were problems with access modifiers, code navigation, and others. In total, the implementation of the ATL rules consisted of more than 9000 lines of code [13].

F. On the automated transnational execution of the action language for foundational UML

In [5], the authors chose a different approach to this problem. No rules have been created to transform an ALF model into another model, but a tool has been created that generates C++ code from an ALF model. This is the first solution that automatically generates code directly from the ALF language. Their solution allows the translation of ALF behavior concepts within the minimum syntactic match. It provides a subset of the ALF language that can be used to describe behavior within the UML model. This includes only the options available in the procedural programming [19]. It also allows the translation of ALF units used to describe the structure of the model (namespaces, packages, classes, operations, and properties). It also provides a memory management system based on the smart pointers principle, a type deduction mechanism, and a scope mechanism. The transformation process can take place in two scenarios.

- **Scenario 1** - Structure and behavior are written using the ALF language. In terms of structure, code is directly generated from ALF units, and types are derived using a deduction mechanism. Three actions can be performed to generate behavior. In the case of the behavior described in ALF, the generator starts transforming the model into text, which results in the C++ code. If the behavior is defined in the C++ language, this block is only copied to the resulting file. In the case the behavior is described in another language, the generator will not take any action.
- **Scenario 2** - The structure is defined by UML elements, the behavior is defined using the ALF language. The translation of the structure defined in UML takes place with the help of a transformation, which is not specified in work. To translate the behavior, the generator starts the transformation of the model into text, as in Scenario 1.

ALF syntax transformation is performed by mapping ALF concepts to C++. In the discussed work, the mapping tables were created according to the place where the translation is performed. These mappings are in the form `<ALF code, C++ code>` and include pairs of qualified names, various expressions, name declarations, conditions, loops, class definitions, operations, indexing, and more. The functionality of this generator was tested on a robot system consisting of two classes written in ALF [5].

VI. Evaluation

Regarding the implementation of the conference review system, it is not possible to capture the application's complexity using the ALF language. No work has been found to create web systems or tools to make this possible. What is possible is to create a skeleton in the Papyrus environment, without considerable functionality. Most applications need to manipulate the data stored in the database. For these tasks, it is necessary to have libraries that allow such operations, but none have been found. Following an unsuccessful search, an inquiry was raised with OMG, which confirmed that there were no libraries to connect to the database or other subsystems.

At the beginning of ALF's development, there were plans to design a Ruby on Rails-style version of ALF that would allow the development of Service-Oriented Architectures (SOAs). Still, due to other business priorities, it was abandoned over time. The only option would be to implement the libraries manually. Another problem is that there are no freely available tools to generate code from the ALF language. So even if the whole system could be described in the ALF, it would be necessary to implement either your own transformation rules to convert the ALF model to model X or to design your code generator.

Communication with OMG revealed an Interaction Flow Modeling Language (IFML) for modeling web-based user interfaces. Furthermore, the communication showed that OMG managed to demonstrate the IFML frontend connection to the back-end business logic implemented using unspecified xUML in a simulated environment. So far, the possibilities of these technologies are the subject of discussion and active research. There is currently no solution on how to generate web systems directly from ALF code or UML models.

Continuous testing of technologies, a study of materials, communication in various discussion groups, communication directly with OMG, and technical support of MagicDraw, it was found that it is impossible to create and generate complex systems using the ALF language. Although there are studies where it was possible to generate functional code from the ALF language, for this to be possible, it is necessary to implement your tools or transformation rules that would allow this.

VII. Future Work

One of the fundamental questions for the successful adaptation of MDE techniques for real software projects is the connection of standard and already used modeling techniques with tools to support simulation verification, preferably in real conditions, and generate complex pieces of code in the implementation language.

Adapting standard techniques, such as UML models or simulation of state diagrams, will facilitate the transition from conventional practices to MDE. Designers will not be faced with the question of entirely new techniques. At the same time, tool support must be available to support the above concepts, ideally combined with existing development environments. As mentioned in the article, the basics of these tools often exist as a plugin to existing tools. Still, they are not very connected to the original environment, and it is always necessary to learn an entirely new concept or formalism for modeling and design.

Another problem is the different variants of the new specification languages, which should allow universal use for different target environments. This approach seems difficult to implement. An important aspect is a possibility of incorporating a programming language into specification models, which will facilitate their comprehensibility and subsequent transformation. Thus, it is not necessary to create new specification languages but to allow existing ones to describe the system behavior, which could, if necessary, be replaced by another one. Although the design system conceived in this way lacks universality, on the other hand, it increases its practical applicability and applicability to a broader part of the community of software system developers.

VIII. Conclusion

The ALF language can be used to simulate models in SysML, which is its primary use now. It is also possible to implement simple programs using two approaches, either alone based on the reference implementation of ALF or in combination with ALF and UML. However, this language is not suitable for implementing complex systems due to limited capabilities and missing tools.

The ALF language is relatively clumsy, necessary libraries offer limited capabilities, and there are no third-party libraries to facilitate development. Due to the fact that ALF is not very widespread, the only reliable guide is the official standard of ALF and academic studies that have dealt with this language. There are also only a limited number of environments in which ALF can be developed. These environments alone are insufficient, so various extensions need to be installed. Combining these environments is much more complicated than programming. Due to limitations, the ALF language cannot describe the whole system, but only part of it. There are no libraries that allow, for example, authorization, database connection, or communication via the REST API. If we look at the development in terms of time, the case study's preparation and implementation using a standard approach took about a month. In the case of the ALF approach, exploring its possibilities, studying the issue, finding relevant resources, reading various studies, and testing multiple technologies and environments took over three months.

Regarding the implementation of the conference review system, it is impossible to capture the application's complexity using the ALF language. No work has been found to make this possible. What is possible is to create a system skeleton, without considerable functionality. The ALF language can be used to simulate models in SysML or to implement simple programs. However, this language is not suitable for implementing complex systems due to limited capabilities and missing tools. Adapting standard techniques, such as UML models or simulation of state diagrams, will facilitate the transition from conventional practices to MDE. At the same time, tool support must be available. Another problem is the different variants of the new specification languages, which should allow universal use for different target environments. It is not necessary to create new specification languages but to let existing ones to describe the system behavior.

Acknowledgment

This work has been supported by the internal BUT project FIT-S-20-6427.

References

[1] J. Bezivin, "Model Driven Engineering: An Emerging Technical Space," Generative and Transformational Techniques in Software Engineering, GTTSE. Lecture Notes in Computer Science. Springer, Berlin, Heidelberg, vol. 4143, 2005, pp. 36–64.

[2] Object Management Group, "Meta Object Facility (MOF) 2.0 Query/View/Transformation Specification," https://www.omg.org/spec/QVT/1.0/PDF, [online; retrieved: September, 2022].
[3] S. J. Mellor and M. J. Balcer, Executable UML: A Foundation for Model-Driven Architecture, 2002.
[4] T. Mayerhofer, P. Langer, and M. Wimmer, "xMOF: Executable DSMLs Based on fUML," Software Language Engineering, SLE. Lecture Notes in Computer Science. Springer., vol. 8225, 2013, pp. 56–75.
[5] F. Ciccozzi, "On the automated translational execution of the action language for foundational uml," Software and Systems Modeling, vol. 17, no. 4, 2018, doi: 10.1007/s10270-016-0556-7.
[6] S. S. Nejati and M. Maleki, "Report on How to Use ALF Action Language and fUML execution/debugging with Moka," https://wiki.eclipse.org/images/5/5a/ALF_fUML_Moka.pdf, [online; retrieved: September, 2022].
[7] "ALF Reference Implementation," http://modeldriven.github.io/Alf-Reference-Implementation/, [online; retrieved: September, 2022].
[8] "ALF Language - Getting started," https://docs.nomagic.com/display/ALFP185/Getting+Started, [online; retrieved: September, 2022].
[9] "Code Engineering," https://docs.nomagic.com/display/MD190/Code+Engineering, [online; retrieved: September, 2022].
[10] E. Seidewitz and J. Tatibouet, "Tool paper: Combining alf and uml in modeling tools an example with papyrus," in 15th Internation Workshop on OCL and Textual Modeling, MODELS 2015, pp. 105–119, [online; retrieved: September, 2022]. [Online]. Available: http://ceur-ws.org/Vol-1512/paper09.pdf
[11] S. Guermazi, J. Tatibouet, A. Cuccuru, S. Dhouib, S. Grard, and E. Seidewitz, "Executable modeling with fuml and alf in papyrus: Tooling and experiments," in 1st Internation Workshop on Executable Modeling, MODELS 2015, pp. 3–8, [online; retrieved: September, 2022]. [Online]. Available: http://ceur-ws.org/Vol-1560/paper1.pdf
[12] Z. Micskei, R.-A. Konnerth, B. Horvth, O. Semerth, A. Vrs, and D. Varr, "On open source tools for behavioral modeling and analysis with fuml and alf," in 1st Workshop on Open Source Software for Model Driven Engineering, MODELS 2014, pp. 31–41, [online; retrieved: September, 2022]. [Online]. Available: http://ceur-ws.org/Vol-1290/paper3.pdf
[13] T. Buchmann and A. Rimer, "Unifying modeling and programming with alf," in SOFTENG 2016: The Second International Conference on Advances and Trends in Software Engineering, 2016, pp. 10–15.
[14] F. Ciccozzi, A. Cicchetti, and M. Sjdin, "On the generation of full-fledged code from uml profiles and alf for complex systems," in 12th International Conference on Information Technology - New Generations, 2015, pp. 81–88.
[15] "Eclipse Model To Text Project," https://www.eclipse.org/modeling/m2t/?project=xpand, [online; retrieved: September, 2022].
[16] "Eclipse Xtext Project – A Framework for Development of Programming Languages," https://www.eclipse.org/Xtext/, [online; retrieved: September, 2022].
[17] "Eclipse Xtend – A Flexible and Expressive Dialect of Java," https://www.eclipse.org/xtend/, [online; retrieved: September, 2022].
[18] "Eclipse ATL – A Model Transformation Technology," https://www.eclipse.org/atl, [online; retrieved: September, 2022].
[19] OMG, Action Language for Foundational UML, Version 1.1, 2017, [online; retrieved: September, 2022]. [Online]. Available: https://www.omg.org/spec/ALF/1.1/PDF